White Ibis

Keith L. Bildstein

White Ibis

WETLAND WANDERER

SMITHSONIAN INSTITUTION PRESS

Washington and London

The epigraph to Chapter 10 is an excerpt from "Old Man
Goes South Again Alone" from *Delusions, etc.* by John
Berryman. Copyright 1969, 1971 by John Berryman.
Copyright 1972 by the Estate of John Berryman.
Reprinted by permission of Farrar, Straus & Giroux, Inc.

Copy Editor: Deborah Sanders
Production Editor: Duke Johns
Designer: Alan Carter

Library of Congress Cataloging-in-Publication Data
Bildstein, Keith L.
White ibis : wetland wanderer / Keith L. Bildstein.
      p.   cm.
Includes bibliographical references (p.   ) and index.
ISBN 1-56098-223-3
1. White ibis. 2. Ibis. I. Title.
QL696.C585B54   1993
598.3'4—dc20   92-38961

British Library Cataloguing-in-Publication Data is available

Manufactured in the United States of America
00 99 98 97 96 95 94 93   5 4 3 2 1

⊗The paper used in this publication meets the minimum
requirements of the American National Standard for
Permanence of Paper for Printed Library Materials
Z39.48-1984

For permission to reproduce illustrations appearing in this
book, please correspond directly with the owners of the
works, as listed in the individual captions. The
Smithsonian Institution Press does not retain
reproduction rights for these illustrations individually, or
maintain a file of addresses for illustration sources.

For Joe, Tom, and Fran

the first for introducing me to birds

the second for introducing me to science

and the third for introducing me to the field

Contents

Preface

I saw my first American White Ibis—which I call the White Ibis throughout this book—in mid-December 1977. I was in the middle of my final year of doctoral research, a four-year study of the wintering ecology of Northern Harriers and other open-habitat raptors wintering on Ohio farmlands. (The Latin names of plants and animals mentioned in the text can be found in Appendix 1.) Tom Grubb, my thesis adviser, and I had planned to do some birding during a quick trip to the Florida Everglades, an area I had not yet visited. On the way, Tom was first to spot and identify the wavering skein of 30 adult White Ibises flying over our pickup along a stretch of Interstate 95 in coastal Georgia.

Our curiosity was aroused. Perhaps these birds were breeding nearby and were flying between their nests and feeding grounds. Or, considering the time of year, perhaps they were flying from a day roost to their feeding grounds or vice versa, or even traveling between feeding sites. As we drove, we discussed the species in general. Our conversation centered on our recollections of a series of papers that National Park Service biologist Jim Kushlan had just published. Kushlan, then a researcher with the Park Service's South Florida Research Station near Homestead, Florida, had been studying White Ibises since his dissertation research in the early 1970s. Within the past few years, Jim had unveiled many details of the species's biology to the scientific community. His contributions had made the White Ibis one of the best known of all wading birds. Tom and I agreed that Kushlan had "covered the waterfront" to a great extent and that there appeared to be little more to learn about this most abundant of Florida's wading birds.

Our limited knowledge exhausted, our talk turned to the Everglades, whether we would arrive in time to secure a campsite (we didn't) and what we would do when we got there (we slept in the back of the truck). Although we repeatedly saw flocks of White Ibises during our trip, we paid them little attention, concentrating on the more spectacular birds we encountered: Brown Pelicans, Bald Eagles, Wood Storks, Roseate Spoonbills, and the like. All too soon we were back in dreary Ohio, where I finished my fieldwork and began to put together the first of many drafts of my dissertation. White Ibises quickly faded into the backwaters of my ornithological consciousness.

But not for long. I saw the species again in May of 1979 during a weekend visit to the North Inlet Estuary in coastal South Carolina, where I encountered large flocks of White Ibises flying between inland feeding sites and a coastal breeding colony. During that visit, I met University of South Carolina graduate student Elizabeth Henderson, who had just begun studying the feeding behavior of this population of ibises. Shortly thereafter, I volunteered to serve as an outside reader on Elizabeth's master's thesis. Later that fall, I was invited to join the University of South Carolina's Baruch Institute for Marine Biology and Coastal Research as an ornithologist at the North Inlet Estuary field site. Although I did not know it then, my second encounter with ibises was to have long-term consequences.

Over the years, albeit slowly at first, my research efforts have shifted from harriers to coastal wading birds, eventually focusing on White Ibises. In retrospect, the transition seems logical. As a neophyte graduate student interested in studying the ecology of foraging behavior, I had decided to work on harriers for three reasons. First, harriers are relatively common open-habitat hawks whose active hunting style is easy to observe and document. Second, gender- and age-specific differences in their plumage allowed me to determine both the sex and, although to a lesser extent, the age of individuals I was watching. Third, the species raises its young in readily accessible ground nests, so studying the link between foraging behavior and breeding success is relatively easy.

White Ibises, I learned, offer all of the same benefits and then some. Not only do they feed in open habitats, they also do so in large flocks, making it possible to collect data on several individuals simultaneously. As a result, I have been able to assess the extent of gender- and age-specific differences in the hunting behavior of this species in a much more direct fashion than I had been able to accomplish with harriers. Ibises also breed in large assemblages. Where I study them, for example, thousands of individuals nest near the ground in grassy vegetation at a single colony site, greatly simplifying the task of assessing the impact of their foraging behavior on breeding success. But the most intriguing aspect of my ibis research was unanticipated. Throughout much of their range, White Ibises nest in brackish marshes, mangrove swamps, and other coastal habitats. My studies revealed that this is only part of the story. I came to learn that, because of a physiological bottleneck, the species is equally dependent upon inland freshwater habitats. The book that follows provides an account of how I reached this conclusion, as well as how this limitation affects the overall ecology and conservation of these intriguing nomads.

But first I need to give credit to those who have helped make all of this possible. Jim Kushlan's sage advice, together with his enthusiastic support of my efforts, greatly eased my transition from harriers to wading birds. Peter Frederick's serious studies of the courtship and mating behavior of White Ibises, along with his not-so-serious nature, provided an essential introduction to the vagaries of working in the North Inlet Estuary. Bobbie McCutchen took the time to show me how to get into and, more importantly, out of the many tidal meanders at the site. Elizabeth Henderson developed a sampling scheme that I have been using for the past decade for observing feeding ibises. F. John Vernberg and Dennis Allen have provided me with a comfortable home-away-from-home at the coast. Environmental physiologist Jim Johnston and I have developed an intellectually fulfilling mutualism: Jim concentrates on studying ibises from the skin-side in, while I focus on studying them from the skin-side out. Will Post's work with White Ibises breeding near Charleston, South Carolina, has considerably broadened my perspective. An all-too-brief but nevertheless productive collaboration with I. Lehr Brisbin enabled me to incorporate studies of captive ibises into my research.

Master's degree candidates Melissa Frix, Andrea Dinep, Barbara McCraith, and Katie Golden, and doctoral candidate Toni De Santo, have filled my summers with enjoyable comradery and reciprocal learning. For several years, Susan McDowell cared for and maintained a flock of captive White Ibises at the Savannah River Ecology Laboratory in Aiken, South Carolina. I could not have sustained my enthusiasm for the project had it not been for the assistance and support of a number of industrious summer interns. To these individuals, all of whom worked long hours at low pay, while encountering many more insects and chiggers than ibises, I extend my gratitude: Dan R. Petit (1984); John Edens, Heidi Koefer, and Robin Hughes (1985); Ed Ceva and Mark Hostetler (1986); Mike Carl

(1987); Alan Harris and Barbara McCraith (1988); Darrin Bauer and Scott Miller (1989); Tanja Crockett, Michelle Davis, and Philippa Shepherd (1990); and Lauri Michel and Renee Pardeick (1991). Many aspects of the fieldwork described within this book were carried out almost entirely by these individuals. Scientific research is considerably more communal than Nobel prizes and other accolades would indicate. My frequent use of the first-person plural in this book is testimony to this fact.

Artists Michelle Davis and Pamela Cowart-Rickman prepared the many illustrations that grace the book. Pictures are often said to be worth a thousand words. Theirs are even more precious.

Albert Conway, Jim Kushlan, and Uldis Roze carefully read and critiqued the entire manuscript. I thank them for their thoughtful comments, many of which helped clarify my writing. Various administrators at Winthrop University, my primary meal ticket during the course of this study, have provided much appreciated collegiality, encouragement, and logistical support through the years. They include Robin Bowers, Anthony DiGeorgio, Phil Lader, Al Lyles, Tom Morgan, Mike Smith, Dan Pantaleo, and especially my Department chair, Luckett Davis.

Too often, inadequate funding is the limiting factor in science. I have been relatively fortunate. The Winthrop University Research Council and Faculty Development Fund have provided continual support for the project, and both the Southern Regional Education Board and the American Philosophical Society have provided intermittent funding. Several local groups, including the Hilton Head, Columbia, and Waccamaw Neck chapters of the National Audubon Society, have sponsored summer interns. The Wilson Ornithological Society and American Ornithologists' Union have provided stipends to graduate students working on the project. The Savannah River Ecology Laboratory has aided my research in a number of ways, most notably through its National Environmental Research Park Program. The National Science Foundation, especially through its Long-Term Ecological Research Program, has been an essential supporter of my studies. More recently, the South Carolina Commission on Higher Education's Cutting Edge Initiative has been a source of funding. Finally, I thank the Whitehall Foundation of West Palm Beach, Florida, for providing three and a half years of substantial financial support, as well as for allowing me to be flexible in expending those funds.

I have had a passionate relationship with White Ibises and Hobcaw Barony for some time. I am especially grateful that the Smithsonian Institution Press and its science acquisitions editor, Peter Cannell, have afforded me the opportunity to share my experiences with a broader audience than has heretofore been possible. Copy editor Deborah Sanders helped improve my written presentation considerably. Both Peter and Deborah have been patient shepherds of my wanderings. I can only hope that the publication of my experiences and insights will provoke similar studies of wetland ecosystems, and that people will come to realize the value of these important habitats.

1   A Historical Primer

And the Lord spoke to Moses and Aaron, saying: Of birds these
are they which you must not eat, and which are to be avoided by
you: The eagle, and the griffon, and the osprey. . . . The screech
owl, and the cormorant, and the ibis . . .

Lev. 11:1, 13, 17

Ornithologists often forget that they are not alone in their abiding interest
in birds. Indeed, much of what scientists know about the world's 23 living
species of ibises, including the White Ibis, comes not from the field notes
and computers of modern biologists, but from a variety of ethnographic,
religious, and historical sources. Although such sources typically lack
complete documentation, they often provide the only information available and, if nothing else, indicate gaps in our own knowledge. Such
sources offer rare glimpses into various societies' views of the natural
world. Finally, and perhaps most intriguing of all, I find such historical,
religious, and literary accounts of ibises a welcome relief from overly
concise technical literature.

   Although ibises are certainly not as well known outside of ornithological circles as are their more famous wading-bird cousins, the storks
and flamingos (to my knowledge no society links ibises to the delivery of
human infants or places plastic models of them in their gardens), ibises
have had numerous historical and cultural encounters with human populations.

Old World Ibises

Sacred Ibises in Ancient Egypt

Egyptians no longer hold the Sacred Ibis in such high esteem as its name indicates. Indeed, this species was hunted for food to the point of extirpation from the region during the late 1800s. Such was not always the case, however. The word *ibis*, which occurs in both Greek and Latin, is almost certainly of Egyptian origin (Choate 1973), and the Sacred Ibis was once one of the most highly regarded and revered birds in all of northeastern Africa. Ancient Egyptians honored the species, which appeared frequently as a hieroglyph (Figure 1.1), as the earthly manifestation of the Egyptian moon deity Thoth. This deity was considered to be the spirit of learning and wisdom, and the scribe of the gods (Boylan 1922). As a result, Sacred Ibises occur throughout Egyptian art, most often as crouched effigies ranging in size from small amulets and figurines to nearly life-sized statues of wood, bronze, gilded silver, and other metals (Houlihan 1986) (Figure 1.2).

As Greek historian Herodotus remarked, the species was held in such high esteem that during the fifth century B.C. in Egypt, killing an ibis, even unintentionally, was a crime punishable by death. During the so-called late Dynastic and Greco-Roman periods of Egyptian culture (approximately 700 to 30 B.C.), enormous cemeteries dedicated to the burial of carefully mummified remains of ibises and their eggs were established at several locations along the Nile, the most famous of which is the Saqqara necropolis near Memphis. Even conservative estimates place the number of ibises interred at this one site alone at over 1.5 million birds. An extraordinary religious cult that was centered around Thoth peaked during this time, creating a spiritual industry in which high priests and their lowly minions hand-reared tremendous numbers of domestically bred ibises. Their efforts were assisted by large ovens in which eggs were incubated artificially. Once grown and fully feathered, ibises were offered for purchase to religious pilgrims wishing to pay homage to the deity. After being put to death, the birds were wrapped in elaborate layers of linen bandages and decorated with appliqués of the god they symbolized, modestly depicted as having the body of a human and the head of an ibis (Figure 1.3). Mummies were then placed in ceramic vessels for burial in subterranean catacombs. Although the impact of such activities on wild populations of ibises is unclear, most of the birds offered to Thoth appear

Figure 1.1. Hieroglyphic epithet of Thoth, the Egyptian moon god, translated as "the excellent one" (Boylan 1922). Drawing by P. Cowart-Rickman.

Figure 1.2. Gilded wood and silver Sacred Ibis statue that adorned the sarcophagus of a mummified ibis. Drawings by P. Cowart-Rickman.

to have been produced from domestic stock (Figure 1.4). There is no indication that free-ranging populations were heavily persecuted at this time. Indeed, the species was still common in Egypt throughout the 18th century (Etchecopar and Hue 1967).

Ancient Egyptian references to the bird's religious status apparently are responsible for the current English vernacular name for that species, and, although to a considerably lesser degree, the Sacred Ibis is venerated even today. Nineteenth-century British ornithologists were so enamored with the Sacred Ibis that they named their professional journal *The Ibis* in honor of the species and chose an illustration of the bird to grace its cover. (This journal is still in publication.) Furthermore, as I found to my somewhat uncomfortable delight when I first attended their annual meeting in 1990, members of the British Ornithologists' Union

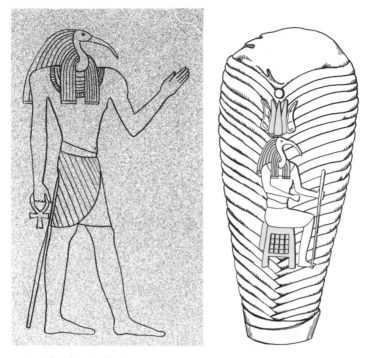

Figure 1.3. *Left:* Thoth, the Egyptian god of wisdom and knowledge, was usually depicted as a man with the head of an ibis. *Right:* Ibis mummy that came from Saqqara and has an appliqué representing Thoth. Drawings by P. Cowart-Rickman.

fondly toast deceased colleagues as "absent ibises" at the end of each year's banquet.

Although the Sacred Ibis is by far the most commonly depicted ibis of Egyptian antiquity, it was not the only ibis employed by artisans and writers of the time. Using deductive logic more typically associated with Victorian detectives, egyptologists have proposed that ancient Egyptian artists included at least three distinct species of ibises in their works. Apparently two other indigenous species, Glossy Ibis and Waldrapp (or Northern Bald) Ibis, appear as hieroglyphs and in art. Artisans devised several techniques to distinguish the three species. Glossy Ibises, which were often thought of as symbols of "sorrow, grief, and uncleanliness" (Kumerloeve 1984), were painted black throughout, whereas a Sacred Ibis was depicted with its distinctive black head, neck, and wing feathers outlining a white body. Appropriately enough, because Waldrapp Ibises

Figure 1.4. Feeding the Sacred Ibises.

were considered to be standards of "excellence, glory, honour, and virtue" (Kumerloeve 1984), they were given red heads, bills, legs, and feet, and blue wings, tails, and body plumage. Artisans further distinguished the Glossy Ibis by inserting a series of small circular feathers in relief on its shoulder, highlighting the location of the species's characteristic iridescent plumage. Waldrapp Ibises were given an accentuated neck ruff, a diagnostic feature for this species, at least in northern Africa (Figure 1.5).

Unsophisticated by more modern standards of naturalistic art, Egyptian depictions of ibises nevertheless provide a rich source of ecological information. Such works, together with the fossilized remains of these species, offer an exciting glimpse of the past, which scientists can use to compare the ecology of today's populations with those of birds from thousands of years ago. For example, the fact that both Sacred and Glossy ibises are usually shown among the umbels of Papyrus thickets and in other wetland settings, whereas Waldrapp Ibises are usually portrayed in upland vegetation, suggests that habitat use by the three species has changed little over the past 5,000 years. Similarly, scenes in which apparently tethered or tamed ibises are feeding near hunters' clap-traps demonstrate that ibises were used as lures to capture waterfowl. Thus, 20th-century observations of ibises and waterfowl feeding in mixed-species flocks most likely reflect an ancient, rather than a recent, symbiotic relationship.

Tragedy is also evidenced by this art. The frequent use of both Sacred and Waldrapp ibises in Egyptian art and hieroglyphs, in contrast to the current rarity of these two species in North Africa, painfully emphasizes the decline of these ibises in the area and their extirpation from modern Egypt. These declines are most likely the result of habitat destruction by growing human populations. Fortunately, sizeable populations of Sacred Ibises occur elsewhere in Africa and Asia. However, such is not the case for the Waldrapp Ibis, a species that in the wild has been reduced to several isolated populations in North Africa, representing an estimated total of less than 500 individuals.

Gesner's Fantastic Forest Raven

Ancient Egyptians were the not the only people who fancied the Waldrapp Ibis. The range of this species once included most of the Mediterranean Basin (hence the species's Swiss-German dialect name of Waldrapp), and

Figure 1.5. Egyptian hieroglyphs of ibises: *left*, Waldrapp Ibis, distinguished by its neck ruff; *right*, Glossy Ibis, whose iridescent shoulder plumage was artistically represented by small circular feathers. Drawings by P. Cowart-Rickman.

the bird has had numerous associations with humanity in the region. Frequently featured on Greek coins during the fourth and fifth centuries B.C., the Waldrapp Ibis also appeared in myth as a result of a brief encounter with the Argonauts on the island of Dia (Desfayes 1987). This species was first described scientifically by 16th-century German naturalist Konrad Gesner (1516–65), who referred to it as a forest raven breeding in the vicinity of Salzburg. Earlier, in the Middle Ages, when the species bred commonly on cliff faces along the Danube, Austrian nobility favored the nestlings as a delicacy. The ibis's growing reputation as a gourmet item (even Gesner commented on its flavor) was not without cost. Despite proclamations by both King Ferdinand and the Archbishop of Salzburg banning entry into ibis colonies for the purpose of collecting young, Waldrapp Ibises disappeared from the area by the middle of the 17th century. Their very existence drifted into myth, and several 18th-century ornithologists, unable to find for themselves what apparently were dwindling populations of the bird elsewhere in its range, suggested that Gesner may have invented this seemingly apocryphal species (Grzimek 1968), his excellent painting of the bird notwithstanding. Not until more modern-day ornithologists rediscovered Waldrapp Ibises near the Red Sea in 1832 were Gesner's original observations at last confirmed.

Although the species has since been extirpated from Asia Minor, the Turks once honored it as a harbinger of spring and as an earthly manifestation of the souls of their kin. Legends grew of ibises guiding pilgrims during their 3,500-kilometer round trip peregrinations to and from Mecca each year. In another legend, ibises transmigrated the souls of the recently deceased to this holy city. Turkish inhabitants also revered Waldrapp Ibises as the lineal descendants of Abu Mengal, the black-plumed ibis that Noah had released to herald a new era of earthly fertility, the same bird that led him and his sons from landfall on Mount Ararat to the bountiful valley below (Schreiber et al. 1989). Not surprisingly, the species's presence near certain towns, including its last Asian stronghold, Birecik, on the upper Euphrates, was much appreciated. For a time, local inhabitants celebrated the bird's annual return each spring by reviving the ancient rite-of-spring festival, *kelaynak yortusu* (Kumerloeve 1984). Unfortunately, neighboring Syrians believed that the sacred powers of the bird were transferable to anyone eating it, and not surprisingly, Waldrapp Ibises began to disappear from Syrian portions of their range. The recent immigration of large numbers of Syrians into Birecik, together with the species's tendency to defecate on human habitations constructed near its traditional cliff-face colony site, may have hastened the demise of Wald-rapp Ibis at the site (Mallet 1977).

Why ibises figure so prominently in systems of human belief is unclear. Perhaps it is their social nature or their somewhat upright stance that draws human admiration. Whatever the reason, people have been honoring these birds for a long time.

Other Biblical References

Both the Old and New testaments contain numerous references to birds. Unfortunately, the limited taxonomy of the day and the fact that translating ancient Hebrew into more modern languages is something of an inexact science cloud the issue of species identity for many biblical references. Nevertheless, several Old Testament translations, including the Greek Septuagint, the Douay Version, and the Revised Standard Version, place the ibis, or "horned one," among the "birds of abomination." These birds, God told Moses, are unfit for human consumption (Lev. 11:13–19)—presumably because they prey on and scavenge other animals. Some scholars suggest that an ibis, perhaps the Glossy Ibis, is one of several haunting birds of doom, whose plaintive cries and nomadic wanderings the prophet Isaiah used to conjure visions of utter desolation (Isa. 34:11–16) (Holmgren 1972).

Ibises in the New World

Scarlet Ibises in South America

The most spectacular ibis in South America, or indeed anywhere in the world, is the appropriately named Scarlet Ibis. Because of its brilliant plumage, as well as its tendency to nest in accessible colonies of thousands of individuals, the Scarlet Ibis has long figured in the human history of both South America and the Caribbean Basin. The Tubinamba Indians of what is now the southern coast of Brazil traditionally constructed elaborate body-length capes from the flight and contour feathers of Scarlet Ibises for the exclusive use of their chiefs. (Although such royal mantles must have been spectacular when first constructed, the first one I saw was a hideously tattered and faded example displayed in a dimly lit room in an archeological museum in Florence, Italy.) Because of the food value of ibises, Tubinamba tribes maintained property rights over traditional ibis colony sites. As a result, many of the villages and rivers within the region include the Tubinamban word *guara*, or ibis, as part of their name. Although it is unclear whether these tribes also collected ibis eggs for food, they most certainly collected nestlings and hunted adults for their meat (Antas et al. 1990).

Spanish and Portuguese colonization of the region fostered egg collection and the hunting of adult Scarlet Ibises on a much grander scale, and may have caused the current disjunct distribution of the species along the Atlantic coast of South America (Teixeira and Best 1981). Even today, numerous eggs, as well as young and adult ibises, are removed from many colonies. Although ibises congregate to breed at such sites for only a few months each year, poachers have learned to preserve the carcasses by salting, so they harvest the birds in large numbers for later consumption. Prefledged young are collected at colony sites by shaking nest trees until the chicks tumble to the ground, where they are gathered for eventual sale, both as pets and for food. Up to 90% of an ibis colony's offspring may be collected in this manner. An artificial-flower industry that used feathers of ibises, as well as feathers of egrets, herons, and parrots, also was operating in French Guiana at least through 1988 (Dujardin 1990).

The Scarlet Ibis was considered a legal game bird in several South American countries well into the 1980s, and even today eggs and nestlings are not protected in Guyana (Ramsamujh 1990). As recently as 1984 a daily bag limit of 10 birds per person per hunt existed in French Guiana;

however, lax enforcement of game laws enabled individuals to collect as many as several hundred birds per hunt. Although the bird is now officially designated as a nongame species in most countries, insufficient enforcement of existing laws is often the rule rather than the exception, and reports of poaching at colony sites are numerous. Indeed, poaching appears to be an all-too-common occurrence in much of the species's range, even in so-called protected areas (Bildstein 1990). (For example, see Chapter 10 for details on the current status of the Scarlet Ibis in Trinidad.)

White Ibises in Colonial North America

When Mark Catesby, a scion of prominent English heritage, arrived in Charleston, South Carolina, in 1722, European settlers had written little about the birds they had encountered in the New World. Catesby filled the void with a benchmark publication that was to become the standard text of New World birds for over 150 years. His *Natural History of Carolina, Florida and the Bahama Islands* (Catesby 1731–47) appears to have been an immediate success. Sensing a continental market for illustrated news of wildlife in the American colonies, Mark Catesby wrote a brief but descriptive text that was accompanied by his detailed paintings of 109 birds he had seen, many of which were depicted against a backdrop of native vegetation. Two of the species Catesby claims to have encountered in coastal South Carolina, the White and Brown curlews, are of interest to us here. Even without his painting of the White Curlew (Figure 1.6), Catesby's succinct description of this bird leaves little doubt as to its true identity:

> This is about the size of a tame pigeon. The bill is six inches and a half long, of pale red color, channelled from the base to the point. The iris of the eyes are gray. The fore part of the head, and round the eyes, is covered with light red skin. Four of the largest wing feathers have their ends dark green. All the rest of the bird is white, except the legs and feet, which are pale red. The flesh, particularly the fat, is very yellow, of a saffron color. When the great rains fall, which is usual at the latter end of summer, the birds arrive in Carolina in great numbers, and frequent the low watery lands.

The cock and the hen are alike in appearance. (Catesby 1731–47, 7)

Few ornithologists have managed a more careful description of an adult White Ibis. Catesby almost certainly used the English name *curlew,* and placed the bird in the same genus *(Numenius)* as the local curlew species, the Whimbrel, because of the superficial resemblance of both species to the Eurasian Curlew, a large shorebird with a similarly decurved bill.

Catesby's descriptions of ibises do not end with the White Curlew. He also painted and described a bird he called the Brown Curlew (Figure 1.6). Again, an excerpt from his brief description of the bird captures the essence of both its anatomy and its ecology:

> This is about the size of the White Curlew. It has the same sort of bill, with red round the base of it, and eyes like the White Curlew. The rest of the head and neck are of a mixed gray. The upper part of the back, wings, and tail are brown. The lower part of the back and rump are white, as is the under part of the body. . . . They [White and Brown curlews] both feed and associate in flocks, yet the White are twenty times more numerous than the Brown kinds. Both these kinds, accompanied with the Wood Pelicans [Wood Storks] come annually about the middle of September, and frequent the watery savannahs in numerous flights, continuing about six weeks, and then retire; and are no more seen until that time next year. . . . (Catesby 1731–47, 8)

Because of the Brown Curlew's striking similarity in appearance and in distribution to the White Curlew, Catesby at first suspected the two birds might represent different sexes of a single species. However, after carefully examining specimens of the two variants and finding testes in both, this meticulous scientist declared them to be two distinct species. Unfortunately, he had failed to consider the possibility that the two color morphs represented different age classes (rather than genders) of a single species, which, in this instance, is precisely the case. Throughout most of their first year, White Ibises basically are brown birds (Catesby's so-called Brown Curlews). It is only during the following spring, when they begin to molt into adult plumage, that they become what Catesby referred to as White Curlews. Although he never suggested in his writings that he entertained this possibility, Catesby came tantalizingly close; he had the

Figure 1.6. Mark Catesby's drawings: *left,* Brown Curlew (now known to be a juvenile White Ibis) (Figure 83 in Catesby 1731–47); *right,* White Curlew (currently, adult White Ibis) (Figure 82 in Catesby 1731–47).

appropriate clues, at least. In his account of the Brown Curlew he mentioned finding clusters of eggs in white hens, whereas he did not indicate such a finding in the brown hens he examined (because they were, in fact, immature forms). An intrepid naturalist, Catesby was also the first to note that young White Ibises feed on crayfishes, a fact that has considerable implications for the breeding ecology of the species.

Had Catesby lived to read William Bartram's widely circulated *Travels through North and South Carolina, Georgia, East and West Florida, etc.* (Bartram 1791), he could have taken some comfort in the fact that this most prominent naturalist also described juvenile and adult White Ibises as being two separate species, but with the single vernacular name of Spanish Curlew (p. 137). Bartram was the first to report that the species flew in "large flocks or squadrons, evening and morning, to and from their feeding places or roosts" and that they were "esteemed excellent food." He, like Catesby before him, linked the White Ibises taxonomically to the curlews, and he too remarked on their dependency upon crayfish prey. A keen observer, Bartram was also the first to note the communal aerial displays that typically precede courtship and mating. Although he failed to recognize these flights for what they were, he did link their occurrence to periods of rain, a connection that was not rediscovered until recently.

The next naturalist to discuss the White Ibis was Alexander Wilson (1766–1813), the father of American ornithology. Wilson, a Scotsman, had been a weaver, schoolteacher, and poet, as well as a self-taught naturalist, before William Bartram prompted him to update and expand Catesby's then dated accounts. Regrettably, his description of the White Ibis (Wilson 1840, 564–65) drew heavily upon Bartram's earlier account (Bartram 1791), thus providing little new information. Although Wilson did not discuss the juvenile color morph, he did describe the Scarlet Ibis, a bird that he claimed might represent a color morph of the White Ibis, rather than a separate species (a taxonomic conundrum that eludes ornithologists even today). Wilson's opening remark in his account of the Scarlet Ibis—the statement that "this beautiful bird is found in most southern parts of Carolina, also in Georgia, and Florida"—remains controversial, especially in light of his later pronouncement that the species is "found only on our most remote southern shores" and his admission that he could not procure enough specimens to explore the possibility of sexual dimorphism.

Although Scarlet Ibises indeed may have occurred in the region, they were probably not as common in Wilson's time as his initial statement suggested (Simpson 1988). A scant several decades later, when John James Audubon studied the region's avifauna, the Scarlet Ibis was a rare bird in the southeastern United States (Audubon 1840–44). Today, although still common in portions of its South American range (Frederick et al. 1990), the Scarlet Ibis is all but nonexistent in the United States. Objects of any recent sightings probably represent escapees from zoos (Belser 1989). Despite what may have been a limited occurrence of Scarlet Ibises in the region, Wilson correctly described the species's dark nestlings (which White Ibises also have); surprisingly, however, he erroneously suggested that fledglings are white and that they then gradually change to red by their third year. How he arrived at such a conclusion baffles the imagination, especially since he correctly described age-related segregation during feeding, a finding that had to await rediscovery by 20th-century ornithologists.

Audubon, America's most artistically gifted 19th-century naturalist, was the first to detail both the anatomy and the ecology of the White Ibis (Audubon 1840–44). Audubon's account is an order of magnitude longer than those of his predecessors, and in it he offered considerable information on the species's breeding biology, including clutch size, nesting phenology, and nestling development, as well as accounts of both external and internal anatomy. Audubon's painting of the species, although not among the most remarkable or prized of his works, remains an alluring depiction of an adult and juvenile ibis (Figure 1.7). Although most of his account is quite rigorous, a portion of Audubon's description of the species's feeding behavior borders on the fantastic:

> The bird, to procure the cray-fish, walks with remarkable care toward the mounds of mud which the latter throws up while forming its hole, and breaks up the upper part of the fabric, dropping the fragments into the deep cavity that has been made by the animal. Then the Ibis retires a single step, and patiently waits the result. The crayfish, incommoded by the load of earth, instantly sets to work anew, and at last reaches the entrance of the burrow; but the moment it comes in sight, the ibis seizes it with its bill. (Audubon 1840–44, 57)

I have watched both White and Scarlet ibises feeding at dozens of locations and on many types of prey, including crayfish, but I have yet to see anything resembling this strategy. Although it may occur in certain areas, Audubon's description of foraging behavior is at best an exceptional, rather than typical, hunting style.

Audubon, who ate both the eggs and meat of White Ibises, remarked that the eggs "afford excellent eating, although when boiled they do not look inviting, the white resembling a livid-colored jelly, and the yolk being of a reddish-orange, the former wonderfully transparent, instead of being opaque like that of most other birds" (Audubon 1840–44, 55). Although he found the meat to be extremely fishy, he notes that the species was often sold in southern markets and was regularly eaten by native Americans. Even today in parts of rural Florida (what little of it remains) the bird is commonly called the chuckalusky chicken in reference to its culinary role. And in Cajun Louisiana, where the species is known locally as the *bec croche* or *petit flaman*, and where these birds habitually feed along the edges of commercial crayfish ponds, many eventually find their way into someone's pot, after being dispatched as presumed pests.

An Identity Crisis: One Species or Two?

Biologists describe species as groups of interbreeding or potentially interbreeding organisms that are "reproductively isolated" from other organ-

Figure 1.7. John James Audubon's drawings of White Ibis. Note the crayfish in the lower left corner. Reprinted, by permission, from Audubon (1840–44). Copyright 1981, 1991 by Cross River Press, Ltd.

isms. Species, then, consist of groups of individuals that are capable of breeding with one another. In most instances this seemingly straightforward biological definition works without problems—but not always. A case in point involves White and Scarlet ibises. Whether or not these two distinctive groups of birds represent one or two species has long been in dispute (Hancock et al. 1992). Historically, weak evidence suggested that the two forms failed to interbreed in northern South America where their ranges overlapped and, consequently, most taxonomists concluded that the two were separate species. On the other hand, White and Scarlet ibises are so similar anatomically, ecologically, and behaviorally (Palmer 1962; Ramo and Busto 1985a, 1985b; Frederick and Bildstein 1992) that, were it not for the obvious difference in plumage, the two forms would be indistinguishable in the field. As a result, several researchers have suggested that White and Scarlet ibises are simply color variations within a single species (American Ornithologists' Union 1983, Ramo and Busto 1987).

Support for this argument is growing. Recent studies have confirmed that individual White and Scarlet ibises often interbreed, not only in captivity—where loneliness may play a role (Rutgers and Norris 1970, Archibald et al. 1980)—but also in the wild (Ramo and Busto 1982, 1987). Indeed, the two color morphs appear to be entirely interfertile. As a result, the most recently published comprehensive treatment of the biology of the world's 23 species of ibises, the monumental *Storks, Ibises, and Spoonbills* by Hancock et al. (1992), sets forth the following conclusion: "The clearest concordance of the evidence with taxonomy is to recognize a single species . . . of American White Ibises with two subspecies: a slightly larger-bodied North American subspecies of white birds, and a slightly smaller-bodied South American subspecies of both white and red individuals" (pp. 154–55). Thus, White Ibises can be either white or red, and for the remainder of this book I will consider both color morphs to be a single species. (Appendix 2 provides a more complete pedigree for the White Ibis.)

2　Focusing on the White Ibises of Hobcaw Barony

Any scientist who is not a hypocrite will admit the important part that luck plays in scientific discovery . . .

Peter Medawar, 1984

Serendipity in Science

When I moved to South Carolina in the fall of 1978, I had no idea I was about to commit a major portion of my professional career to a study of White Ibises. At the time, my immediate professional goals included no wading-bird ecology whatsoever. My first priority consisted of writing the lectures I needed to survive my first full year of teaching. Then I planned to sit down at a typewriter (those were pre-word-processor days) and complete my doctoral dissertation on harriers. Somehow, I managed to accomplish both of these goals before Christmas, and by spring of 1979 I was looking for a summer project. I eventually decided to return to central Wisconsin to finish some work on harriers. But before I did, I volunteered to spend a weekend in May working on a project at the field site of the University of South Carolina's Belle W. Baruch Institute for Marine Biology and Coastal Research at Hobcaw Barony, near George-town, South Carolina.

Researchers at the site were in the midst of a multidisciplinary study of energy flow on the institute's property at the North Inlet Estuary, and I, together with 60 other individuals, had offered to help collect water and plankton samples as tidal forces filled and drained the site. Aside from an embarrassing case of sun poisoning, my trip to the Baruch Institute ranked as an unqualified success. The visit provided me with considerable insight into how large-scale ecosystem science is performed in the field. But more significantly, I had an opportunity to meet with F. John Vernberg, the director of the Baruch Institute, who asked me to consider becoming involved in the project. John's offer was too good to resist, and that fall I agreed to direct the collection of field data needed to assess the role that birds played in energy flow at the site.

Although bird communities have long been recognized as one of the most conspicuous components of estuarine ecosystems, studies of their distribution and abundance at specific estuaries have rarely been undertaken—and with good reason. The study I had agreed to oversee involved censusing, twice a month for two years, the entire avian community inhabiting a 3,000-hectare salt-marsh site. My first thought was that the marsh, with its sparse vegetation, level terrain, and seemingly well-placed creeks, would make the job of censusing birds easy. But I had forgotten to consider the tides. High tides made walking straight transects, even at the highest elevations, difficult at best. And low tides repeatedly left us stranded in tidal meanders. Even after I threw out the book on bird censusing, surveying the marsh's bird community required a good bit of compromise.

During our two-year travail, Bobbie McCutchen, my field technician, and I counted 95 species of birds that used the estuary (Bildstein et al. 1982). Our analysis of the data indicated that more species used the site during fall and spring, when many migratory populations passed through the area (Figure 2.1). About one-third of the species sighted on the marsh were seen breeding on or near the site, including all but 1 of the 12 species of wading birds seen. On an annual basis, breeding species constituted most of the avian biomass (the combined mass, or weight, of the avian community), in large part because of the multithousand wading-bird colony site at the southern edge of the estuary on Pumpkinseed Island.

Two groups of birds, long-legged waders (herons, egrets, and ibises) and rails, made up half of all of the birds seen and more than half of the avian biomass (Table 2.1). And two species alone, White Ibises and Clapper Rails, made up 47% of all individuals recorded, as well as 45% of the avian biomass (Bildstein et al. 1982).

In late 1980, Bobbie and I began to enter our data into a mathematical model that simulated energy flow through the community. The model, despite its complexity, greatly simplified interpretation of avian energetics

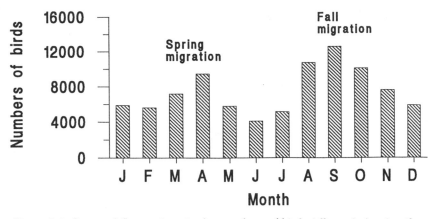

Figure 2.1. Seasonal fluctuations in the numbers of birds (all species) using the North Inlet Estuary. Monthly averages are based on data collected from fall 1978 through fall 1980.

and population dynamics at the site, while providing a reasonable estimate of the avian-induced energy flow there. (For a more thorough explanation of the value of such models, I recommend reading James and McCullough 1985.)

The results of this early effort—my first study of birds at the North Inlet Estuary—provided me with a much-needed feel for the size and structure of the area's avian community. More importantly, the results of this study emphasized the decided ecological importance, at least in terms of relative energy flow, of two of the most common species of birds

Table 2.1 Ordinal composition of the avian community at the North Inlet Estuary, 1978–80

Avian order	Individuals (%)	Biomass (%)
Rails (Gruiformes)	42	30
Shorebirds, gulls, and terns (Charadriiformes)	29	20
Perching birds (Passeriformes)	16	5
Wading birds (Ciconiiformes)	10	33
Ducks (Anseriformes)	1	4
Others (Gaviiformes, Podicipediformes, Pelecaniformes, Falconiformes, and Coraciiformes)	1	7

at the site: the White Ibis and the Clapper Rail (Dame et al. 1986). Indeed, our calculations revealed that the White Ibis was responsible for 10%, and the Clapper Rail for 40%, of all of the energy flowing through the avian community. If I intended to become a part of the Baruch Institute's long-term studies of ecosystem function at the site, concentrating my efforts on at least one of these ecologically significant species seemed reasonable.

At first, I briefly entertained the notion of studying both White Ibises and Clapper Rails. I soon realized, however, that the kind of detailed studies I envisioned would require significant field efforts and I could afford to focus on only one of the two species. But which one?

Clapper Rails were attractive options because they alone were responsible for 40% of the avian-induced energy flow at the estuary. A quick perusal of the literature, however, revealed that rails, although little known and seemingly ripe for exploration, would be difficult to study. The species builds cryptic nests, feeds secretively, and is difficult to follow without the use of radiotelemetry. No wonder it was little known. (See Meanley 1985 for an overview of what *is* known about the ecology of Clapper Rails.) Although White Ibises were far less important in terms of energy flow, and although in other regions the species had already been well studied—some might even say "worked over"—by Jim Kushlan (Kushlan 1974, 1976, 1977a, 1977b, 1977c, 1977d, 1978, 1979a, 1979b), studying White Ibises had its strong points. Individual White Ibises were extremely conspicuous at the site, both when feeding on the marsh and when breeding on nearby Pumpkinseed Island. Their conspicuousness made them easy to census, not only on the ground but also from the air. Studying details of ibis breeding ecology and nesting success was especially convenient because the entire breeding population nested near the ground and close together as a single colony on tiny Pumpkinseed Island.

At the same time that I started thinking seriously about White Ibises, two graduate students, Peter Frederick at the University of North Carolina and Elizabeth Henderson at the University of South Carolina, also initiated detailed studies of White Ibises at the site. Peter planned to concentrate his efforts on the species's courtship and mating behavior at Pumpkinseed Island (see Frederick 1985b), whereas Elizabeth had devised an effective sampling scheme for studying ibis feeding behavior on a small portion of the marsh near the field lab (see Henderson 1981). After lengthy discussions with both students, I decided to embark on an ambitious long-term study of White Ibis breeding and feeding ecology. Although I was not exactly certain what I was stepping into, by the summer of 1980 I began to work in earnest on the feeding ecology of White Ibises, the species that would be the focus of my field efforts throughout the 1980s.

Having just invested four years of my life studying harriers, I initially resisted the change in the direction of my fieldwork. Compared with what I knew about harriers, I knew next to nothing about wading birds. True, I had read most of Jim Kushlan's papers about White Ibises, but my memory of their contents was fuzzy at best. There was also the question of White Ibises' appearance. One of my colleagues commented that the species's droll, downturned bill recalled visions of French Resistance leader Charles de Gaulle. In my mind ibises were not so pompous: I thought they resembled the late vaudevillian Jimmy Durante. Either way, ibises finished a distant second to the more stately harriers that I had been studying. Nevertheless, they were relatively large birds, and as was the case with harriers, I could study their feeding and breeding behavior at great distances. More importantly, ibises were extremely abundant at the North Inlet Estuary, and I quickly found that working with the species allowed me to collect data at a rate more than 10 times that to which I had been accustomed while working with harriers. I decided that maybe the appearance of ibises was not so funny after all.

My involvement with the topic of White Ibises has grown to include intensive studies of the feeding and breeding behavior of ibises at the North Inlet Estuary site, and of more than a dozen hand-reared captive ibises, as well as briefer studies of free-ranging ibises in Trinidad and Venezuela. The results are detailed in the remaining chapters of this book. But before moving on to my studies, I need to describe the setting: my South Carolina study site.

An Ecological Tour of Hobcaw Barony

My principal research site for ibis studies has been Hobcaw Barony, a 7,500-hectare (27-square-mile) tract of coastal land in northeastern South Carolina, several kilometers due east of the coastal port of Georgetown, 90 kilometers northeast of Charleston. Geographically, Hobcaw Barony occupies the southernmost portion of Waccamaw Neck, a narrow peninsula of Pleistocene and Holocene sand dunes that parallels the mainland and is separated from it by the Waccamaw River. Mud Bay, a shallow and appropriately named muddy northeastern extension of Winyah Bay, borders the property directly to the south, and the Atlantic Ocean lies directly to the east (Map 2.1). Pumpkinseed Island, an isolated 9-hectare chunk of salt marsh in the center of Mud Bay, annually hosts a multi-thousand-pair, mixed-species colony of wading birds. Although at least eight other species of wading birds nest on the island (Table 2.2), the colony is dominated by numerous nesting White Ibises, which typically constitute 50 to 80% of the breeding birds at the site (Bildstein et al. 1982).

The southeastern third of Hobcaw Barony consists of the North Inlet Estuary, a well-mixed, high-salinity, cordgrass ecosystem typical of the region's coastal plain (Pritchard 1967). The remainder of the site consists of southern maritime forests in well-drained upland areas and tupelo–cypress swamps in the lowlands. As for the details of the salient physical and biological features of the area, perhaps the best way to describe them is to offer an imaginary summertime tour of the site, similar to the one I was taken on when I first visited the area in 1979:

Binoculars and refractometer in hand, we smear our skin and clothes with insect repellent. (The local favorite is a particular brand of skin softener that seems to work as well as the more traditional repellents containing deet and certainly smells nicer.) Our boat trip begins on a rising tide in late May at Dirleton, an antebellum rice plantation, several kilometers north of the barony on the Pee Dee River. With headwaters in central North Carolina, the Pee Dee is the longest of four rivers (the Sampit, Waccamaw, and Black rivers are the other three) that join to form Winyah Bay before discharging into the Atlantic Ocean. Before leaving the dock, shortly after eight o'clock in the morning, we take our first water sample. The refractometer, an optical device that measures the refraction of light at a glass–water interface, allows us to estimate the water's salt content. Our sample reads 0%, indicating that we are in fresh water. Later, we will see the salinity increase as we approach the ocean-strength (i.e., 3.5%) salt water of the Atlantic.

The property around us is currently managed for wintering waterfowl. During summer the only waterfowl to be seen are Wood Ducks, a species whose cylindrical nesting boxes dot the flooded fields, and an occasional Mottled Duck, a nonmigrating American Black Duck look-alike that state wildlife officials have introduced to the area in an attempt to improve the fall hunting season. In late fall, these two species will be joined by several migratory species that breed further north. As we shove off from the landing we notice numerous wooden gates scattered along

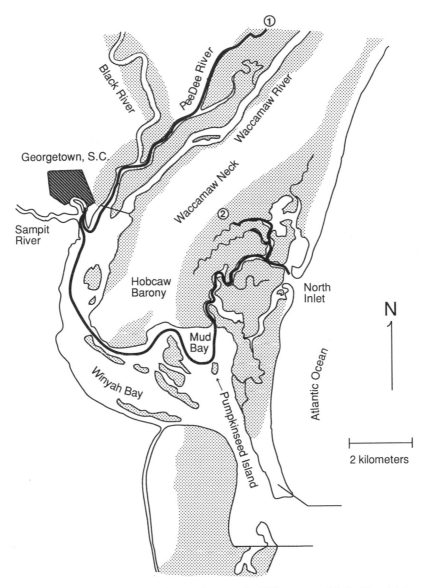

Map 2.1. Hobcaw Barony, at the southern end of Waccamaw Neck. The thick solid line traces the route of our hypothetical boat trip from the origin (number 1) to the end point (number 2). Stippled areas represent freshwater and brackish marshes.

Table 2.2   Species of wading birds nesting on Pumpkinseed Island, 1979–90

Species and breeding status	Yearly abundance
Super-abundant breeder	
White Ibis	Usually at least several thousand nests
Abundant breeder	
Great Egret	Usually at least several hundred nests
Snowy Egret	Usually at least several hundred nests
Tricolored Heron	Usually at least several hundred nests
Glossy Ibis	Usually at least 50 nests
Common breeder	
Little Blue Heron	Usually 10 to 30 nests; may not breed in some years
Black-crowned Night-Heron	Usually 10 to 30 nests; may not breed in some years
Occasional or rare breeders	
Cattle Egret	Up to five nests
Green-backed Heron	Only one nest found in only one of the study years
Least Bittern	Possibly breeds at site; no nests found, but adults frequently seen there during the breeding season

the diked area to our left. The impoundments, originally cypress swamps and tidal marshes, were converted to rice-producing fields with slave labor in the early 1800s. The wooden gates, still assiduously maintained, represent the lineal descendants of cleverly devised weirs that use tidal forces to flood and drain the fields. The impoundments' dikes, covered with Southern Bald Cypress, Elderberry, Marsh Mallow, Giant Reed, Poison Ivy, and various grasses, look hospitable enough. But as we pull in for a closer view, several large snakes, one of which appears to be a rather fat-bellied Eastern Cottonmouth, slither over the steep bank, and we decide not to disembark. Representatives of several species of mosquitoes and biting flies hover overhead as we rev the engine and continue downstream.

Half an hour later, the tea-colored, tannin-rich, oligotrophic waters of the Black River join us to the west as we travel through expansive horizons of 2- and 3-meter-tall Common Reeds, a cosmopolitan exotic that does well in disturbed wetlands. The refractometer reads 0.2% as we pass under a derelict concrete bridge that was once U.S. Highway 17, an important coastal artery, and is now a fishing pier for local residents. Several hundred meters farther, we reach a current four-lane span that was built in the 1970s in anticipation of the region's growing human population. A marina is to our left; its fleet of more than 30 deep-sea fishing boats, replete with oversized flying bridges, each festooned with the latest in electronic fish finders, signals the occurrence of the annual billfish tournament. The watercourse quickly widens as the more tidally influenced Waccamaw River joins us to our left. The intracoastal waterway is spotted with an intermittent stream of pleasure craft, as well as red and green U.S. Coast Guard channel markers. Precariously perched atop one of the markers is a huge stick nest, over the sides of which two nestling Ospreys are peering as they eagerly await their next meal. A mullet-laden adult screams while circling overhead, and we make a hasty retreat. As we go, we notice that at least six of the many cypress snags along the shoreline are also capped with Osprey nests, several of which appear to have been damaged by Hurricane Hugo, a catastrophic tropical storm that struck the area the previous fall.

Deciding to break for lunch, we cut back across the Pee Dee and Black rivers, and proceed up the Sampit River, the shortest of the bay's four arteries. Rounding a point of land to our right, we come upon Georgetown, a historic South Carolina seaport whose skyline reveals an odd mixture of 18th-century widow's walks and 20th-century steel and paper mills. Six shrimping trawlers, each with a characteristic white-tipped mast, are unloading to our right. The conspicuous tips, we are told, enable the local seafarers' deity to pinpoint and rescue sinking vessels. We tie up at the long dock and take another water sample. The refractometer reads 0.6%. After dining at a seafood restaurant, we visit the small but informative Georgetown Rice Museum. Then we return to the boat and cross the bay to Hobcaw Barony. It is already early afternoon, and we still have much to see.

The salty air suggests the approaching ocean. To the left pass the contiguous marshlands of Hare and Rabbit islands, beyond which we spot the roof of Bernard Baruch's Hobcaw House, a steel-framed brick edifice nestled amid a grove of Live Oaks. Loblolly Pine and oak cover most of the upland. The marshes along the bay are dominated by salt-tolerant Giant Cordgrass and by Black Needlerush. The former superficially resembles Common Reed, whereas the latter is a stiff 1- to 2-meter vegetative cover to which I almost lost an eye in 1984. Our refractometer reads 0.9%. We pass Frazier's Point, site of a Civil War battery, and weave among the Marsh Islands toward Pumpkinseed Island's wading-bird colony in Mud Bay.

As we approach Pumpkinseed Island, the fetid smell of addled eggs, recently drowned young, and wet guano belies the presence of a multithousand-nest colony of wading birds. Turning north, we pass within 100 meters of the site, stopping momentarily to watch herons, egrets, and ibises intermittently flying to and from the island, ferrying food to developing young. Several Royal Terns are fishing the bay, while a raft of adult and juvenile Brown Pelicans floats nearby. Although there is less than a meter of water under our bow, any people jumping over the side would find that keeping their heads above the waterline for long is impossible. Mud Bay's soft bottom consumes all. Our refractometer reads 1.6%.

Minutes later, we enter the pristine 3,000-hectare North Inlet Estuary, a mixture of meandering creeks, mud flats, treacherous oyster bars, and salt marsh. The term *estuary* is derived from the Latin *aestus*, meaning "heat" or "boil," undoubtedly in reference to the shifting tides that characterize such sites. Among formal scientific definitions, Pritchard's (1967) is the most widely cited: "An estuary is a semi-enclosed coastal body of water which has a free connection with the open sea and within which sea water is measurably diluted with fresh water derived from land drainage." North Inlet Estuary opens to the sea through both Winyah Bay and Mud Bay to the south and through North Inlet to the east. The estuary's freshwater input comes from small streams, forest runoff, and groundwater intrusion, as well as from the rivers flowing into Winyah and Mud bays. Representative of estuaries in the region, the site consists of approximately 70% salt marsh, 20% tidal meander, 5% mud flats, and 1% oyster reefs. Mean tidal range at the site (i.e., the vertical distance between average high and low tides) averages 1.5 meters. Most of the marsh is covered with Smooth Cordgrass, a salt-tolerant species capable of withstanding regular soakings of almost sea-strength brackish water. Its less salt-tolerant cousin, Giant Cordgrass, is limited to the southernmost sections of the marsh, areas that are closer to, and more heavily influenced by, freshwater input from the bay. Saltwort, Black Needlerush, Groundsel Bush, and Marsh Elder fringe the marsh in higher, less frequently inundated areas.

We enter the estuary through No Man's Friend, an appropriately named tidal meander with an ominous deltaic sandbar lurking below its surface. The refractometer now reads 2.0%. Several hundred meters further we pass by Oyster Bay, a shallow body of water whose benthic surface consists of a treacherous mosaic of soft mud and oyster reef. To our left, the dorsal fins of a mother Atlantic Bottlenose Dolphin and her offspring cut the surface. The two are working together to herd fishes into the shallows, where these potential prey become considerably more vulnerable. The mother turns and approaches to within several meters of the boat and raises her head in an apparent effort to inspect its contents. Next, the bobbing head of a female Loggerhead Turtle also appears.

We turn into Town Creek on a falling tide, careful to trace a channel marked by the red-topped posts that we and the watermen who crab the area have placed at irregular intervals along the tidal flows. Although the markers work well for the estuary's cognoscenti, their some-what haphazard placement is of little value to more casual visitors, and the area is seldom used by weekend recreationists. Slender Goat Island, a sandy hammock dominated by Live Oak, Red Cedar, and several species of pines, rises abruptly from the marsh to the left. Much of the island's woody vegetation, especially on the seaward side, is dead—a mute testi-mony to the ferocity of last fall's hurricane. Similar stands of dead pines can be seen along the entire edge of the marsh. An 18-meter (60-foot) metal watchtower pierces the island's knurled canopy. Originally erected by game wardens to replace a wooden tower that poachers had burned, the structure serves as an excellent vantage point for observing the feeding behavior of White Ibises. Our refractometer now reads 3.2%, close to full-strength seawater. Following Town Creek to the east, we quickly find ourselves at the North Inlet, the estuary's northern connection with the Atlantic Ocean. Taking another refractometer reading at the mouth of the inlet, we confirm what we already know: At 3.3% the water here is almost ocean-strength. Its salinity is diluted slightly only because the tide is still falling and because the less-dense brackish water tends to "float" atop the denser seawater. We quickly turn about and head for the Baruch Institute's field laboratory. The lab, which is situated at the forested edge of the estuary and is maintained by the University of South Carolina, is our base of operations in the field.

But first we detour into Bly Creek and find ourselves traveling southwest into a staked 66-hectare section of marsh at the base of the watchtower. This structure is my principal site for studying White Ibis feeding behavior. By now the creek is well drained, and tens of thousands of Sand and Mud fiddler crabs can be seen feeding along its muddy banks.

Turning about, we head for nearby Oyster Landing and the field lab. Low tide has arrived (alternate highs and lows follow at intervals of just over 6 hours) and, scraping bottom, we drag the boat the final few meters to the landing, carefully avoiding the pitfalls that would submerge our hip boots. Several hours after starting, our last water sample reads 3.2% salinity. Once ashore, we tour the old lab, a gutted shell courtesy of last fall's hurricane. Currently, all lab activities at the site, including ours, have been cramped temporarily into a trailer at the edge of the marsh, about 100 meters from where we have hauled our boat out of the water.

A three-hour tour along several stretches of the property's 145 kilometers (90 miles) of sandy roads reveals a series of successional pine forests amid the sandy ridges and swales. Areas that are not as well drained host Tupelo Gum and cypress swamps. During the trip, we pass several colony sites of the endangered Red-cockaded Woodpecker that inhabits the uplands. Active sites are easily identified by the greenish-white resin streaming from nesting and roosting cavities excavated on clustered older pines. The birds are nowhere to be seen. We do, however, chase White-tailed Deer, several black and roan Feral Hogs, and even a Gray Fox from the road in front of us. We also spot an Eastern Fox Squirrel. This lumbering larger cousin of the more widely distributed Eastern Gray Squirrel occurs in a variety of pelage patterns at the site, and the one we see is a black-bodied individual with white ear tufts, a white facial mask, and a grizzled tail.

After more than two hours in the uplands we venture into a cypress swamp, where saffron-colored Prothonotary Warblers greet us along an elevated boardwalk and a Pileated Woodpecker calls in the distance. Weaving through the swamp, we search in vain for the skulking alligator, sunning Copperhead, and roosting White Ibises I had guaranteed we would see. Yellowflies, mosquitoes, and no-see-ums abound, however, and we hastily retreat to the vehicle. Minutes later we are back at our starting point at the field station's dormitory complex, checking ourselves for ticks.

Local Weather

With the notable exception of devastating hurricanes, Hobcaw Barony's maritime climate is relatively benign. Winters at the site are mild, with

January daily temperatures averaging a minimum of 3°C (38°F) and a maximum of 14°C (58°F). Summers are notoriously hot and humid, with July daily minimum and maximum temperatures averaging 22 and 31°C (72 and 88°F), respectively (Barry 1980). Maximum temperatures exceed 32°C (90°F) about 30 days each summer. Temperatures in excess of 38°C (100°F) are exceptional, but even these levels are reached during some summers—usually over the course of several days, and all too often in conjunction with oppressively humid conditions. Ibises adjust their behavior at such times (see Chapter 5), and so do human observers, who have been known to scale back their otherwise ambitious schedules, consume incredible quantities of fluids, and complain loudly to lab-based colleagues upon returning from the field.

The area experiences a mini dry season from October through November, followed by increasing rainfall that peaks in March and April. A second, more variable "wet season" occurs from June through early September, when thunderstorms and tropical depressions occur regularly but in a somewhat unpredictable pattern. Sleet and snow are uncommon in the area, especially on the marsh, and ice rarely forms, even in fresh water.

Significant tropical storms and hurricanes occur every couple of years, usually in late summer to early fall, when the accompanying rains are much needed in the coastal plain. Although most storms cause little damage, devastating gales do pass through the area, usually in clusters, as they did during the 1890s, 1900s, and 1950s, when series of damaging hurricanes moved through the region. The most recent destructive storm was Hurricane Hugo, which struck the coast early on the morning of 22 September 1989. Winds in nearby Georgetown were estimated to have peaked at 112 kilometers (70 miles) per hour. In South Carolina alone, 35 deaths were attributed to the hurricane. The storm cut a 100-kilometer (62-mile) path of destruction through the state, where it downed more timber than did Hurricanes Frederick and Camille, the Mount St. Helens volcanic eruption, and the great Yellowstone National Park fires of 1988 combined.

Much more damaging than the wind, however, was the 4.3-meter (14-foot) wall of water that accompanied the storm. Riding atop an already high nocturnal tide at the site, the hurricane's storm surge barreled across the North Inlet Marsh, destroying the field lab at its edge, and penetrating several kilometers into the forest. The resulting saltwater intrusion killed many salt-intolerant trees, including extensive stands of the locally dominant Loblolly Pine. Numerous multihectare stands of pine were destroyed, the result of either windfall, salt spray, or saltwater intrusion. In addition—although now is still far too early to assess all of the long-term effects of the event at the site—it appears likely that a new marsh–forest boundary will be reestablished landward, with a new marsh extending into what was once a forested area.

Adding insult to injury, Southern Pine Beetles have opportunistically invaded the area in the wake of the storm. Although initial attacks of these ravenous insects were directed at stands of storm-stressed trees, the presence of this species at the site threatens adjacent healthy stands as well.

The Human History of Hobcaw Barony

The narrow peninsula of land due east of Georgetown is known as Waccamaw Neck. The area has a long and varied history, having played host to a succession of Amerindians, Spanish explorers, English settlers, French freedom fighters, antebellum indigo and rice plantation owners, and, most recently, 20th-century Wall Street financier and presidential confidant Bernard Baruch. As background for the ibis story, a brief digression into the human occupation of the site is in order. Over the centuries, human occupation and use of the area have so shaped the local landscape that, had humans not occupied the site, I sometimes wonder whether White Ibises would be using it today as they do.

The first Europeans to settle the area were Spanish. In 1521, Lucas Vasquez de Ayllon commissioned a voyage of exploration from Spain's Caribbean stronghold of Hispaniola to what the natives of the West Indies then called Chicora. Five years later, de Ayllon himself journeyed to Chicora and, together with about 500 Europeans, a few African slaves, and 90 horses, established the settlement of San Miguel in the vicinity of Winyah Bay. Although the colony's exact location remains in dispute, several authorities place it at Hobcaw Point on the southern tip of Waccamaw Neck. (Hobcaw is a native American name meaning "the land between the waters.")

Unfortunately for de Ayllon, the colony did not prosper. A malarial climate, poor nutrition, unfriendly natives, and numerous internal disputes doomed the settlement to rapid collapse. After the death of their leader in late October 1526, the 150 colonists who had survived the bitter winter of 1526–27 retreated to Hispaniola's Santo Domingo the following spring. Europeans did not return to Hobcaw for more than a century. And those who came next were English rather than Spanish.

As did the settlers in de Ayllon's time, in 1670 the English found the region to be sparsely inhabited by Winyah and Waccamaw Indians. According to an English census of 1715, the two tribes maintained seven villages in total, each with about 100 individuals. Native Americans ventured from the villages to collect fish and shellfish in nearby estuaries and roots from the surrounding uplands. Even today, remnants of their lengthy tenure at the site can be found, along with ample evidence of their impact on the landscape. Pottery shards abound on area beaches after storms buffet the area each fall. More importantly, the dozens of Red Cedars and Live Oaks that were uprooted by Hurricane Hugo's high winds and storm surge exposed a series of extensive oyster shell middens along the estuary's edge, confirming what many had suspected. The massive accumulations of shells, the result of routine oystering by indigenous Americans and more recent European inhabitants, have almost certainly stabilized the shape of the estuary's edge, enhancing the growth of trees along its borders and hammocks. White Ibises frequently use these trees as roosting sites during the day, and I suspect that human use of the site hundreds of years ago affects how ibises use the marsh today. Pumpkinseed Island also includes a large midden of oyster shells, on top of which many White Ibises nest each year.

Despite a pre-European history of stability, native American use of the area ended rather abruptly in 1715, after an unsuccessful insurrection against the English. Weary of what they believed to be unscrupulous trading practices, and fearing that the census conducted earlier in the year presaged widespread enslavement—not an unreasonable concern given that the English proprietors had granted their colonists the privilege of taking indigenous Americans as slaves in 1683—Waccamaw Neck's native inhabitants participated in a bloody but abortive regional uprising later known as the Yamesee War. As a result of their unsuccessful attempt to overwhelm the growing population of British colonists, many Winyah and Waccamaw Indians were killed outright. Those who survived and failed to slip away inland were captured and shipped to slavery on West Indian sugar plantations (Swanton 1946).

In 1718 when King George II, in an effort to solidify his grip on the throne, granted Lord Carteret the 7,500 hectares of land known as

Hobcaw, few indigenous inhabitants remained (Jones 1971) to contest his ownership of the land. Carteret, one of eight Lord Proprietors of the Carolinas, did not keep "Hobcaw Barony" for long, but sold the tract, sight unseen, to land speculator John Roberts in 1735. Roberts, in turn, subdivided and sold the property to "developers," individuals interested in the site's potential economic value. Initially, Hobcaw's forested uplands yielded what were then referred to as "naval stores" (pitch, tar, turpentine, rosin, and the like), essential supplies for the maintenance of Great Britain's vast colonial empire. But by the fall of 1777, when a hero of the French Revolutionary War, the Marquis de la Fayette, passed through the area on his way to Yorktown from his landing point on nearby North Island (Smith 1913), most of the site's uplands had been cleared for grain crops, indigo, and pasture. When upland agriculture proved too difficult on such sites, tidal wetlands bordering the Waccamaw River were diked and drained for what proved to be a fabulous rice culture (Porcher 1976).

Slave labor on a scale rivaling that of ancient Egypt, and the use of tidal floodgates, ensured extraordinary profits. On the eve of the American Civil War, Hobcaw held the crown jewels of southern antebellum agriculture: 13 major rice plantations, each producing about one-half million pounds of rice annually. Similarly productive plantations extended miles upstream, along tidal reaches of three of the region's major rivers. By the 1850s, nearby Georgetown was exporting as much rice as principal Asian ports in India and China (Rogers 1970).

The Civil War ended the era of low-cost labor and, with it, the region's economic prosperity. Rice plantations were severely crippled by the loss of their slaves, who made up 85% of the county's population in the mid-19th century and who literally provided the backbone of this economy. Eventually, even the largest and grandest plantations succumbed, the final blows being administered by a series of hurricanes that devastated the area in the 1890s and early 1900s.

As the plantations withered and died, "a second yankee invasion" coincidentally occurred (Rogers 1970). Wealthy northerners, many of whom had first seen the area during their service in the Civil War, began to acquire many of the derelict plantations as vacation retreats. Word quickly spread that opulent homes, together with some of the finest duck-hunting sites on the continent, could be had at bargain prices. One of the new aristocrats was South Carolina-born and New York-educated Bernard Baruch. Baruch, a wonder boy of his age, was a Wall Street partner at 25 and a millionaire at 30 (Baruch 1957). Adviser and confidant of U.S.

presidents from Woodrow Wilson to John Kennedy, Baruch's attraction
to coastal South Carolina was representative of his genre:

> In this hectic age of distraction, all of us need to pause every now
> and then in what we are doing to examine where the rush of the
> world and our own activities are taking us. . . . Having acquired
> this habit, I naturally grasped the opportunity to acquire a verita-
> ble Shangri-La in my native South Carolina—famed Hobcaw Bar-
> ony, whose sandy beaches and salt marshes once offered the
> finest duck hunting in the United States, with four rivers and a
> bay abounding in fish, vast stretches of almost primeval forest,
> and—no telephone. (Baruch 1957)

The aspects that attracted this financier to the barony—its naturalness,
the magnificence of its marshes and beaches, and perhaps most of all, its
seclusion (right down to the lack of a telephone)—are precisely what
attracted me to the site. The one difference was in our level of involvement:
Baruch purchased this backwater retreat and demanded its exclusive use.

Between 1905 and 1907, Baruch acquired 7,500 contiguous hectares along the southern tip of Waccamaw Neck, almost all of the original
barony granted to Carteret nearly 200 years earlier. Baruch maintained
his barony as a private hunting reserve, even to the point of stretching a
chain across the inlet to prevent trespassing from the ocean side. Much
of the land was left untouched, except for most of the woodland, which
Baruch allowed to be logged as a patriotic gesture during the early 1940s.
Most of all, Hobcaw was Baruch's getaway, a place where he could wile
away the hours, entertaining such luminaries as Winston Churchill,
Franklin Roosevelt, George Marshall, Omar Bradley, Jack London, Walter
Huston, and Billy Rose, as well as his many financial cronies. According
to newspaper accounts, the property was, at the time of its acquisition by
Baruch,

> the wildest part of South Carolina . . . like the tropics. . . . In the
> old reserve giant alligators have their homes and around it in tall
> pines Bald Eagles built their nests. Around the margin for miles
> turkeys and deer are found in abundance. In the winter it is a
> resting place for ducks and the shooting is often good. Every kind
> of marsh bird is found there, from herons wading on stilts to
> divers and bay birds. The Spanish curlew [White Ibis] is shot
> along the strand and yellowleg snipe, together with plover and

other species too numerous to catalogue, are all found there. . . .
An ornithologist or botanist would find here full exercise for his
faculties and field for endless research. (Anonymous 1905)

By the end of the Second World War, Baruch's interest in the property
began to wane, and he rarely visited the site, preferring instead to spend
time at Little Hobcaw, a more modest retreat some 65 kilometers (40 miles)
inland. However, his daughter, Belle, an avid equestrian and aviator,
remained an ardent fan of the barony and devoted much of her life to
maintaining its naturalness. Although she reluctantly permitted duck
hunting, Belle insisted that deer and other wildlife be allowed to roam
unharmed. Belle first purchased a portion of the property from her father
in the 1930s and finally acquired title to the entire barony by 1956. At the
time of her unexpected death in 1964, her father, who survived until 1965,
named in *her* honor the foundation that she had intended to establish in
his name.

Today, per Belle's wishes, Hobcaw Barony is managed by the
Belle W. Baruch Foundation as a natural laboratory for teaching and
research in forestry, marine biology, and conservation, in connection with
colleges and universities in the state. Two research institutes—one in
marine science and affiliated with the University of South Carolina, and
one in forestry and associated with Clemson University—attract numerous researchers and students who work on the uplands and marshes of
the site, as well as in the offshore waters nearby. During the mid-1980s
the National Science Foundation designated the barony as a Long-Term
Ecological Research Site, one of a group that eventually will include about
20 research sites in various ecosystems throughout the world.

3 Pumpkinseed Island and the Breeding Biology of White Ibises

A whimsical solution to a scientific conundrum:

> Long before the people without color arrived on their wooden is-
> lands pulled by billowing clouds caught in the branches of leafless
> trees, but not before liars had been forced into the bodies of fiddler
> crabs and condemned to walk sideways forever, North Inlet Salt
> Marsh was invited to a party celebrating the birth of his niece.
>
> At first North Inlet refused to go. He explained to his
> wife he had nothing to offer the daughter of his brother Hobcaw
> Forest. North Inlet was still smarting from the ridicule he had
> suffered one year earlier when he presented the baby's mother
> with a heart-shaped cordgrass wedding basket filled with black,
> sulfurous mud. Never again would he be embarrassed by such a
> meager gift.
>
> Later that day North Inlet's wife devised a secret plan.
> Revealing her husband's dilemma to her sister-in-law, she pointed
> out how empty the celebration would be if the baby's only uncle
> failed to attend. Later that night Hobcaw Forest learned of his
> brother's plight.
>
> After consulting with his uncle, Waccamaw River, Hob-
> caw commanded that all of the herons, egrets, and ibises living
> on his lands immediately transfer their nests to tiny Pumpkinseed
> Island in North Inlet. As soon as they did, their droppings began
> to fertilize the once barren marsh. Almost immediately numerous
> animals began to flourish in the marsh's tidal meanders. Shortly
> thereafter, the estuary was producing mountains of oysters,
> crabs, and shrimps, which North Inlet then bartered for the lum-
> ber he needed to build a cradle for his niece. At the same time,
> North Inlet's wife began to weave an accompanying mattress of

salt-marsh hay, while Pumpkinseed's wading birds plucked their feathers to provide down for a pillow.

Even now the winds whistle with news of this handsome gift, and of the bountiful land that produced it. The birds were so proud of the role they had played that, after holding council, they decided to return to Pumpkinseed Island to breed the following year. They continue to do so even now.

K. L. Bildstein

History of Pumpkinseed Island's Colony

Reports of White Ibises in coastal South Carolina date from Catesby's sightings in the early 18th century (Catesby 1731–47). Nevertheless, it was not until 1922 that the species was documented as breeding in the state. In that year, a noted amateur ornithologist and egg collector, Arthur T. Wayne, discovered approximately 100 pairs of ibises breeding on a derelict rice plantation north of Charleston (Wayne 1922). Wayne had been searching South Carolina for ibises and their eggs for decades. Twenty years after Wayne found the colony, it had grown to about 700 pairs and a second site was established in the Santee Delta, less than 30 kilometers (20 miles) south of Pumpkinseed Island (Sprunt 1944). Jim Parnell of the University of North Carolina at Wilmington first documented White Ibises breeding on Pumpkinseed Island when he recorded 2,000 pairs in 1968 (Parnell 1968). Local watermen suggest that ibises started breeding at Pumpkinseed many years earlier.

In the mid 1970s, Pumpkinseed Island and Drum Island (in Charleston Harbor, 90 kilometers [56 miles] southwest of Pumpkinseed) played host to about a quarter of the Atlantic Coast's breeding population of White Ibises (Osborn and Custer 1978). By the late 1980s, Pumpkinseed Island hosted the largest ibis colony north of Florida. Despite sporadic ibis breeding in the Okeefenokee Swamp during recent years (Stinner 1983), no large coastal ibis colonies have been found in Georgia. Since 1987, when ibises ceased using Drum Island, a colony on Battery Island in the mouth of the Cape Fear River in coastal North Carolina (approximately 100 kilometers [60 miles] north of Pumpkinseed) has been the only other multithousand-bird site in the region.

My initial trip to Pumpkinseed Island reminded me of the time my grandfather took me to a turkey farm. Even before Peter Frederick and I had landed on the island late one afternoon in May of 1980, my nose confirmed what I should have anticipated based on Peter's photographs of the site. In a good year, more than 10,000 pairs of White Ibises, together with thousands of other wading birds, crowd the tiny 9-hectare (22-acre) colony. From the air the island appears to be an enormous, but slightly misshapen, nonpareil candy—its dark brown organic mud speckled with countless white birds. On the ground, the sights, sounds, and smells quickly overwhelm human intruders.

Pumpkinseed Island is what ornithologists call a mixed-species colony. Thousands of nesting White Ibises share the site with other wading-bird neighbors, including Glossy Ibises, Great Egrets, Snowy Egrets, Cattle Egrets, Tricolored Herons, Little Blue Herons, Black-crowned Night-Herons, and Green-backed Herons. Other neighbors are Marsh Wrens, Boat-tailed Grackles, Common Moorhens, Clapper Rails, and even the notoriously elusive Black Rail. White Ibises are by far the most common species of breeding birds on the island. In most years this species easily outnumbers all other species combined.

Having spent three of the previous five summers diligently, and often unsuccessfully, searching for a few dozen cryptic Northern Harrier nests on an expansive 16,200-hectare (40,000-acre) marsh in central Wisconsin, I stood at the edge of the island in awe of what lay before me. There, quite literally, were thousands of nesting White Ibises, most of them incubating eggs or brooding chicks. The activity of dozens, if not hundreds, of nests could be seen and monitored from a single elevated blind. Studying the breeding biology of White Ibises was going to be quite different from studying Northern Harriers.

The number of White Ibises breeding on Pumpkinseed Island varies considerably from year to year. During the course of our studies, for example, estimated maximum numbers have ranged from no nesting pairs in 1990 to slightly more than 20,000 nesting pairs in 1987 (Figure 3.1).

Over the years, we have used several methods to census White Ibises. By far, our most accurate technique has been to have volunteers walk back and forth in a broad swath across the island, counting each nest (Figure 3.2). This procedure, however, is not only logistically difficult and physically strenuous for the surveyors (several volunteers have fainted during sweltering heat waves) but also disruptive to the birds. Therefore, we have also done aerial surveys, photographing the nesting colony from about 300 meters overhead. We then project the photographs

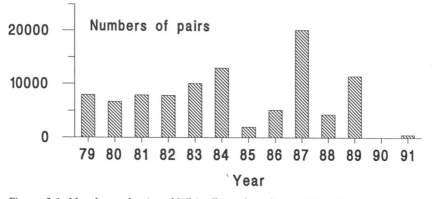

Figure 3.1. Numbers of pairs of White Ibises breeding on Pumpkinseed Island yearly, 1979–91.

Figure 3.2. Workers censusing nests on Pumpkinseed Island.

onto a paper-covered wall and mark and count each nest. Because Pumpkinseed Island is basically flat and its vegetation is low, almost all nesting White Ibises are visible from the air. The accuracy of the technique is quite high compared with the accuracy of ground counts (Frederick 1987a).

Population fluctuations similar to the ones we have observed are typical of White Ibises breeding elsewhere. The species is a nomad—a wetland wanderer—especially when it is selecting breeding sites. Although individual colony sites are traditional in the sense that many are used repeatedly, sometimes for decades, their use each year depends upon both the availability of local prey and the breeding conditions at other sites. Ibises hedge their bets. Like the prospective vacationer who, in an effort to maximize time in the sun, reserves space at several resorts and then waits for last-minute forecasts before deciding where to go, ibises apparently decide where to breed each spring only after investigating several alternatives.

The vacation analogy fits in all but one point: Ibises actually are looking for rainy weather, not trying to avoid it. For members of the family Threskiornithidae, significant rainfall determines not only the location but also the intensity of each year's breeding effort. Ibises in southern Africa (Bald Ibises) and in northern Africa (Waldrapp Ibises) typically forgo breeding during dry periods because reduced grazing and proscribed burning at these times reduces the availability of important insect prey (Robin 1973; Manry 1982, 1985a, 1985b). Individuals that do breed during dry years lay fewer eggs and are more likely to desert their young than are birds that breed in wetter years. Elsewhere in Africa, Sacred Ibises breed only after the beginning of the rainy season (Urban 1974a, Clark and Clark 1979). Nomadic breeding is also common to the several ibis species in Australia: These birds shift colony sites regularly, nesting only in areas with heavy flooding (Carrick 1962, Waterman et al. 1971, Woodall 1985). The same appears to be true for many neotropical ibis species (ffrench and Haverschmidt 1970, Luthin 1983), as well as for the nomadic Whitefaced Ibis in western North America (Ryder 1967).

Breeding White Ibises also respond to local rainfall (Bildstein et al. 1990). Perhaps the best example of the extent to which the species is dependent upon local rainfall comes from Jim Kushlan (1976), who reported that southern Florida's breeding population of White Ibises increased 35-fold in a wet year over what it had been during the previous drought year. We have documented similar, albeit less spectacular, fluctuations among White Ibises breeding at Pumpkinseed Island. Since 1979, ibis breeding intensity at this site has been closely correlated with the amount of precipitation occurring during the 6-month period preceding egg-laying season each May (see Chapter 7). In this region, abundant winter and early spring rainfall increases the amount of flooding in bottomland hardwood forests, which, in turn, enhances crayfish activity in the area. Because ibises at

Pumpkinseed Island depend heavily upon crayfishes as food for their young, rainy Carolina winters typically presage extensive breeding activity at the site. Dry winters are followed by reduced breeding.

Jim Kushlan discovered an intriguing phenomenon concerning the extent of White Ibis breeding activity in southern Florida. During the early 1970s, most ibises in the region bred at inland sites in and around the Florida Everglades, and only a small portion of the population nested along the coast. However, the smaller *coastal* colonies were more consistently successful from year to year than were the considerably larger *inland* colonies. Kushlan concluded that, whereas inland colonies served as the major recruitment source for the region's population, especially during wet years, coastal colonies ensured a continued source of young during drier years (Kushlan 1974). My analysis of Carolina's coastal colonies revealed that coastal colonies also exhibit greater annual stability than do southern Florida's inland colonies (Table 3.1). Furthermore, coastal colony sites show relatively greater stability regardless of their size (the coastal colonies of the Carolinas are considerably larger than the coastal colonies of southern Florida, but all are more stable than the inland colonies). Coastal colonies thus must be acting as safety nets for breeding ibises during hard times inland (i.e., droughts). This principle has important implications for the management and conservation of White Ibises: Coastal sites, regardless of their relative size, need to be protected to ensure the continued survival of regional populations of ibises.

How regional are ibis populations? Recently, I have come to suspect that ibises breeding in southern Florida belong to the same nomadic population as the birds I have been studying at Pumpkinseed Island. Evidence for this idea comes in the form of reciprocal fluctuations in the numbers of ibises breeding in southern Florida and at Pumpkinseed (when ibis numbers in South Carolina are low, those in southern Florida are high, and vice versa; see Bancroft 1989). Genetic studies of ibises breeding both South Carolina and Florida have supplied additional evidence (Stangel et al. 1991). If my suspicions are correct, the species will need to be managed across state boundaries to ensure its continued viability.

Courtship and Mating

White Ibises are extraordinarily conspicuous when they court and mate, and consequently this portion of their breeding cycle has been well stud-

Table 3.1   Annual variation in the numbers of White and Whitefaced ibises breeding at various colony sites

Species and location	Years Range	N	Mean	Number of pairs per year Range	CV[a]
White Ibis					
The Everglades, Fla.[b]	1958–73	16	2,231	0–12,400	186%
Battery Island, N.C.[c]	1963–85	10	2,604	6–4,849	57%
Drum Island, S.C.[d]	1958–86	7	6,907	387–20,000	106%
Pumpkinseed Island, S.C.[e]	1968–89	14	5,793	1,976–20,158	67%
Whitefaced Ibis[f]					
Knudsen Marsh, Utah	1968–79	10	273	0–950	119%
Bear River Club, Utah	1968–79	10	1,753	0–4,980	94%
Bear River Refuge, Utah	1968–79	9	669	0–2,560	77%

[a]The coefficient of variation (CV) of a sample (i.e., standard deviation × 100/sample mean) enables direct comparisons of the extent of variation in samples with substantially different means (Sokal and Rohlf 1969).
[b]Based on data in Kushlan (1974) for ibises breeding at several colonies near and in the Everglades National Park.
[c]Based on data in Adams (1963), Custer and Osborn (1977), Parnell and Soots (1979), Allen-Grimes (1982), Shields (1985), and Bjork (1986).
[d]Based on data in Beckett (1965), Osborn and Custer (1978), and Post (1990).
[e]Based on data in Parnell (1968), Osborn and Custer (1978), Bildstein et al. (1990), and my unpublished data.
[f]Based on data in Steele (1984).

ied. Indeed, the scientific literature is crammed with detailed accounts of ibis reproductive biology. (Those interested in learning more about this aspect of the species's life history should consult Palmer 1962, Kushlan 1974, Rudegeair 1975, or Frederick 1985b and 1987b.)

The first White Ibises usually return to Hobcaw Barony each spring in mid-March. Within days, small flocks of several dozen to several hundred individuals can be seen engaging in elaborate display flights, the sine qua non of ibis courtship. Typically, such flocks coalesce above the eventual colony site at Pumpkinseed Island, then the birds depart in all directions while engaging in prolonged series of aerial acrobatics. This display can only be likened to mass pandemonium. Courtship flights are most common between late morning and late afternoon, especially on turbulent days following heavy rains. Although ibises are quite capable of flying in strict formation when they choose to do so, little if any flock coordination is apparent during courtship. Individual birds can be seen rising though the amorphous three-dimensional flock, before turning and, with partially folded wings, plummeting toward the ground in an erratic and seemingly uncontrolled gyre. Such maneuvers may help synchronize the reproductive behavior and physiology of the birds.

Within a week of such flights, small flocks of "bachelors" can be seen flying slow and low over Pumpkinseed Island, their long bills pointed downward, searching for nesting sites. Groups of males often land during this time, presumably to inspect potential breeding locales more thoroughly. At first, most landings are brief, but gradually flocks settle in certain areas and males begin to engage in ritualized display preening, head rubbing, and bill popping. Male ibises are uncharacteristically aggressive at this time, and numerous fights ensue, many of which result in extensive bloodletting. A hand-reared male ibis named Willard behaved similarly. Although our captive flock has been generally demure and unassuming, Willard, one of our larger hand-reared males, was so aggressive when courting each spring that he physically attacked his keepers whenever they entered the aviary to feed him and his mate. Fortunately, by the time his chicks hatched, Willard's enthusiasm waned somewhat, and the keepers once again could clean the area under his nest with minimal disturbance.

Female ibises, which are notably smaller than the males (Kushlan 1977d, Bildstein 1987) and have conspicuously shorter bills (Figure 3.3), are somewhat cautious at this time when approaching prospective mates. Nevertheless, they too are combative, although decidedly less so than their mates. On rare occasions, females will fight with one another, sometimes viciously, especially when two of them are simultaneously attracted to the same displaying male.

Among White Ibises of either sex, aerial disputes are rare. Most confrontations are brief skirmishes lasting but a few seconds. However, on several occasions, I have watched especially pugilistic males engage in prolonged bouts of feather pulling and bill dueling. One such bout resulted in bloodied faces for both participants. Eye injuries, facial scars, and crippled legs, all of which are more common among male ibises (Kushlan and Bildstein 1992), attest to the volatility of these encounters.

In addition to being more aggressive during courtship, White Ibises also take on a decidedly different appearance at this time. Although the species does not produce the elegant courtship feathers, or "aigrettes," that are characteristic of many wading birds, White Ibises do undertake a substantial make-over of their own. Except during the 2- to 3-week courtship period, the bill of an adult ibis is a somewhat drab salmon pink or flesh color, as are its legs and the unfeathered portions of the face and

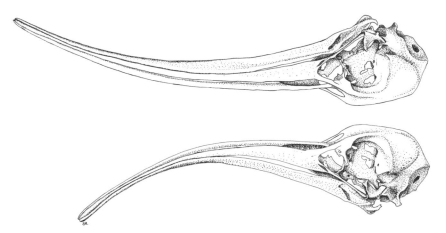

Figure 3.3. Skulls of White Ibises: *top*, male; *bottom*, female. Drawing by M. Davis.

head. All of that drabness changes during courtship. Within days, the pale face, legs, and bill deepen to a radiant geranium. Shortly thereafter, the bill begins to darken, and the tip becomes ebony-colored (Figure 3.4). (Some White Ibises breeding in the Venezuelan llanos develop entirely jet black bills, as do Scarlet Ibises in that region [Ramo and Busto 1985b]). Both male and female ibises undergo this color metamorphosis, which is accompanied by the simultaneous development of an exaggerated gular pouch, or throat sack. The pouch, which consists of a mass of sagging facial skin projecting from the base of the lower mandible (Figure 3.4), has been reported to be larger overall in females than in males (Kushlan 1974, Rudegeair 1975). Even so, several of the captive males we have kept through breeding age developed pouches that were as least as large as those of the females. Although the exact function of the gular pouch is unknown, Rudegeair suggested that it might be useful visually during courtship displays or that it might serve to alter the pitch of honking vocalizations at these times. Whatever its purpose, this striking feature vanishes shortly after the time of egg laying, almost as quickly as it appears.

The precise mechanisms responsible for these physical changes are unknown. Presumably, the transformation is mediated by hormones, the release of which may be triggered by environmental conditions (Kushlan 1976), display behavior, or both. Research in this area is almost nonexistent. However, as a result of a serendipitous phone call that I

Figure 3.4. A female White Ibis: *top*, in courtship coloration and with gular pouch; *bottom*, out of courtship coloration. Drawing by M. Davis.

made in 1986, I now know that diet plays at least a supporting role in the color changes.

During the summer of 1986, my colleague Jim Johnston, graduate student Toni De Santo, and I had collected several recently hatched chicks to monitor their growth and development under different dietary regimes (see Chapter 8). We had also decided to try breeding some of these birds in captivity. Maintaining birds in captivity for long periods is hard enough, but keeping them in such good shape that they will breed is even more difficult. The four aviaries available to us at the Savannah River Ecology Laboratory near Aiken, South Carolina, seemed spacious enough. The climate was right. And we appeared to have enough birds to induce breeding. But what about their diet? Unless the birds were fed a proper diet, successful breeding would be unlikely. I then thought of Ron Morris, Curator of Birds at the North Carolina State Zoo. Ron was managing a small breeding colony of Scarlet Ibises in his collection. I called and asked for help. Ron was adamant about the diet he fed his birds, and Jim, Toni, and I decided to adopt all of his suggestions.

In January of 1987, we began feeding our captive flock a mixture of fish meal, shrimp meal, dog food, and horse meat, together with vitamin and mineral supplements. On top of all this we added Ron's secret ingredient, a dash of canthaxanthin. Canthaxanthin is one of the beta carotenes, a group of vitamin A precursors responsible for the pink and red colors found in many of the invertebrates that ibises typically feed on in the wild. Ron had suggested adding this pigment to the diet because trial and error had taught zookeepers that a diet supplemented with beta carotene prevented brightly colored wading birds such as Scarlet Ibises and flamingos from gradually losing their colorful plumage in captivity. The pigments are manufactured by numerous plants, fungi, and bacteria, but most animals, including birds, are unable to construct them de novo from their constituent elements. Therefore, such animals must include these pigments in their diet, if they are to use them.

Painstaking examinations of the blood and feathers of Scarlet Ibises and flamingos revealed that canthaxanthin was a major beta carotenoid in these species (Fox 1975). If Ron's dazzling flock of Scarlet Ibises was any example, the beta carotene supplement worked well, at least in that color morph. But what would this treatment do for *White* Ibises? Aside from providing them with an important precursor for vitamin A, would it also enhance the color changes that occur when these birds court each spring? I hoped so. Research had suggested that beta carotenes were responsible for the vibrant leg and facial skin of flamingos, as well as for their colorful feathers (Fox 1975), and the assumption that the same would be true for White Ibises seemed reasonable. A modest experiment was in order.

Susan McDowell, who was then in charge of maintaining our captive flock, and I decided to test this simple hypothesis. We did so by splitting the flock into two groups, each containing roughly equal numbers of males and females, and each maintained in a separate aviary. One of the groups (our treatment flock) was given a diet with canthaxanthin, while the other (our control flock) received the same diet but without the carotenoid. We began our experiment in January of 1988.

Our results, although based on an extremely small sample size, suggested that canthaxanthin did intensify the color changes that occur in the bills, legs, and faces of White Ibises at the time of courtship. During the spring of 1988, for example, all seven of the birds on the pigmented diet clearly showed more color when courting than did the seven birds on the unsupplemented diet. In fact, none of the birds without canthaxanthin ever assumed the brilliant colors typical of courting ibises, and none appeared to court as persistently as did their more pigmented counterparts. Furthermore, whereas four of the individuals on the canthaxanthin diet eventually paired and produced eggs that spring, none of the control birds managed to do so. Much the same occurred in 1989, when again the only birds to produce young were those receiving the carotenoid.

We have not yet been able to determine whether color change alone was responsible for the differences in breeding activity, or whether canthaxanthin acted indirectly by augmenting circulating levels of vitamin A. Either way, our results demonstrate that the presence of carotenoids in the diet of White Ibises increases the likelihood of successful mating in the species. Whether or not free-ranging birds expressly select prey with high levels of beta carotenes specifically to achieve this effect awaits further study.

Once a male White Ibis establishes his display territory, he begins to solicit females in earnest. Each male does so with a repertoire of ritualized presentations, which usually includes the bill-snap display, head bobbing, head rolling, display preening, and feather ruffling. Enticed by these antics, a female cautiously approaches in a crouched posture with her feathers compressed and slicked back, the antithesis of the displaying male, apparently in an attempt to avoid eliciting an aggressive response. Initially, the female is rebuffed by the seemingly schizophrenic male. Eventually, however, the male relents, signaling acceptance by holding his bill agape, softly honking, and slowly raising and lowering his head. Shortly thereafter, the male extends his neck over the female's and drapes his bill over hers in what appears to be an attempt to entwine the two. Having courted, the pair copulates repeatedly over the course of the next several weeks (Figure 3.5).

On Pumpkinseed Island, White Ibis courtship and mating, which peak in April or May each year, are highly synchronized within "neighborhoods" (Frederick 1987b); as a result, most eggs hatch within days of the nearest neighboring eggs. Nevertheless, late arrivals on the breeding scene, as well as birds whose eggs and chicks had been flooded earlier (as discussed below), can sometimes be seen courting and laying eggs well into June.

Ibis Infidelity

It had long been assumed that White Ibises, like most birds and unlike most mammals, were monogamous in their mating habits. That is, it was

Figure 3.5. White Ibises courting and copulating on Pumpkinseed Island. Photographs courtesy of P. Frederick.

thought that male and female ibises, at least within individual courting and mating periods, paired with a single member of the opposite sex and remained faithful to that mate during the nesting cycle. No observers had noticed a pattern in this species of bonding with two or even three mates simultaneously (i.e., bigamous or trigamous behavior) or mating with several individuals in close synchrony without the formality of courtship (i.e., promiscuous behavior). We now know otherwise. Jim Kushlan's (1973a) provocatively titled article "Promiscuous Mating Behavior in the White Ibis" dismantled the somewhat Victorian notion of the trustworthy ibis spouse. Kushlan's account described several incidents of promiscuous mating among five pairs of ibises that were nesting close to each other. Since that initial report, what have come to be called "extra-pair copulations," or EPCs, have been seen on numerous occasions by several researchers (Kushlan 1973a; Frederick 1987b, 1987c).

The promiscuous behavior of White Ibises on Pumpkinseed Island has been studied in considerable detail by Peter Frederick (1985b) during the breeding seasons of 1979–83. Peter's work, together with my observations at the site, leaves little doubt as to the lack of fidelity among White Ibis mates. Even relatively brief observations of individual ibis neighborhoods soon take on all the trappings of a daytime soap opera. Peter has estimated that between one-third to one-half of all copulation attempts on Pumpkinseed Island occur between members of different pairs of ibises and that, in an average year, over 95% of all individuals (male and female) take part. Although females sometimes "protest" the advances of males to whom they are not paired, and although males sometimes peck at, pull feathers from, and even bloody females about the head before engaging in EPCs, most females offer little, if any, resistance during most copulation attempts. When females do resist, males typically walk to the next nest and try again. But EPCs are not without risk. A male is more likely to be interrupted—either by other interlopers or by the female's own mate—when performing an EPC than when copulating with his own mate, and lengthy brawls often ensue. As a result, we often see bloodied males throughout the courtship period.

Customarily, a male White Ibis reduces the chance of cuckoldry by remaining close to his mate throughout most of her fertile period, even though this often means forgoing regular feeding trips off the island. As is often the case in other species, it is the male's nearest neighbors, rather than intruding males from more distant locations, that pose the greater threat.

How successful are EPCs? Peter's observations suggest that about one-quarter of the White Ibis females he watched were involved in at least one EPC that could have produced a fertile egg. Overall, however, he estimates that a maximum of 6% of all fertilizations occurred as a result of EPCs. Male ibises expend considerable time and effort protecting the paternity of the chicks they help rear by closely guarding their mate throughout her fertile period. However, there is no indication that males with especially promiscuous mates are less likely to care for their putative offspring than are males with more chaste partners. Also, there is no evidence that especially promiscuous males attend to offspring other than those in their home nest, or that they pay less attention to their young than do more faithful males.

Why do White Ibises behave promiscuously instead of remaining faithful to their mates? One possibility is that especially promiscuous males produce more young. In a study where genetic markers were used to determine paternity in Red-winged Blackbirds, researchers found that as many as half of the nests they examined contained at least one EPC-produced nestling—a finding that suggests that, in this species at least, males achieve more than 20% of their reproductive success by such promiscuity (Gibbs et al. 1990). However, even if ibises had similar reproductive success through EPCs, if all males were equally successful in their endeavors to copulate outside of their pair bonds, none would gain any obvious advantage over the others. The variation among individual ibises in the number of EPCs they perform, and the costs they accrue as participants, needs to be examined in greater detail.

On the other hand, several researchers have hinted that female White Ibises might increase their fitness in such a system, because multiple parentage within clutches increases the genetic variability therein. However, increased variability within clutches also might produce greater competition among nestlings, which, in turn, could increase nestling mortality within broods. Another possible explanation is that especially attractive males might be a limited resource at the site. In such a case, females might pair with the less attractive males—thus deceiving them into caring for the future offspring—but actually copulate with only the more attractive extra-pair males. Any, all, or none of these hypotheses may be responsible for the way that ibises mate (Frederick 1987b). Whatever the reason (or reasons), EPCs appear to be an established way of life among the White Ibises of Pumpkinseed Island.

Selection of the Nest Site

Although I have had difficulty predicting exactly how many individuals of each species will nest at Pumpkinseed Island in any given year, predicting in which type of vegetation each species will nest has never been difficult. Each year the colony's inhabitants settle into discrete neighborhoods at the site, with different species or groups of species characteristically occupying different vegetation types. Great Egrets, Snowy Egrets, Cattle Egrets, and Black-crowned Night-Herons, for example, almost always build their nests in and under the Marsh Elder that grows along the northeastern edge of the island, whereas White Ibises and Tricolored Herons nest almost exclusively in herbaceous vegetation, usually in Black Needlerush, Saltmarsh Bulrush, or Giant Cordgrass. Glossy Ibises nest in both Marsh Elder and herbaceous vegetation, usually in areas where these two vegetation types intermingle.

The nests of White Ibises are not intermingled as much with those of the other species, but the nests of many of the other birds are, and the results are often surprising. Consider, for example, the intriguing relationship that exists between Great Egrets and Snowy Egrets nesting at the site. Each spring Great Egrets arrive several weeks earlier than Snowy Egrets. After briefly courting, most Great Egrets construct nests high in the Marsh Elder canopy, usually about 0.5 or 1.0 meter above the ground. By the time the Snowy Egrets arrive several weeks later, most of the seemingly prime upper canopy of Marsh Elder is teeming with nesting Great Egrets. Snowies proceed to build their nests lower in the canopy, and many breed directly on the ground. A similar vertical partitioning of the nesting resource between these two egrets occurs at other colonies as well, including nearby Drum Island. At first I believed that this vertical stratification was simply the result of the earlier nesting and larger Great Egrets taking the best sites, and Snowy Egrets nesting at whatever sites remained. That Snowy Egrets actually might be choosing to nest below Great Egrets, rather than being forced to do so by their larger cousins, became apparent only after a hurricane rearranged the island's vegetative cover.

In late September 1989, Hurricane Hugo stripped Pumpkinseed Island of almost half its Marsh Elder, thereby creating numerous isolated patches of vegetation where a continuous stand once had been. The number of nesting Great Egrets declined substantially the following year, apparently because of the loss of potential nest sites. The next spring, most of the surviving Marsh Elder was quickly crowded with nesting Great Egrets, but several isolated patches remained unused. Additional birds nested on portions of a huge detrital wrack that the storm had deposited on the island, and a few nested directly on the ground, usually in places where Marsh Elder had existed the previous spring. When Snowy Egrets returned en masse several weeks later, I expected them to place their first nests in the Marsh Elder that had been left vacant by the Great Egrets. However, none did so. What they did was crowd in and build almost all of their nests underneath existing Great Egret nests, even though this scheme required that most of the nests be located directly on the ground. The choice was not without cost: A month later, all but a few of these ground nests were washed away during a series of especially high spring tides that swept across the island, while most raised ground nests (including almost all of the Great Egret nests) remained intact. The only conclusion I can draw from these observations is that Snowy Egrets actively choose to nest in the immediate vicinity of Great Egrets, perhaps because the larger size of the Great Egrets affords the smaller snowies a degree of protection from such avian predators as crows and gulls. Support for this notion comes from the fact that Glossy Ibises, Cattle Egrets, and Black-crowned Night-Herons, too, tend to place their nests under those of the larger Great Egrets, although these three species appear to be far less slavish than Snowy Egrets in doing so.

We frequently find the nests of four, and sometimes even five, species of wading birds clustered within several meters of one another in the island's shrub thicket. Regrettably, all is not the peaceable kingdom that such a scene initially suggests. The Black-crowned Night-Heron has an alternative, or at least an additional, reason for building its nest close to those of other species of wading birds. Nestling Black-crowned Night-Herons—which, gram for gram, rank among the most belligerent and pugnacious birds I have ever handled—are notorious for their habit of eating the nestlings of other wading birds. Almost as soon as nestling night-herons are ambulatory, usually at about 2 to 3 weeks of age, they begin to walk through the colony, looking for unattended young. Nestlings of this species are the ultimate ground-based nursery bullies. Although I have learned to respect night-herons for what they are, I do admit having felt a bit of righteous indignation the first time I saw a nestling skulking about with the toes of a Snowy Egret extending from its stuffed gape. Adult night-herons pose an even greater threat because they are airborne and can cover the entire island to search for their victims.

Indeed, one of the problems my students and I have faced while working in the colony is that of Black-crowned Night-Herons taking advantage of our presence to pluck temporarily unprotected nestlings from their nests.

The White Ibises of Pumpkinseed Island rarely nest close to other species of wading birds, nor do they appear to do so at other mixed-colony sites (Spendelow and Patton 1988). Groups of several dozen to several thousand White Ibises typically nest in tight subcolonies, usually within several meters of their nearest neighbor, and at considerably greater distances from most of the other species of wading birds nesting at the site. At Hobcaw Barony, White Ibises usually arrive several weeks after most of the other species have already begun to breed. Most of the population settles among the island's grassy vegetation, often in low-lying areas. That they continue to do so even during years when patches of the more substantial Marsh Elder are unoccupied leads me to suspect that White Ibises actually prefer to nest in grassy vegetation at the site. Indeed, the few White Ibises that do nest in woody vegetation at the site are usually the last individuals to arrive. On Pumpkinseed Island most ibises build their nests in clumps of Black Needlerush, although in recent years Giant Cordgrass and Saltmarsh Bulrush have also been used extensively. Nests are usually constructed close to one another, and at this site small groups of several dozen to almost 100 pairs of ibises tend to build in close synchrony. Different portions of the island are used in different years (Map 3.1), and although some areas of the island appear to be regularly favored or avoided, I have been embarrassingly consistent in my inability to predict where the first subcolonies will be built each year.

Building and Filling the Nest

Once a pair of White Ibises bonds, and regardless of who eventually fertilizes the eggs, nest building begins in earnest. Rudegeair (1975) suggested that in Florida the female chooses the actual nest site, which is usually located near the display site, and then proceeds to build most of the nest by herself. My observations on Pumpkinseed Island are similar. Construction, which occurs throughout the day, is usually completed within a week. Not to be outdone by their mates, many males assist in nest construction, even to the point of stealing material from neighboring nests while doing so. Fighting for nest material, which can be ferocious,

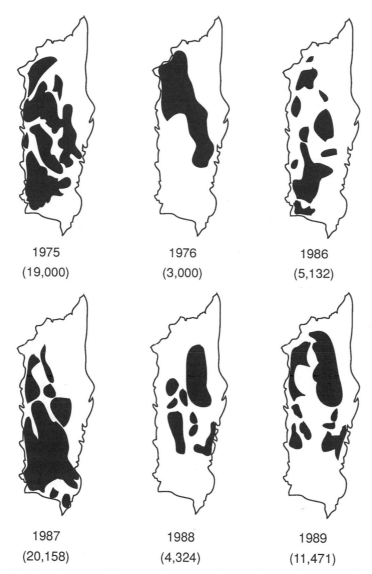

1975
(19,000)

1976
(3,000)

1986
(5,132)

1987
(20,158)

1988
(4,324)

1989
(11,471)

Map 3.1. Locations (and, in parentheses, numbers) of pairs of nesting White Ibises on Pumpkinseed Island, 1975–76 and 1986–89.

is frequent at this time, even when nesting material appears to be plentiful nearby. Some of the more lengthy encounters, which typically include prolonged bill dueling, draw blood. At Pumpkinseed Island, nests are vulnerable to pilfering even after eggs have been laid. And in the absence of either parent, a nest can be dismantled, and its eggs destroyed, within minutes. Hence, breeding pairs rarely leave their nests unattended once building begins.

Throughout much of their range, White Ibises fabricate their nests primarily from twigs (Hammatt 1981, Kushlan and Bildstein 1992). At Pumpkinseed Island, however, most nests are constructed from herbaceous vegetation. Many are built almost entirely from live vegetation growing in the immediate vicinity of the nest. Almost all are supported by rooted clumps of grassy vegetation that the ibises simply weave together, apparently in the same manner as ibises nesting in saw grass in the Florida Everglades construct their nests (Kushlan 1973b). The edifice is often bolstered with twigs and additional herbaceous vegetation brought in from other areas at the site. Human-manufactured items, including paper, burlap, rope, lumber, Styrofoam, and the all-too-ubiquitous and potentially lethal plastic six-pack ring, also appear regularly in nests. Indeed, certain ibises inexplicably accumulate large caches of such items.

Mated pairs exhibit considerable variation in their building efforts. At Pumpkinseed Island each year, at least a few individuals construct nests that are fully four to five times taller and somewhat wider than those of their nearest neighbors. Nevertheless, most White Ibis nests are modest see-through affairs, resembling more closely the ramshackle platforms built by Mourning Doves than the well-crafted cup nests of more industrious species such as the American Robin. The nests measure between 20 and 35 centimeters in diameter, and are usually placed about half a meter from the ground. Each year, however, many nests are built directly on the ground, and others that are built in shrubs hover more than a meter above the surface of the marsh. Elsewhere, researchers have reported that ibises line their nests with live mosses and cypress leaves before egg laying (Wayne 1922, Stephens 1950). I have never seen them do so at Pumpkinseed Island, perhaps simply because such items are not available at the site.

Within neighborhoods, nests are built in close synchrony, typically within 4 to 7 days of each other. As a result, portions of the island that are devoid of nests one week can be teeming with life the next. On Pumpkinseed Island, nearest neighbor distances (measured from the center of one nest to the center of the next) average between 50 and 80 centimeters (Frederick 1985b, my unpublished data), just far enough to be out of pecking range. Similar high-density nesting has been reported at other colony sites (Rudegeair 1975, Girard and Taylor 1979).

White Ibises often steal material from each others' nests, especially when initiating construction. Reciprocal theft of nesting material is common, with individuals alternately playing victim or thief, depending upon who is and who is not at the nest. Even so, I have never seen previously flooded and abandoned nests, which are typically abundant after catastrophic spring tides, reused by other birds. Whether such nests are ignored because they often contain decaying carcasses, the remains of which might pose a health threat, because persistent ectoparasites reside therein, or simply because their flood-prone nature has been revealed, is unknown. An extensive search of the literature produced a single account of ibises reusing their nests: Allen-Grimes (1982) reported that 12% of the nests she studied at Battery Island in coastal North Carolina were reused, and that young did fledge from such sites.

Once a nest is complete, egg laying begins within the week. Eggs are laid at 1- to 2-day intervals, usually before dawn. On Pumpkinseed Island, clutches tend to be larger earlier in the season, when many females lay four or five eggs, and then later two-egg clutches become more common. On rare occasions, we have found six, and even seven, eggs in a single nest. A close inspection often reveals two sets of three or four slightly different eggs. This evidence suggests that two females have been involved, a phenomenon referred to as egg dumping. We have not yet had the time to follow the course of such nests in detail. However, we have never counted more than five young in a single nest, so perhaps larger "clutches" meet with only mixed success.

Unlike the other nine species of wading birds nesting on the island—all of which lay uniformly colored eggs that are pale bluish green (Great Egret, Green-backed Heron, Little Blue Heron, Snowy Egret, Tricolored Heron, Black-crowned Night-Heron, Least Bittern), light blue (Cattle Egret), or glossy green (Glossy Ibis) (Palmer 1962)—White Ibises lay cream to pale bluish-green eggs covered with distinctive light to dark brown splotches that often vary from clutch to clutch. Although this remarkable incongruity has greatly simplified our task of identifying the nests of White Ibises, it has also caused some consternation. Why are White Ibises so different, even from Glossy Ibises, in this respect? Had White Ibises suffered heavier egg predation than any other species at the site, and had egg splotching hence evolved as camouflage to reduce this mortality factor?

To test this hypothesis, two of the students working on the project during the summer of 1990 decided to conduct an experiment. During June and July, Tanja Crockett and Philippa Shepherd spent several days staining chicken eggs they had bought at a local market. Half of the eggs were dyed to resemble the uniformly bluish-green eggs of the Great Egret, and the others were dyed cream and then speckled with dark brown to resemble the eggs of the White Ibis. Several days later Tanja and Pippa carefully placed the eggs in 30 abandoned Glossy Ibis nests located in a stand of Giant Cordgrass on the island. Fifteen nests each received a "clutch" of two Great Egret egg look-alikes, and another 15 received a clutch of two ibis egg look-alikes. The students returned to note the fate of the eggs 2 and 4 days later. However, this initial run might have been compromised somewhat because several of the Glossy Ibis nests were in denser vegetation than others, and eggs placed therein probably had been less visible to aerial predators than eggs placed in other nests. For this reason, we carried out two additional runs of the experiment several weeks later, using abandoned Great Egret nests that were all clearly visible from above. The results of all three runs were similar. There was no hint of an advantage for splotched eggs (i.e., all statistical probabilities of a significant difference were greater than 0.10). In fact, in one of the runs splotched eggs were slightly, although not significantly, *more* vulnerable to aerial predation than were unsplotched eggs.

Why did our experiment fail to produce the expected result? One possibility is that aerial predation at Pumpkinseed Island simply was not great enough to produce the anticipated species effect. Or splotching may be a response to ground predation, which rarely occurs on the island. On the other hand, splotching may have nothing to do with predation. For example, female ibises may use these marks to personalize their eggs, thereby increasing their ability to detect and avoid egg dumping. A final possibility is that splotching has no adaptive function in White Ibises. Our current inability to explain this aberrancy indicates that, even after my 11 years of White Ibis studies, much remains unknown about this species.

4   Colonial Nesting

For every complex problem there is a simple answer *and it is wrong*.

H. L. Mencken

As soon as I laid eyes on the wading-bird colony on Pumpkinseed Island, an irritating series of questions began to rattle my brain: Why do White Ibises nest colonially (and why so close to one another)? And why do they usually nest with other species of wading birds? How did Pumpkinseed Island come to be used as a colony site (and why was this site chosen from among many possible islands)? Below, I attempt to answer each of these questions in turn.

Why Do Birds Nest in Colonies?

Approximately 87% of the world's 9,000 species of birds nest in solitary pairs (Lack 1968). Nevertheless, colonial nesting does occur in birds, and in some taxonomic groups it is quite common. Well over half of all wading birds, for example, nest colonially, as do as at least two-thirds of the world's ibises (Krebs 1978, Archibald et al. 1980, Luthin 1983). Indeed, in many species of ibises, individual pairs rarely nest alone.

Current explanations for why some birds nest in colonies originate from the suggestions of British ornithologist David Lack (1966, 1968). Lack suggested that two major selective factors favored colonial nesting: (1) increased avoidance of predators, and (2) the more efficient exploitation of food resources. Several cogent modifications and expansions of Lack's ideas have since been proposed. (For more thorough, although not necessarily more enlightening, reviews of the topic, interested readers should consult Ward and Zahavi 1973, Krebs 1978, Burger 1981, Kharitonov and Siegel-Causey 1988, and Siegel-Causey and Kharitonov 1990.)

One of Lack's suggestions was that solitary foragers would nest colonially only if such an action were to decrease the risk of nest predation. For example, a species would be expected to nest colonially if nesters could deter approaching predators better by acting as a group at the colony site than by acting alone at a solitary nesting site. Another advantage to nesting colonially and breeding synchronously (as usually occurs among colonial nesters) is that of "predator swamping." The argument is that colonial nesters provide such an abundance of potential food (i.e., their eggs and young) in such a small area over a brief period of time that they overwhelm (or "swamp") the ability of local predators to seriously threaten individual nests within the colony. Lack also proposed that colonial nesting would be expected when certain types of extremely limited habitats afforded better protection from nest predators than did the other possible habitats. In such instances, coloniality would be "passive": Individuals would nest in colonies, not because nesting close together was favored, but because safe nesting habitat was severely limited.

Lack went on to suggest that selection might favor colonial nesting outside of the context of predator avoidance. For example, a species might be expected to nest colonially if, in so doing, individuals were better able to follow other individuals to appropriate feeding sites (i.e., if colony sites functioned as "information centers" [as defined by Ward and Zahavi 1973]), or if birds feeding together were better able to exploit food resources than were individuals foraging on their own. Coloniality might also occur when food resources are available only in widely dispersed clumps, near which nesting aggregations would form.

What about ibises? Within the family Threskiornithidae, species that feed alone nest alone, and those that feed in groups nest in groups (Krebs 1978). This principle, along with the fact that White Ibises feed almost exclusively in flocks (Wrege 1980; Bildstein 1983, 1984), strongly suggests that colonial nesting in White Ibises is linked to flock feeding. Although this conclusion seems to be a logical one, and one with which I am somewhat comfortable, I cannot help wondering whether the sequence of factors was the other way around (i.e., perhaps colonial nesting came first, possibly as an antipredator tactic [see below], and then flock feeding followed as a consequence). Such evolutionary conundrums have managed to keep me awake on numerous evenings. That many of my colleagues also claim insomnia offers little comfort.

Why Do White Ibises Nest with Other Species?

The mixed-species nature of the Pumpkinseed Island colony site is typical of other sites with White Ibises (Spendelow and Patton 1988, Kushlan and Bildstein 1992). Both Drum Island 90 kilometers to the southwest and Battery Island 100 kilometers to the northeast have also supported other wading-bird species in addition to White Ibises (Shields and Parnell 1985, Post 1990). Indeed, mixed-species nesting is reported in 9 of 12 species of ibises for which sufficient data exist (Krebs 1978); these findings suggest that mixed-species nesting is the norm within the family. But why is this so? One possibility is that nesting habitat that is relatively predator-free is limited in certain areas. Thus, different species nest together not because they are attracted to each other, but rather because they are attracted to a similar safe haven for raising their young. This reasoning does not explain the situation at Pumpkinseed Island, however, because other marsh islands nearby seemingly could provide the same type of refuge from ground predators but remain unused.

A more complete scenario for mixed-species nesting has been proposed by Rutgers University biologist Joanna Burger (1981). Burger suggested that by nesting in large mixed-species colonies, individuals derive the same antipredator benefits of nesting in large single-species assemblages, but they do not incur an increased cost that accompanies nesting in large aggregations of one's own species, the cost of greater direct competition for nesting and food resources. Of course individual ibises would not need to realize the method in their madness for mixed-species nesting to occur. Natural selection could achieve this end simply by enhancing the reproductive output of those individuals who make the correct choice. If the decision to nest near other species has a genetic basis, and if the benefit suggested by Burger is real, then the tendency to nest in mixed-species colonies would quickly spread through the population. In much the same way that recently fledged ibises learn how to fly without understanding the principles of aerodynamics, colonial nesters perhaps are programmed to make the correct choices without even realizing why they are doing so.

Because they nest at some distance from the other species of wading birds nesting at the site, White Ibises appear to benefit little, in terms of group defense of their eggs or young, from these neighbors. Also, because ibises feed on different prey and in different habitats than do the other species of wading birds nesting on Pumpkinseed Island, feeding advantages associated with mixed-species nesting also seems to be quite low. Thus, although Burger's (1981) scenario may apply for some of the wading birds that nest on Pumpkinseed Island, its use as an explanation for mixed-species nesting in White Ibises is not so apparent.

Why Do Wading-Bird Colonies Form at Certain Localities?

Why is Pumpkinseed Island a colony site? A simple explanation is that White Ibises are traditionalists in choosing a place to nest, so having chosen Pumpkinseed Island sometime in the past, they continue to return the colony site in subsequent years. Although this explanation may be correct, it leaves another question unanswered: How do such traditions begin?

Historical evidence presented in Chapter 3 suggests that White Ibises first extended their breeding range into South Carolina earlier this century. A more speculative possibility, however, is that ibises merely *reextended* their breeding range back into the region after the area recovered from a series of devastating hurricanes that struck near the turn of the century. The "initial" colonization that Arthur T. Wayne reported (Wayne 1922) actually may have been a recolonization. Ibises can survive for at least 16 years in the wild (Clapp et al. 1982) and for considerably longer periods in captivity (Spil et al. 1985), so the birds that Wayne saw in 1922 may have been the remnants of an earlier regional breeding population. But even if Wayne's observations do represent a real range expansion, the question of initial colony site choice remains.

Repeated sightings of recently fledged White Ibises north and east of colonies in the Carolinas (Francis 1978, McNabb 1978) suggest that at least some juvenile White Ibises disperse outside the current breeding range of the species. Whether such individuals return to these dispersal sites later and attempt to breed is unknown; however, several fledglings initially wing-tagged at Pumpkinseed Island in the early 1980s eventually nested 100 kilometers northeast of the site in coastal North Carolina. Similar extrarange postfledging dispersal is known to occur in Roseate

Spoonbills (Robertson et al. 1983) and Great White Herons (G. V. N. Powell and R. Bjork, personal communication), as well as in several species of gulls and terns. But still, even if those who first decide to use a colony site are young novices rather than experienced breeders, why choose Pumpkinseed Island? Why not somewhere else?

My guess is that, regardless of the experience level of the breeders who initiated the first breeding attempt on Pumpkinseed Island, the birds chose the site because it provides the essential mix of safety from predators and proximity to food. Freedom from predation appears to be especially important for ibises (see Stahlecker 1989). Most ibis colonies are on islands, presumably to reduce predation from ground predators (see Frederick and Collopy 1989). Marsh islands like Pumpkinseed are ideal in this regard. The only resident mammal on Pumpkinseed Island, aside from the occasional researcher, is the ubiquitous Cotton Rat, a species whose population is held in check by flooding tides, and against which parental White Ibises can successfully defend their eggs and young.

Although many other mammals, including Raccoons and River Otters, inhabit nearby salt marshes, Pumpkinseed Island's small size and low elevation apparently preclude permanent habitation by viable populations of these species. Even visits by such species are unlikely, because travel to and from the island requires a 2-kilometer swim in sometimes treacherous waters. (Aerial predators are not deterred by Pumpkinseed Island's insular nature, and several species of birds do affect egg and nestling survival on the island; see Chapter 5 for details).

Mammalian predators are not the only ground threats White Ibises face while raising their young. American Alligators also can cause problems for the species. Whether or not they do so depends upon local rainfall, which in turn affects the salinity of Mud Bay. Because alligators have a lower tolerance for brackish areas than do their more aggressive cousins, the crocodiles (Taplin et al. 1982), they are rarely seen in and around Mud Bay. Their appearances are limited to the wettest years. Even when alligators do occur on the island, most stay for less than several weeks. That their appearance is abbreviated is lucky for the birds, as well as for any humans in the area. A 1.5-meter (5-foot) gator consumes an abundance of eggs and nestlings. And unexpectedly disturbing one at close range is enough to impress even the most jaded old-timer. The first time that I encountered a gator in close quarters while I was slogging hip-deep in heavy waders through a mire, I all but flew out of my boots. Only after about 20 meters of struggle did I realize how odd I must have appeared to the boatload of locals fishing nearby. Fortunately, the American Alligator belongs to the cowardly side of the family Crocodilia, and most retreat quickly when encountering humans. Indeed, despite their noticeably superior agility, on such occasions alligators appear to be at least as frightened of us as we are of them.

Audubon's account (1840–44, 58–59) of an alligator attempting to prey upon a White Ibis in Bayou Sara, Louisiana, recalls the biology of a bygone era:

> . . . the ibises had all departed for the Florida coasts, excepting a few of the white species, one of which we at length espied. It was perched about fifty yards from us in the center of the pool, and as the report of one of our guns echoed among the tall cypresses, down to the water, broken winged, it fell. The exertions which it made toward shore seemed to awaken the half-torpid alligators that lay in the deep mud at the bottom of the pool. One shewed [sic] his head above the water, then a second and a third. All gave chase to the poor wounded bird, which, on seeing its dreaded and deadly foes, made double steps towards the very spot where we stood. I was surprised to see how much faster the bird swam than the reptiles, who, with both jaws widely opened, urged their heavy bodies through the water. The ibis was now within a few yards of us. It was the alligator's last chance. Springing forward as it were, he raised his body almost out of the water; his jaws nearly touched the terrified bird; when pulling three triggers at once, we lodged the contents of our guns in the throat of the monster . . . the ibis, as if in gratitude, walked to our very feet, and there lying down, surrendered itself to us. I kept this bird until the succeeding spring . . . when after its long captivity, I restored it to liberty, in the midst of its loved swamps and woods.

Although individual alligators may pose a threat to individual ibises, this predator's overall impact on White Ibises may, in fact, be positive. I have often wondered whether one of the major reasons that islands serve so admirably as colony sites for ibises is because the alligator-infested waters surrounding them deter mammals from entering therein (Jenni 1969).

Pumpkinseed Island appears to be a good choice of nesting locations not only because of reduced predation risk, but also because of prey availability. The island's location in Winyah Bay (Figure 2.4) at the confluence of three major rivers (the Black, Waccamaw, and Pee Dee rivers), as well as its proximity to a fourth (the Santee River), places it within striking distance of a number of both freshwater and saltwater feeding habitats— important ingredients for successful breeding. In this regard, Pumpkin- seed Island bears a striking resemblance to the other two large colony sites in the Carolinas. Both Drum Island to the south and Battery Island to the north also are relatively small coastal islands near the mouths of important river drainages (Map 4.1). At all three sites, ibises are known to feed in the freshwater swamps associated with these rivers, as well as in closer brackish marshes. (See Chapters 7 and 8 for additional details.)

Although Pumpkinseed Island may be an ideal site in terms of predator avoidance and proximity to food, White Ibises nesting at the site have another problem with which to contend: The nests they build are prone to flooding. As a result, periodic high tides substantially affect nesting success on the island. Although average high tides pose only a modest threat, twice a month the moon, sun, and earth are aligned in what astronomers call *syzygy* (a bizarre combination of vowels and consonants that is far harder to spell than to say: "sizz-a-jee"). The phe- nomenon takes two forms: *conjunction,* which occurs during the new moon, when both sun and moon are on the same side of the earth; and *opposition,* which occurs during the full moon, when the earth is directly between the two. Usually the alignments are far from being exact; if they were, the earth would bear witness to monthly solar and lunar eclipses. But even without such exactitude, during conjunction and opposition the sun and moon reinforce each other's gravitational pull, thus producing a series of "spring tides," during which the low tides are lower than normal and, more importantly, the high tides are higher than normal. (The term *spring tide* has nothing to do with the season of spring but rather is derived from the German word *springen,* which means to leap up.) By comparison, so-called "neap tides" are twice-monthly events that occur during the two half-moon periods of each lunar cycle when sun and moon are in quadrature, or at right angles to each other, and when their gravitational forces tend to dampen each other (Wylie 1979). In coastal South Carolina, tidal range, or amplitude of successive high and low tides, is often twice as great during spring tides as it is during neap tides.

On Pumpkinseed Island, high spring tides can completely cover the island with more than 30 centimeters of water, especially when high onshore winds conspire to accentuate the phenomenon. Because most White Ibises build their nests within centimeters of the ground on Pump-

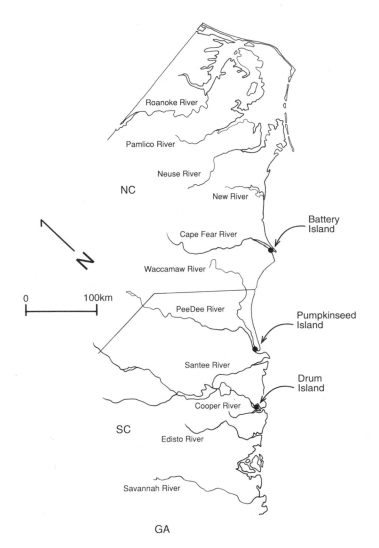

Map 4.1. The locations of the three largest White Ibis colony sites in North and South Carolina.

kinseed Island, such flooding has the potential to substantially affect breeding success. Peter Frederick alerted me to this source of mortality in 1980, but not until 1985 did I witness the phenomenon first hand. Over the brief course of 3 days in early May of that year, I watched in horror as high spring tides washed away half of the contents of the nearly 2,000 ibis nests that were being used at the time. But even that event left me unprepared for the devastation my associates and I witnessed in early June 1988.

Throughout the 1980s White Ibises had faithfully returned to the area in large numbers by mid-March each year and had initiated egg laying several weeks thereafter. Indeed, from 1979 through 1987, ibises returned to Pumpkinseed Island like clockwork, each year beginning egg laying within 4 days of 1 April. In 1988, however, the birds were late. In fact, they were very late. After visiting the island repeatedly between mid-March and early April and seeing no more than 50 ibises—all of which were noncourting—at any one time, I began to wonder if the birds would breed at all that year. Just as I was about to give up all hope, several dozen birds began to nest at the site. On 27 April my much-relieved colleague and graduate student, Toni De Santo, called to let me know that the first eggs—although more than 3 weeks behind schedule—had been laid. After breathing sighs of relief, Toni and I quickly turned to our tide charts.

As luck would have it, the next potentially devastating series of spring tides was scheduled to begin on Friday, 13 May. If the weather held, most of the breeders might be successful after all. Although all of the birds would still be incubating, their relatively impermeable eggs would be better able to withstand these high tides than would their more vulnerable and wettable nestlings. Peter Frederick (1987a) had demonstrated that eggs could survive more than an hour of tidal inundation and still hatch. Of course, if the weather did not hold and wind-assisted tides swept over the island, eggs, nestlings, and indeed, entire nests might be lost. All Toni and I could do was hope.

The 13th came, the weather held, the nests survived, and 4 days later nestlings were hatching out. Although the 1988 breeding season had got off to a late start, I was beginning to think it might be successful after all. The charts indicated that the next set of spring tides should be less dramatic than the one that had just passed, and that it would not occur for several weeks. I figured by that time many of the nestlings would be capable of surviving a soaking. I was mistaken.

Lulled into thinking that the worst was over, I made plans to return to my office in Rock Hill for a couple of days. I left Baruch late on the afternoon of 31 May, the day before the next series of especially high tides was scheduled to occur. As it had been for almost a week, the weather was sunny and hot, with light, variable winds and 60-centimeter-high (2-foot-high) seas. The birds would be safe. The day after I left, the weather began to change. The winds shifted to the northwest, and the seas increased to 1 meter (3 feet). Over the next two days a cold front passed through the area. Temperatures dropped from 22 to 11°C (from 72 to 52°F) and a little over 1 centimeter of rain fell on 4 June. But more importantly, steady 15- to 20-knot northeasterly winds heaped additional water into Winyah Bay. As a result, low tides scheduled for 2 and 3 June never occurred, and two exceptionally high nocturnal tides swept over the island on successive evenings. By the time I returned to Hobcaw and visited the colony on the morning of 4 June, most of the impacted nestlings were already dead. A combination of repeated midnight soakings and 11°C (52°F) temperatures had proved to be too much for even 2-week-old chicks, and many nestlings on the island were younger than that. In some areas every nest had been inundated and every bird had been killed. Many of the nestlings that we found were no longer in their nests but strewn about in the mud. Some were floating offshore. Whether these individuals had attempted to flee the rising waters, or whether they had merely floated from their platforms after dying of exposure was unclear. Others were still in their nests. Few appeared to have actually drowned. Many had apparently huddled together with their siblings as the waters rose around them.

Within a few days, the putrid stench of decomposing bodies could be detected half a kilometer from the island. Almost overnight, Pumpkinseed had turned into a death trap. More than 1,000 nestlings had perished.

Most of the colony site was now devoid of breeding activity. At least 90% of the nests had been destroyed. In a few short days, the breeding season had turned from marginal to nightmarish. My initial disbelief gave way to numbness and, eventually, to tortured speculation. If only the birds had returned on time. If only they had concentrated their nesting efforts in the Black Needlerush instead of in the lower lying Giant Cordgrass. If only the cold front had not moved through. If only the winds had not shifted.

The devastation of early June 1988 drove home just how tenuous the situation was for White Ibises nesting on Pumpkinseed Island. The birds, quite literally, were putting all of their eggs in a single basket, and by extension, so was I.

After the devastation, I began to research the situation. For most of this century, sea levels have been rising along the South Carolina coast at the rate of about 2.5 millimeters a year (or about an inch a decade), helped in part by subsidence of the local coastal land mass (Hicks et al. 1983, Kana et al. 1988). As a result, Pumpkinseed Island has suffered considerable erosion since 1872, altogether losing its adjacent sister island to the south (Figure 4.1). Overall, the island complex appears to have lost more than 50% of its surface area in little over a century. A twice-daily buffeting by the tides, the effects of which are exacerbated by hurricanes, tropical depressions, and "nor'easters" such as the one described above, appears to be the major culprit. Because White Ibises that nest at the site do so in close proximity to the ground, tidal flooding poses a constant and most serious threat to eggs and small nestlings. Between 1980 and 1984, annual losses to tidal inundations ranged from 43 to 100% of the nests (Frederick 1987a).

As might be predicted, losses were greater in years when, because of either astronomical alignments or local storms, tides were especially high. In 1985, I began monitoring the effects of tidal washouts on the breeding success of ibises nesting on Pumpkinseed Island. The results

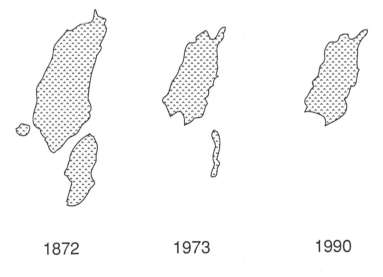

1872   1973   1990

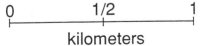

Figure 4.1. Approximate sizes of Pumpkinseed Island in 1872, 1973, and 1990.

Table 4.1   Timing and effect of tidal washout events in relation to
White Ibises' breeding attempts on Pumpkinseed Island, 1979–89

Year[a]	Breeding pairs before washout	Nests washed out (%)	First egg laying	Washout
1979[b]	7,933	ND	5 Apr.	ND
1980	6,669	96	2 Apr.[c]	8 May
1981	7,887	48	7 Apr.	16 May
1982	7,814	100	30 Mar.	18 June
1983	10,035	63	30 Mar.–4 Apr.	20–25 June
1984	12,973	43	30 Mar.–12 Apr.	16 May
1985	1,976	50	5 Apr.	5 May
1986	5,132	53	4 Apr.	8–15 May
1987	20,158	40	2 Apr.	12–14 May
1988	4,324	90	27 Apr.	1–2 June
1989	11,471	47	22 Apr.	3–7 May

[a]Data for 1979–85 are from P. Frederick; some of these data appear in Frederick (1987a).
[b]ND = no data recorded.
[c]First laying date was derived from first courtship date.

were not comforting. Between 1985 and 1989, annual losses of nests continued to range between 40 and 90% (Table 4.1).

Human-induced global warming may exacerbate the problem. Climatologists suggest that global warming will be accompanied by an increase in the number of high-energy coastal storms, as well as by ever-increasing rates of sea level rise. If these projections hold, White Ibises may have little breeding time remaining on Pumpkinseed Island.

Six other islands are in Winyah Bay within 3 kilometers of the current colony site, and several of these are larger and somewhat higher than Pumpkinseed Island. Although none of these is known to have been used as a colony site in the past, the time may come when White Ibises and other wading birds nesting at Pumpkinseed Island will defy tradition and shift their breeding activities to one of these sites. To date, I have seen no indication that the shift is underway.

Although some colonial-nesting birds promptly desert traditional breeding sites in the face of increasing predation, there is no indication of similar desertion strategies in response to repeated tidal washout (Burger 1982). Presumably, greater site tenacity occurs in the face of tidal inundation because site-specific tidal washouts are less predictable than predation intensity across years (at least during periods of stable sea levels).

5   On Becoming an Adult

Every living thing comes from an egg.

William Harvey (1578–1657)

Contributing to the next generation of ibises is the most difficult thing an ibis does. To accomplish this feat, prospective parents must realize three goals. First, each must find a compatible, fertile, and capable mate. Second, the two mates must secure a relatively safe, predator-free nesting site. And third, both parents must incubate their eggs and provide sufficient food to their developing young. Ibises that regularly fail to accomplish one or more of these tasks jeopardize their ability to pass their genes on to the next generation.

In Chapter 3, I described how the White Ibises of Pumpkinseed Island achieve the first and second of these reproductive goals. The third goal, how they manage to safeguard their eggs and nourish their young, is the subject of this chapter.

Precarious Beginnings as an Egg

Shortly after being fertilized in the female's infundibulum, the rose-colored eggs of developing ibises are launched on a peristaltic journey through the oviduct. After a brief pause in the magnum to gather a small amount of gelatinous albumen, embryos are pushed into the uterus, or so-called shell gland, where each is encased in a semipermeable, calcium carbonate shell. This shell will be the embryo's home-away-from-home for the next 3 weeks. The shell receives a splotchy coat, and the completed egg is deposited into its nest. If all proceeds according to plan, the entire journey takes less than 2 days.

Female ibises typically lay one egg per day early in the morning on alternate days, and incubation begins several days before the last egg of a clutch is laid. Although both parents incubate their young, on Pumpkinseed Island female ibises provide most of the effort, particularly at night. Even so, different pairs exhibit considerable variation in the degree to which each member incubates the eggs, and on Pumpkinseed Island at least, it is often difficult to predict which parent will be at the nest at any given time. One certainty is that parental ibises are remarkably tenacious incubators, especially in cold and rainy weather. Some individuals have even been seen attempting to incubate eggs that were floating in the nests during storm tides (Frederick 1987a).

Aside from wanting to protect their eggs from the physical environment, expectant ibises have another reason for being especially tenacious while incubating. Breeders covet each other's nests with a passion; when eggs are left unguarded, even for relatively brief periods of time, interlopers routinely poke and crush the eggs as they pirate nesting material or as they attempt to usurp the nest itself. The rapidity with which this destruction can occur became apparent during the breeding season of 1989 when we removed the male and female first from one nest containing eggs and small young, then from another, to place radio telemeters on the parental birds. Although each pair had been away from the nest for less than 45 minutes while being fitted with their transmitters, in both instances their eggs had been crushed, their chicks killed, and their nests disassembled.

Although neighboring conspecifics pose the greatest threat, other species of wading birds, especially Great Egrets, also harass incubating ibises. In early May of 1987, for example, I watched a particularly pugnacious Great Egret construct the better part of its nest from twigs it had pilfered from the nests of at least three pairs of White Ibises. More than a dozen times within an hour, the egret simply flew or walked to an ibis's nest, pushed the occupant off, and proceeded to extract a piece of nesting material. In each instance, the displaced ibis, which usually waited several meters away, returned to the nest and resumed incubation as soon as the egret had left.

Incubating and brooding ibises spend a considerable amount of time warming their eggs and young, especially at night, when temperatures at the colony site can dip below 16°C (60°F). Sometimes, however, ibises actually need to cool their eggs and young. Cooling is especially necessary late in the breeding season, when afternoon highs frequently exceed 35°C (95°F). At such times, adults often stand up in their nests and crouch over their eggs with their backs to the sun, their wings partially spread, and their feathers ruffled. On many such occasions ibises engage in *gular fluttering*, the rapid and often resonant vibration of the bones and muscles of the throat (Lasiewski 1972). Gular fluttering, the functional equivalent of panting in mammals, cools its practitioners by increasing the rate of evaporation along the moistened surfaces of the digestive tract. (Feathers, together with a lack of sweat glands, substantially reduce an ibis's ability to cool itself by means of evaporation across its skin.)

Eliminating excess heat, or *heat dumping*, is usually a communal affair. On one especially hot and hazy afternoon in early June of 1987, for example, all but 3 of the 100 nest-tending adults I was monitoring were squatting and fluttering over their nests, slowly turning in unison as they tracked the sun's path across the sky. Although the 25 nestlings I was watching at the time were also squatting with wings spread, less than half were orienting themselves away from the sun. (I concluded that they had not yet learned that orientation, as well as posture, is an important determinant of success in this endeavor.)

Emergence of an Individual

If all goes well, White Ibises hatch after about 21 days of incubation. Hatching is a rather arduous affair, and in some instances it can take more than 2 days to accomplish. Although hatchlings and adults communicate vocally throughout this 2-day period, hatchlings are not assisted by their parents as they struggle to extricate themselves from their shells. As is true of most birds, a hatchling ibis departs its egg by skillfully chipping a small air hole in the shell with its egg tooth, a horny protuberance located near the tip of the upper mandible. Over the next day or so, the hatchling pivots its cramped and contorted body in the shell and repeatedly snaps its head backward, thus enlarging its exit. Only after completely separating the blunt and pointed ends of the shell is the chick finally able to pry itself free.

When they emerge from their shells, hatchlings are blind, nearly naked, cold-blooded, wobbly-necked, 39-gram weaklings that bear a closer resemblance to their reptilian ancestors than to the parents who bore them. If all goes well, in less than 2 months these feeble beings will be fully feathered young birds, flying from the colony site to begin an independent existence beyond the reach of parental care.

What is perhaps most visually surprising about hatchling White Ibises is the fact that they are not white (Figure 5.1). Although the skin of hatchling ibises, which is especially loose-fitting about their face and eyes, is a light pinkish color at birth, their heads and necks are covered with a dense, shiny, jet black down that slicks distinctively toward the rear of the bird. The rest of the body is sparsely covered with light gray down on the ventral side and dark gray down on the dorsal side (De Santo et al. 1990). Except for a few minor differences about the head and neck, hatchling White Ibises rather closely resemble hatchling Glossy Ibises, but this superficial similarity quickly fades as the birds age. Furthermore, the behavior of these two species is decidedly different. As chicks, White Ibises are far more belligerent than their glossy counterparts.

The only white feathering on hatchling White Ibises is a variably sized (1- to 5-millimeter) topknot, and it occurs on only about one-third of all young. Although the frequency of this feature within each year's cohort of young ibises has proved to be remarkably constant (occurring in 31% of the hatchlings in 1987, 30% in 1988, and 38% in 1991, the only years in which my students and I have measured it), the appearance or absence of the topknot among siblings is apparently random.

In addition to lacking their parents' distinctive white plumage, hatchlings also lack their parents' characteristic decurved bills. The bills of young chicks are basically short and straight and, except for a dark gray tip, flesh-colored. It is not until the birds are several weeks old that their bills begin to turn distinctively downward (Figure 5.2). The nestling's conspicuous white egg tooth, so essential to the escape from the shell, is sloughed within 5 to 9 days of hatching.

For a person who handles recently hatched nestlings repeatedly, it is almost impossible not to compare them with human figures. Hatchling Tricolored Herons, for example, are recognized by my students as punk rockers, in large part because of the species's seemingly spiked and erratically projecting burnt-orange head feathers. On the other hand, hatchling White Ibises, with their droopy eyes and slick black head feathering, evoke the droll image of the late Shemp Howard of Three Stooges' fame.

One of the most remarkable aspects of each nestling's appearance is its striking individuality. Young ibises differ not only from their parents, but also among themselves, even among siblings. Most of the distinguishing traits of an individual are limited to the head and neck region, principally to the bill and face, and to the amount of white feathering in the topknot (if any). The pied bill, which is present at hatching and continues to develop over the course of the first 4 weeks of life, is particularly variable, even among birds of identical ages (Figures 5.2, 5.3).

Uniqueness in appearance is especially marked at about 2 weeks of age, the very time that the young first begin to venture from their nests on a regular basis. Other species of colonial-nesting wading birds, including Little Blue Herons, Tricolored Herons, Yellow-crowned Night-Herons, and Snowy Egrets, show somewhat similar degrees of individual variation (McVaugh 1972, 1975), and I believe that the same is true for Glossy Ibises. Researchers have recently suggested that such variability functions as a so-called *signature trait* for nestlings, especially in species whose adults tend to build their nests close together and whose roving juveniles are often found in large assemblages. Signature traits are believed to help parents single out and selectively care for their young (Stoddard and Beecher 1983, O'Connor 1984). The fact that I was able to use this variation to recognize captively reared nestlings supports this notion. Although my students and I have not yet had the opportunity to test this hypothesis in the field, it seems reasonable to assume that distinctive differences in the appearances of nestling White Ibises function in much the same manner at the Pumpkinseed Island colony site.

Essentials of Nestling Life

Growth

An unfortunate rule of thumb among birds is that growing up is the most dangerous part of life (Lack 1954). White Ibises are no exception to this rule. Because they are initially small and unable to fly, recently hatched ibises are decidedly more vulnerable to most environmental forces than are their parents. Take predation, for example. The smaller size of nestling ibises makes them not only easier to catch but also easier to swallow than adults. Unfortunately, the effort of growth and development also increases a nestling's susceptibility to nutritional stress. Because of such problems, nestling ibises "attempt" to grow out of this stage of life as

Figure 5.1. *Counterclockwise from upper left:* Developmental stages of a nestling White Ibis from hatching through fledging. The entire sequence takes between 7 and 8 weeks, during which time the bird increases in weight from less than 40 grams to over 600 grams. All stages are not drawn to the same scale. Drawings by M. Davis.

Figure 5.1. *Continued.*

rapidly as possible. In 1985, Jim Johnston and I decided to monitor the rate at which they accomplish this goal.

Each year since 1985, we have tracked the growth and development of several dozen nestling White Ibises at the Pumpkinseed Island colony site. To assess growth, we recorded the weight of each bird, as well as the length of its "leg" (or tarsometatarsus), middle toe, toe pad (measured as the distance between the tip of the middle toe and hallux, or hind toe), bill (or culmen), and next-to-outermost flight feather (or primary) (Figure 5.4). We began measurements as soon after hatching as possible. Because we knew that sibling rivalry might affect the rates

Figure 5.2. Bill and facial markings of a single hand-reared White Ibis nestling between 7 and 32 days old: *upper left,* day 7; *upper right,* day 15; *lower left,* day 26; *lower right,* day 32. Drawing by M. Davis.

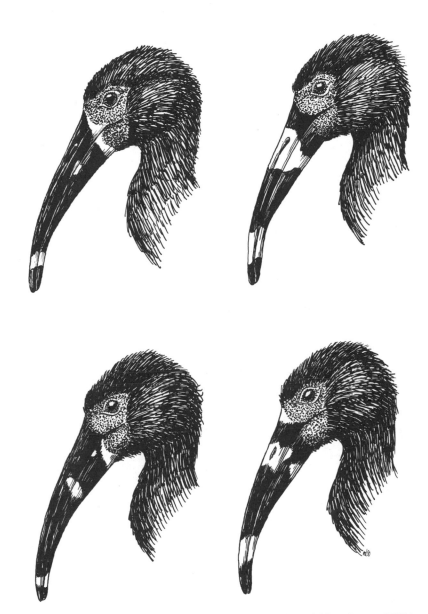

Figure 5.3. Bill and facial markings of four 27- to 31-day-old hand-reared White Ibis nestlings. Note individual variation in bill markings. Drawn by M. Davis from photographs of actual birds.

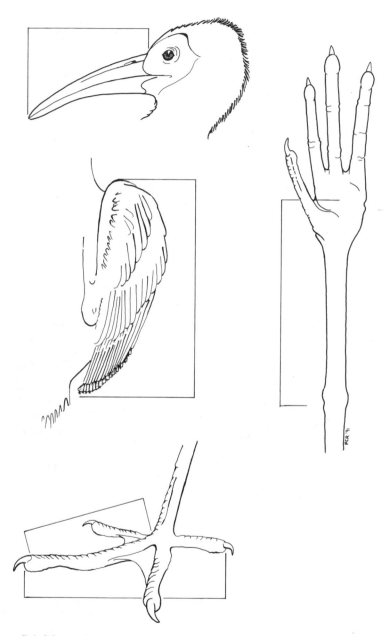

Figure 5.4. Measurements of nestling ibis anatomy for assessment of growth: *upper left*, bill or culmen; *middle left*, flight feather or primary; *middle right*, "leg" or tarsometatarsus; *lower left*, middle toe and toe pad. Drawing by P. Cowart-Rickman.

78

at which first-, second-, and third-hatched young in a nest grew and developed, we restricted our measurements to the oldest sibling in each nest. Once we started measuring a bird, we made every attempt—weather and tides permitting—to remeasure the bird at approximately the same time on alternate days, until it was about 2 weeks old. After that point, the birds became increasingly difficult to relocate.

As is true of most birds, the growth of nestling ibises follows a sigmoidal or S-shaped growth curve—that is, increases in size are initially modest, then they become more rapid, and eventually they level off at what are often referred to as asymptotic, or adult, values (O'Connor 1984) (Figure 5.5). Although all of the body parts that we measured followed this overall trend, those associated with walking and running (i.e., the leg, middle toe, and toe pad) developed far more rapidly and reached asymptotic values considerably sooner than did the one associated with flight (i.e., the flight feather). The bill grew slowest of all (Figure 5.6). I presume that these differences—which occurred consistently in both hand-reared and parent-reared birds, and which Jim Kushlan (1977a) had noted earlier in nestling White Ibises in Florida—reflect the fact that different selective pressures are acting on different parts of the nestling's body. The rapid development of the nestling's legs and feet, for example,

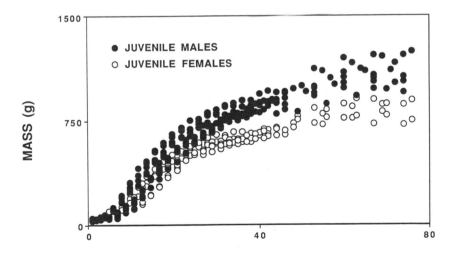

Figure 5.5. Body weights (in grams) of female and male nestling White Ibises. Each circle represents one measurement.

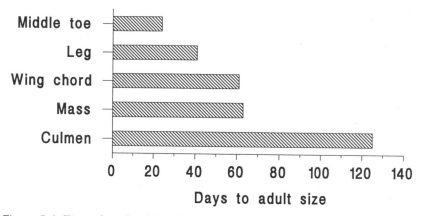

Figure 5.6. Times from hatching (day 0) to asymptotic (adult) values for various growth variables in White Ibises.

apparently serves two functions. First, it increases the nestling's ability to run for cover when potential danger appears; and second, it increases the nestling's ability to track down its parents and secure prey from them as they return to the colony with food.

The rather retarded development of the nestling's bill, which grows to only about two-thirds of its adult length by the time of fledging (i.e., readiness for flight) also serves two purposes. First, up until fledging, the nestling's shorter, stouter bill almost certainly facilitates the juxtaposition of the juvenile's gape with that of its parent during food transfers, thereby increasing the efficiency of prey delivery from parent to young. And second, after fledging, the bill's shorter length probably makes it easier to maneuver and "mandibulate" than a longer bill. Several human examples support the latter suggestion: Downhill skiers and stilt walkers often begin on short, stubby appendages before graduating to longer, more graceful ones. Individuals unaccustomed to using a hammer often begin by grasping this tool closer to the head than the handle's length makes necessary.

There is, however, a trade-off involved in having a shorter bill: the proportionate reduction in access to burrowing prey. The fact that recently fledged ibises capture prey at rates that are far below those of adult birds (as discussed in Chapter 6) is probably related to the fact that juveniles have shorter bills than do adults. The deficiency appears to be short-lived. Most of our captively reared birds had full-size, adult-length bills by the time they were 3 months old.

Diet

In addition to measuring the growth and development of nestlings each year, Jim and I also gathered data on nestling diets. Although we sometimes did so by gently massaging the crop of a nestling until it offered a small aliquot of its most recent meal, most of our nestlings voluntarily submitted samples of their diets as soon as they were lifted from their nests, and in some instances even earlier. Each sample was immediately placed in a plastic bag and then on ice for later analysis. Every effort was made to sample individual birds on only one occasion, and in no case did we attempt to induce samples from the birds whose growth and development we were measuring.

After samples of regurgitated food were thawed, they were analyzed in two ways. First, each sample was spread to a uniform thickness on a glass plate, and the approximate percentage of each prey type was determined. Second, each sample was placed in a centrifuge to separate its liquid and solid ingredients, and the salt content of the fluid portion was then determined with a rather sophisticated electrical device known as a freezing-point depression osmometer. Jim and I had decided to perform this analysis because we knew that ibises often fed in rather salty environments, and we wanted to know whether or not parents were diluting the salt content of their prey before feeding it to their nestlings.

Throughout their range, White Ibises typically feed upon crustacean prey, so it was no surprise that the bulk of the regurgitant Jim and I collected from nestlings at the colony site typically consisted of two types of crustaceans: crayfishes and fiddler crabs. It also was no surprise that samples rich in crayfishes were significantly less salty than were those dominated by fiddler crabs. After all, crayfishes typically inhabit freshwater wetlands, whereas fiddler crabs are typically found in brackishwater salt marshes. In addition to these two major dietary components, parents also delivered smaller amounts of other species of crabs, as well as fishes, shrimps, spiders, snails, and insects, to their young (Figure 5.7).

Perhaps most important was our discovery that crayfishes, which ibises seemed to prefer over all other types of prey, formed the bulk of

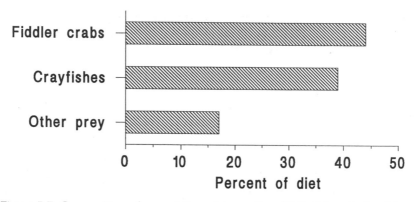

Figure 5.7. Composition of prey delivered to nestling White Ibises during May of 1985. The "other prey" category included other species of crabs, as well as fishes, shrimps, spiders, snails, and insects.

the nestling diet in high-rainfall years, whereas fiddler crabs tended to become a more important dietary item in drought years.

Provisions at the Colony

Hungry Nestlings and Their Contenders

Young ibises develop most rapidly during their first week out of the shell. Hatchlings seem barely prepared for the outside world. Their eyes are wholly or partially closed, and their bodily movements are both uncoordinated and weak. Typically, they sleep through most of the first day and are fed for the first time the next morning. For the first week or so, the young birds spend most of their time either nestled below one of their brooding parents or persistently soliciting a meal. As early as day 2, the chicks are capable of propping their heads on the base of their necks while trilling loudly for food. Although they will eventually learn to do so only when a parent is near, nestlings initially beg for food whenever they are hungry, which for the first week or so seems to be almost all of the time. I often know when chicks have begun to hatch simply by listening for their characteristic calls.

By day 4, the nestlings manage to balance their bodies on rapidly developing feet and shuffle backward to the rim of the nest to defecate. By day 6, most are actively crawling about the nest on a regular basis and jockeying with their sibs for the best position at mealtime. In less than a week, the chicks transform themselves from bashful (but noisy) weaklings into belligerent food-snatching feeding machines whose demands keep both of their parents busy ferrying prey back to the nest for the next 6 or 7 weeks.

When parents return to Pumpkinseed Island with food, the ration they are carrying consists of a rather unappealing and almost unrecognizable slurry of macerated crustaceans, fish, and insects. Parental ibises deliver the partially digested food to their begging young in small boluses, regurgitating these rounded masses from lower in their digestive tracts (Figure 5.8). Nestlings repeatedly poke their parents' bills to entice them to regurgitate. Parents typically disgorge boluses directly down their chicks' throats, and in many instances the transition is so smooth that the only indication it has happened at all is the chick's subsequent gulping behavior. Only infrequently do the parents miss their targets. When they do, the chicks usually scavenge the dropped food immediately from the bottom of

Figure 5.8. Food transfer between a parent White Ibis and its 7-week-old nestling. Photograph courtesy of P. Frederick.

the nest. By the time the chicks are 2 weeks old, most are diving bill-first down their parents' throats and extricating the boluses long before the parents have had an opportunity to bring the boluses up to bill level.

By this time, most nestlings also seem to have learned that begging for food makes little sense unless a parent is near, and the colony becomes a decidedly quieter place. Even so, noisy disputes continue to erupt in isolated pockets throughout the colony, especially when parents are returning to their nests with food. Sometime during their second week, most nestlings begin to flap their wings actively and to thrust their bills emphatically forward while begging for food, in an apparent attempt to emphasize their demands. Shortly thereafter, nestlings begin to place one of their wings over the back and neck of a parent while food is being transferred, seemingly shielding themselves and the parent from competing sibs. Nestlings also begin to beg from each other at this time, usually by grasping, tugging, and generally mandibulating the bill of a recently fed, adjacent sibling. Although nestlings often persist in such matters, I have yet to see one succeed in this behavior.

Recently fed young must also contend with food-begging adults, many of which are successful in inducing nestlings to disgorge their latest meal. Peter Frederick (1985a) was the first to witness this insidious foraging technique at Pumpkinseed Island. Peter explained that piratical adults were likely to strike in one of two ways:

> First, when parents fed young older than 10 days, a "pirate" would stand nearly touching the parent as the young begged and the parent worked a bolus of food up its throat. Just as the parent opened its bill to regurgitate, the pirate would force its bill into the parent's gape, sometimes for the full length of the throat, pulling out and swallowing the bolus of food. If the pirate arrived during or just after a successful feeding, the pirate would force its bill into the gape and throat of the young and extract the food.
>
> Pirates would also walk among unattended resting young (older than 10 days of age) and force their bills into the gapes of the young, extracting food from the crop.

Most piratical adults concentrate their efforts on recently fed nestlings, rather than on the parents who are feeding them. Surprisingly, parents are decidedly passive during such events. Neither Peter nor I have ever seen pirates robbing nestlings that were less than about 10 days old, possibly because smaller nestlings receive less prey from their parents during each meal and are, therefore, less profitable targets than are older individuals. Although I have never seen a pirate transfer food from another's offspring to its own, I can think of no reason why such an event could not occur.

A few adults appear to specialize in food robbery. Peter reports seeing one recognizable individual pirating prey on at least 26 occasions (Frederick 1985a), and I have watched several individuals walk from nest to nest, attempting to shake down the occupants. Only when they were finally successful did these birds fly off to another part of the colony site. Whether individual nestlings suffer substantially as a result of being pirated is not clear. However, several successive robberies could impede a nestling's development, especially during a time when the bird's parents are supplying only marginal amounts of prey. On the other hand, when performed on a regular basis, piracy apparently offers its practitioners a low-cost, high-benefit alternative to finding their own food.

Helpers at the Nest

Whereas some nestlings suffer as a result of coming into contact with nonparental adults, others apparently benefit.

Each year, in addition to serving as a nesting site for thousands of breeding adults, Pumpkinseed Island also hosts several dozen to several hundred nonbreeding, second-year, subadult White Ibises, whose distinctive plumage (Figure 5.9) makes them easily recognizable. Many of these second-year birds spend a significant amount of time attending to nestlings whose parents are off foraging. Ornithologists typically refer to such nonparental birds as "helpers." First observed by Alexander Skutch in 1935, helping behavior now has been reported in 50 families of birds (Skutch 1986). Simply stated, helping occurs whenever a bird directs parental behavior at young that are not its own (Brown 1987). In most instances helpers are relatively young individuals, and often they give such attention only to their younger sibs. Helping behavior typically includes feeding young; however, food provisioning per se is not an essential characteristic of the behavior.

Although I have yet to study this intriguing behavior in detail, helping appears to be an annual event at the colony. Helping was especially prominent during both 1987 and 1989, when I spent a total of about 20 hours documenting this behavior in several small groups of second-

Figure 5.9. Plumage changes of White Ibises between fledging and breeding: *upper left*, summer of first year; *upper right*, winter of first year; *middle left*, spring of second year; *middle right*, late summer of second year; *lower left*, winter of second year; *lower right*, spring of third year. Drawing by M. Davis.

year birds whose molting plumage enabled me to identify them individually. My field notes of the morning of 5 June 1989 are typical:

8:30. Watching a second-year male preening four 12- to 14-day-old nestlings at an unattended nest near the north end of the island. No food is being transferred, but the second-year bird is preening the nestlings, and the nestlings are begging and probing its gaping bill. This is the only second-year bird in the immediate vicinity. Several adults walk within 1 meter of the nest without interacting.

8:50. An adult male ibis walks toward the second-year bird, displaces it, but then returns to a nest 3 meters off.

8:55. The second-year bird returns to the nest and resumes its interactions with the nestlings.

9:02. The second-year bird leaves the nest and walks 3 meters to another nest, where it begins to groom yet another nestling. Almost as soon as it does, it is chased by an adult male back to the original nest where it resumes grooming and intention-feeding [or mock-feeding] the four original chicks.

9:04. The second-year bird is chased from the original nest by another adult male, but returns 30 seconds later after the male has walked off.

9:20. Yet another adult male flies in and bumps the second-year bird from the nest; [the chased bird] then moves 2 meters off to interact with two other nestlings. When it tries to return to the original nest 3 minutes later, it is repulsed once again by the adult male, who 1 minute later begins to feed the chicks that had been tended by the second-year bird.

9:26. The second-year bird flies out of sight to the northwest. [The same second-year bird was seen at the same nest on the following day.]

Why should an ibis help raise another's young? Why not attempt to raise its own young? Is helping an altruistic behavior, or is it actually a selfish act? Although the questions seem simple enough, the answers to them have engendered considerable controversy among ornithologists (see Brown 1987, Koenig and Mumme 1987). Most observers who have studied helping behavior fall into one of two camps: that of "hard-core" altruism or that of "soft-core" altruism (Wilson 1978). The hard-core altruism theory suggests that helpers actually benefit from their seemingly unselfish actions because they typically direct their help only at the offspring of close relatives. Following this line of reasoning, helpers are assisting—albeit indirectly—in the passage of some of their own genes into the next genera-tion. In human terms, helpers could be viewed as childless aunts and uncles assisting in the care of their favorite nieces and nephews. The soft-core altruism theory suggests that the apparent altruistic act of helping benefits its practitioners in a more direct fashion, either by affording them an opportunity to eventually take over the helpee's territory (because they are in the right place at the right time) or by enabling them to practice parental skills that will eventually be of use to them when they begin to breed. But which scenario applies to ibises?

My observations suggest that helpers are likely to help at a num-ber of nests, and that they often move from one part of the colony to another while doing so. Unless the helpers that I watched had many close relatives breeding at Pumpkinseed Island, and unless these relatives were scattered throughout the site, these helpers often assisted young to which they were not closely related. Thus, helper ibises do not appear to be acting as the avian equivalents of human aunts and uncles. Nor do these helpers appear to be attempting to gain access to nesting territories, since the locations of such territories vary considerably from year to year (Map 3.1). Why, then, do second-year birds help? I believe that helping behavior in White Ibises provides younger, less experienced birds with an excellent opportunity to practice the parenting skills they will eventually need to successfully raise their own young. In such terms, helping is more of a selfish deed than an altruistic act.

Departure from the Homesite

The First Steps

Regardless of who is caring for them, by the time the nestlings are several weeks old, they begin to tumble from their nests as humans approach, and my co-workers and I must be particularly careful not to disturb them as we go about our daily chores in the colony site. Five to seven days later, healthy nestlings have developed into what we have come to refer to as "runners," birds that have not yet fledged but nevertheless are no longer confined to their nests. Shortly thereafter runners begin to form *crèches*, or gatherings of similarly aged young, ranging in size from tens to hundreds of birds. Although one or more parental birds can regularly be found in the vicinity of such concentrations, whether or not these adults are actually watching over the crèche remains unclear. What is clear is that nestlings within crèches are continually interacting with one another.

Given the species's gregarious nature, the principal purpose of such gatherings may be to enhance the development of social skills, in much the same manner as school yards do for human young. Most of the nestlings that survive to fledging eventually leave the island in small parties of less than ten to several dozen individuals. Although we have never been able to determine with certainty the long-term stability of such flocks, circumstantial evidence—the sighting of groups of recently fledged young of identical size distributions at particular feeding sites for several days in succession—suggests that the small flocks often consist of young birds that have formed at least short-term relationships. If this companionship indeed exists, then crèches may also be places where young ibises find their "friends." Additional work involving color-marked birds is planned to address this intriguing possibility.

Recruitment to the Flock

Whether they do so with old friends or merely with casual acquaintances, leaving the island for the first time seems to be a rather harrowing experience for young White Ibises. By the time they are 5 to 6 weeks old, chicks are capable of flying 50 to 100 meters or more, and many can be seen sailing over the island in pursuit of food-bearing parents. A week or so later, most will have left the island and begun to feed on their own. (Although I cannot be sure that all ibises first leave the colony site when they are 7 to 8 weeks old, I do know that each of the eight nestlings Toni De Santo and I tracked by radiotelemetry in 1986 and 1987 left for the first time at that age [De Santo et al. 1990].)

Parents hasten the departure of their young by providing them with less and less food as the appropriate departure date approaches, and by attempting to entice them off the island. Many times I have watched an adult fly from the island with a nestling in hot pursuit. More often than not, the nestling quickly returns to the safety of the colony site after briefly looking down toward the waters of Mud Bay. (It is relatively easy to see where an ibis is looking, since it typically turns its head, and thus its long decurved bill, in that direction.) In at least three instances during my observations, the parent also returned to the island at this time and again attempted to lure the hesitant fledglings from the site. Only once have I seen an adult succeed in such an endeavor. And even then, three attempts were required to convince the reluctant youngster.

There is no indication that parental ibises feed their young away from Pumpkinseed Island. Indeed, I have never seen an assemblage of ibises away from the colony site that in any way resembled one or more family groups. Once they have left the colony, juvenile ibises tend to spend most of their time in the company of their peers, even when foraging close to adult ibises.

Recently fledged juveniles do, however, travel to and from the colony together with adults, and by late June of each year flocks of White Ibises traveling between the Pumpkinseed Island feeding grounds to the north and west frequently consist of mixtures of adult and juvenile birds. Ibises typically fly in formation when commuting in such groups. Most of the birds my students and I have observed at such times were flying either in long wavering skeins or in V formations similar to those seen in many species of waterfowl. Traveling in either of these configurations is believed to reduce the energy expenditure of participating birds by improving the aerodynamics of all but the leading individual in each flock (Storer 1948). Presumably the birds benefit by "drafting," as do the trucks that travel in tight convoys along the U.S. interstate highway system.

In 1984, Dan Petit and I decided to study this aspect of ibis behavior in detail (Petit and Bildstein 1986). From late June through late August of that year, Dan and I carefully recorded the relative flight positions of more than 64,000 adult and juvenile White Ibises flying between Pumpkinseed Island and their inland feeding sites. Each bird was classified as flying either in formation or out of formation. A bird was considered to be flying in formation whenever another individual was no more than 2 meters in front of and slightly to the side of the bird in question (i.e., when it was in a position to take advantage of the aerodynamic benefits offered by the lead bird). Although more than 85% of all of the adults we watched were flying in formation when first sighted, most of the juveniles were not. Indeed, for the first month of our observations, more than 75% of all juveniles sighted were flying out of formation. Consequently, whereas most all-adult flocks glided across the sky in highly organized progressions, the flight formations of mixed-age flocks tended to resemble the halftime repertoires of an ill-prepared marching band, with many of the juveniles continually failing to bring up the rear. Not until late August did most of the juveniles master the essential skills of flying in formation.

They may have managed to do so just in time. Many species of birds have notoriously high rates of juvenile mortality (Lack 1954). Ornithologists have suggested that, by traveling together, birds are able to increase their flight distances by as much as 70% (Lissaman and Schollenberger 1970). Most of the nestlings raised at the Pumpkinseed Island colony site migrate considerable distances to Florida and elsewhere each September (Bildstein et al. 1982). Doing so in formation may increase their chances of surviving to adulthood.

Nonwhiteness in White Ibis Development

White Ibises are basically black at birth. The recently fledged young are dark brownish gray dorsally, but white ventrally. Breeding adults are white (Figure 5.9). Why the coloring of ibises is such is not immediately obvious. Although two possibilities—thermoregulation and camouflage—came to mind when I first saw an ibis hatchling, both produced more questions than answers. Consider, for example, the thermoregulation hypothesis. Avian physiologists have known for some time that dark plumage tends to absorb, rather than reflect, incoming solar radiation, and that white plumage tends to have the opposite effect (Hamilton and Heppner 1967). Thus, darkly plumed birds, including nestling White Ibises, should have less difficulty staying warm than nestlings with whiter plumage. Accordingly, darkly plumed birds should be more likely to overheat than their white counterparts. The fact that on hot afternoons recently hatched nestling ibises often pant and gular-flutter in their nests when parental adults are not attending them, and older, more ambulatory nestlings usually seek shelter beneath nearby vegetation, suggests that overheating is, in fact, a problem for nestlings. Also, if dark plumage is so beneficial in a thermoregulatory sense, then why are nestling Sacred Ibises and Little Blue Herons, as well as Great, Snowy, and Cattle egrets, white at hatching? Similarly, my other initial explanation for dark plumage in nestling ibises—that it served to camouflage the young, thereby protecting them from predation—also failed to explain the white plumage of nestling egrets and Little Blue Herons.

Having quickly arrived at two explanatory cul-de-sacs, I decided that I might be asking the wrong question. Instead of trying to figure out why the nestlings did not look like their parents, perhaps I should have been trying to figure out why the parents did not look like their nestlings. Inverting the question was more than a semantic exercise. A number of evolutionary theorists consider an organism's early stages of development to be more "conservative" or evolutionarily stable than its adult stages. (The rationale for this argument is rooted in the 18th-century notion that ontogeny recapitulates phylogeny, or that the history of an individual briefly recapitulates the history of its genetic lineage. Although modern biologists no longer support this theory in its extreme mechanistic form, the notion that juvenile stages of descendants resemble the adult stages of their ancestors is still widely held [Gould 1977].) If this explanation were applied to plumages in ibises, the dark plumage of nestlings would represent the species's ancestral condition, and the light plumage of adults would represent a more recently "derived" or evolved state. Support for this hypothesis comes from the fact that, although nestling Scarlet and White ibises have almost identical plumages (ffrench and Haverschmidt 1970, De Santo et al. 1990), adults of the two color morphs have decidedly distinctive plumages.

But even if this hypothesis is true, why then is it that the two-toned subadults, not to mention the almost-all-white breeding adults, have not maintained their ancestral condition? Although the jury is still out on the value of light versus dark plumage in wading birds (Caldwell 1986), Jim Kushlan has offered a well-reasoned, albeit somewhat complicated, argument for plumage coloration (Kushlan 1978).

Kushlan begins his argument by discounting the importance of both absorptive and predator avoidance roles for dark plumage in most wading birds. He then assumes light plumage will be more cryptic against the daytime sky than dark plumage. He goes on to propose that diurnally active species with light ventral plumage are less visible from below than are birds with dark ventral plumage, and that this reduced visibility enhances the foraging success of such species by making their prey less able to detect and avoid them. He also proposes that diurnally active birds with light dorsal plumage are more conspicuous from above than are those with dark plumage, and that this enhanced conspicuity, in turn, makes them more easily located by other wading birds. The assumption is that by being light dorsally, individuals of flocking species will enhance their ability to find each other. (A series of ingenious experiments that involved placing white and dark models of wading birds in environmental circumstances to test these purported effects support both of these suggestions [Kushlan 1977b, Mock 1981].) Kushlan concludes by predicting correctly that diurnally active, gregarious feeders such as adult White Ibises should have light plumage, both ventrally and dorsally. Unfortunately, his explanation fails to account for the plumage of subadult nonbreeders, which are dark dorsally. Or does it?

Perhaps the conspicuous dorsal plumage of adult ibises evolved to make potential breeders more visible to one another during the breeding season—a time when finding mates and new sources of prey is especially critical—whereas the less conspicuous dorsal plumage of subadults evolved to make birds that have not had a chance to fledge less visible to aerial predators. Unfortunately, like many of my more interesting speculations about White Ibises, such an explanation is virtually impossible to test directly.

6 Feeding Behavior

I cannot agree with Burke when he says it is only our ignorance of nature that causes all our admiration and excites all our emotions.

Alexander von Humboldt, 1848

Throughout their range, White Ibises typically feed on small invertebrate and vertebrate prey in wetland habitats while wading in standing water. They are, after all, "wading birds." But in coastal South Carolina, where ibises feed almost exclusively on several species of fiddler crabs, ibises spend almost all of their time searching for prey on the exposed surfaces of tidal marshes. Since one of the principal goals of my studies has been to document the ecological role of ibises in the salt-marsh ecosystem, most of my observations of feeding ibises have consisted of individuals walking across unflooded portions of the North Inlet Marsh.

White Ibises possess several anatomical specializations that are useful in feeding. Their eyes are positioned so that they focus on the tips of their long, decurved bills. The bills themselves are well innervated and quite sensitive, and they probably close automatically upon contact with prey (Kushlan and Bildstein 1992). In many habitats, individuals feed almost exclusively by tactile probing or groping, rather than by actually seeing their prey. *Probing* consists of relatively rapid and repeated sewing-machine-like movements of the tip of the bill into and out of an area covered in water, whereas *groping* involves holding a slightly opened bill agape in the water and sweeping it from side to side (Kushlan 1978). Even when closed, the decurved bill has near its center a slight but conspicuous gap, which allows the tips of the upper and lower mandibles to operate like tweezers as the ibis attempts to grab and restrain reluctant prey. (Readers interested in learning more about anatomical and ecological adaptations for feeding in other species of ibises, storks, and spoonbills should consult Kushlan 1978 and Hancock et al. 1992 for reviews of the subject.)

Observing Feeding White Ibises in the Field

My principal study plot for watching feeding White Ibises was the 20 or so hectares of the Bly Creek drainage closest to the warden's tower at the North Inlet Marsh, about 5 kilometers north of the Pumpkinseed Island colony site (Figure 6.1). I was not the first biologist to watch ibises feed at this location. Earlier, when she was a graduate student, Elizabeth Henderson had studied several aspects of the foraging behavior of ibises at the site (Henderson 1981). Henderson's sampling technique, which I adopted, was remarkably straightforward. I simply climbed onto my observation perch—the 18.5-meter-tall warden's tower at the northern tip of Goat Island—set up my telescope, sat down on my stool, and scanned the horizon for foraging ibises (Figure 6.2). Once I spotted an ibis, I flipped on my tape recorder, punched my stopwatch, and dictated details of the bird's behavior. Below is a 4-minute excerpt from my field notes from the morning of 20 July 1980, my first day of such observation. In this case, I was describing an adult ibis feeding near the center of a flock:

> . . . probe, *capture, capture,* step, step, probe, *capture, capture,* step, *capture,* step, probe, step, probe, *capture,* probe, *capture,* probe, *capture,* step (1 minute), step, probe, *capture,* probe, probe, probe, probe, step, step, probe (2 minutes), step, probe, probe, probe, *capture,* probe, *capture,* probe, step, step, probe, step, probe, step, probe, step, probe, step, probe, step, probe, *capture,* probe, *capture,* step (3 minutes), probe, step, step, probe, *capture,* probe, step, *capture,* probe, *capture,* probe, *capture,* probe, *capture,* probe, probe, *capture,* probe . . .

Even then, less than 5 minutes into something that was to occupy me for more than a decade, I was impressed: The adult White Ibis I had been watching had captured 19 fiddler crabs in 4 minutes. I had watched Northern Harriers for more than 10 hours from the same tower before I

Figure 6.1. Tower view of the portion of the Bly Creek drainage where ibis feeding behavior was observed.

had seen that species capture as many prey items as this adult ibis had captured in just 4 minutes. Recording the feeding behavior of White Ibises was going to be both fun and profitable, at least on a relative scale.

Each evening after a full day of field observations, I spent several hours replaying the tapes and entering the data on a series of index cards. Although it would have been easy to put off transcribing each day's field observations, I had learned several years earlier that such delay has dire consequences. As a graduate student in the early 1970s, I had spent a fair portion of my meager stipend buying dozens of cassettes and loading them with weeks of observations so I could delay the dreaded task of transcribing them. By the time I did get around to listening to them, I realized that in many instances I had failed to record one or more of an observation's essential details. Because at least several weeks had passed since I had made each observation, there was little hope of recalling such details. But even if I did record everything, the thought of sitting down at my desk in September and listening to hours of old tapes was enough to make me shiver. There are few aspects of field biology that I do not enjoy; transcribing data is one of them.

For each 4-minute observation, I recorded every time the bird took a step, probed the marsh surface or fiddler crab burrow in search of prey, captured prey, and stopped searching and looked up toward the sky. I also recorded the date, the location of the bird on the marsh, the bird's age and gender (whenever possible), the size of the flock in which the bird was feeding, and the bird's location within that flock. I decided to restrict my observations of individual birds to 4 minutes because Elizabeth had discovered through trial and error that watching birds for longer than that was both tedious (eye strain and tongue-tying are but two of the symptoms) and risky (birds were more likely to fly off and negate the data collected during longer observations). Once the data were transcribed onto cards, I summarized the events therein and entered them into a computer for statistical and graphical analysis.

When I have wanted to compare the behavior of two or more classes of ibises (i.e., adults versus juveniles, single birds versus those hunting in flocks), I have done so by collecting "pairs" of 4-minute observations. A paired observation consists of sequentially coupled feeding records of two individuals, one from each class of the comparison, that are foraging near one another. This paired sampling technique has allowed me to compare the behavior of different birds under similar condi-

Figure 6.2. Collecting feeding-rate data from the tower on the Bly Creek drainage, Hobcaw Barony.

tions, thereby reducing the effects of time of day, weather, prey availability, and other extraneous influences.

Over the last 10 years, my colleagues and I have used the 4-minute technique to collect thousands of observations of feeding White Ibises and other wading birds. Throughout this time, I have never ceased to marvel at the efficacy of this simple scheme. It may not be "rocket science," but it certainly gets the job done.

Ibis Prey

White Ibises are crustacean specialists. In freshwater habitats ibises feed mainly on crayfishes (Cambaridae), whereas in coastal habitats estuarine crabs (Ocypodidae) are the principal prey item taken (Bildstein 1983, Kushlan and Bildstein 1992). These two families of crustaceans often constitute more than 90% of the diet of ibises.

But White Ibises also take many other aquatic and terrestrial arthropods, including insects, as well as worms, some snails, small reptiles, and fishes. Indeed, ibises seem willing to feed upon almost any small animal that they can catch that is about 10 centimeters or less in length. Members of our captive flock, for example, not only took all of the 3-centimeter fiddler crabs and 10-to 13-centimeter crayfishes we offered them, but also searched their cages for small tree frogs and Anolis Lizards that haplessly wandered in. In Trinidad, I have seen Scarlet Ibises feeding on bill-length (i.e., 15-centimeter) sandworms. There is even a report from Florida of White Ibises feeding on small Eastern Cottonmouths (Baynard 1913).

White Ibises have a variety of prey available to them at North Inlet (Table 6.1). Most, however, feed exclusively on the Mud Fiddler Crabs and Sand Fiddler Crabs, two species of crabs that make up the bulk of the macroscopic invertebrate fauna of the marsh. (Common Marsh Snails, Mud Snails, and Marsh Periwinkles, all of which are also common marsh inhabitants, are largely ignored by feeding ibises, perhaps because of their thick shells.) Although fiddler crabs are also fed upon by other long-billed birds such as Willets and Whimbrels, on the Bly Creek drainage, the White Ibis is the dominant threat to these prey. Dozens of the tiny arthropods inhabit each square meter of the marsh. The crabs, most of which are less than 3 centimeters across, derive their name from the

Table 6.1 Potential prey species of White Ibises feeding on the North
Inlet Marsh

Group	Species
Mollusca	Marsh Periwinkle
	Mud Snail
	Common Marsh Snail
Crustacea	Sand Fiddler Crab
	Mud Fiddler Crab
	Red-jointed Fiddler Crab
	Blue Crab
	Atlantic Mud Crab
	Brown Shrimp
	White Shrimp
	Grass Shrimp
Vertebrata	Mummichog
	Atlantic Silverside

enlarged claw that the males possess. This claw is waved during courtship
to attract females and is also used as a weapon during disputes with other
courting males (Crane 1975). Female fiddler crabs lack the enlarged major
claw, substituting a second normal-sized feeding claw in its place (Figure
6.3).

Estimating the numbers of fiddler crabs at North Inlet was not
easy. The scientific literature on fiddler crabs indicates that there is only
one way to do so with certainty: Tramp out onto the marsh, dig up a
measured fragment to a depth of about 30 centimeters, haul it back to the
lab, sift through sediment, locate all of the crabs therein, and extrapolate
that number to the marsh as a whole. Since crab numbers were likely to
fluctuate, both spatially and temporally, this absurdly laborious procedure
would have converted us from bird-watchers into crab-watchers, something none of us wanted to become. Fortunately, we discovered a compromise. Earlier studies had indicated that at low tide the number of crabs
feeding on the surface of a marsh is loosely correlated with the total
density of all the crabs, both above and below the ground.

We decided to count only the fiddler crabs on the surface and to
compare these numbers over space and time. Doing so would enable us
to determine the relative numbers of fiddler crabs on the marsh and,

Figure 6.3. Fiddler crabs, White Ibises' main prey on the Bly Creek drainage: *top,* male crab; *bottom,* female crab. Drawing by M. Davis.

eventually, whether or not birds were feeding in areas with the highest crab densities. Our actual survey technique was straightforward, although it probably appeared a bit whimsical to the uninitiated. Once a week, on the day after each dawn-to-dusk count of White Ibises feeding at the site, we counted surface crabs in randomly selected locations on the marsh and compared those totals with the numbers of crabs in areas that had been most heavily used by ibises on the previous day. Each survey consisted of 15 counts in the random areas and 15 in the heavily used areas. For each count, we tossed a square frame, which was made of 2.5-centimeter-thick plastic pipe and was 0.5 meter long on each side, onto the marsh, waited anxiously for about 3 minutes while the crabs that had been feeding on the surface crawled back out of their burrows and returned to the surface to feed, and then counted visible crabs (Figure 6.4).

Our surveys indicated that between 1984 and 1990, the Bly Creek drainage averaged about 25 surface fiddler crabs per square meter. But surface crabs were only part of the story. Numerous crabs also lurked beneath the marsh surface in a network of excavated burrows.

As is true elsewhere in their range, Bly Creek's fiddler crabs excavated two kinds of burrows. Breeding burrows, constructed only by males, were used for mating, whereas intertidal burrows, excavated by both sexes, were used as refuges from the tides that regularly flooded the area. Crabs also sought shelter in both types of burrows when retreating from predators, and it was into such burrows that most of the crabs withdrew whenever they detected approaching White Ibises.

The combined density of surface and subsurface fiddler crabs on the Bly Creek drainage is astounding. During the summer of 1990, graduate student Barbara McCraith attempted to remove all of the crabs from within three 9-square-meter fenced enclosures on the marsh. Barbara and her assistants spent several hours a day patiently extracting crabs as they left their burrows to feed on the marsh surface. Several weeks into the experiment Barbara discovered that she had, on average, removed more than 45 crabs per square meter of marsh, and she never got all of them. These observations suggest that crab densities on the drainage approach half a million individuals per hectare.

Many ecologists consider salt-marsh fiddler crabs to be the ecological equivalents of terrestrial earthworms. Like earthworms, fiddler crabs are thought to play decisive roles in such important environmental processes as increasing sediment "bioturbation" (the rearrangement of sediment by animal activity), mineralization, and oxygenation, as well as in enhancing plant productivity (Montague 1980). In light of their supposed ecological significance, I was especially interested in learning more about

Figure 6.4. Counting fiddler crabs on the Bly Creek drainage.

the crabs and about how their interactions with White Ibises affected their ecology and behavior.

Distribution and Abundance of the Feeding White Ibises

Throughout the breeding season, White Ibises search the marsh for fiddler crabs whenever the tides permit. The birds appear to prefer to feed on uninundated portions of the marsh, but many remain even during especially high tides, when water spills over the banks of tidal meanders onto the marsh and so-called sheet flow covers most of the site. Indeed, between May and August each year, about the only time that ibises are absent from the site is when water covers the surface to a depth of more than 20 centimeters. Even at these times, scattered individuals can be seen attempting to feed along the upland perimeter of the marsh.

Although White Ibises rarely fly onto the marsh to feed after showers begin, individuals that are already feeding when rain begins often continue to do so. Nevertheless, ibises do tend to vacate the site during electrical storms, a phenomenon we have been unable to study in detail because we too retreat at such times. I have yet to have anyone question my thunderstorm protocol: When in doubt, leave the tower. Grounded or not, an 18.5-meter metal tower, jutting more than 5 meters above the surrounding canopy, is not a safe haven in an electrical storm— nor, for that matter, is the marsh. In July 1986, upon my return to the tower after a brief but severe electrical storm that I had weathered at the base of the lookout in a pickup truck, I had trouble seeing one of the meter-high stakes that marked the study grids on the marsh. I felt certain that the stake had been there when I left the tower less than an hour earlier. Later that afternoon, when I hiked out onto the grid to replace the marker, I stumbled across its charred remains several meters from its splintered base. No wonder the birds retire during such events.

Typically, the first White Ibises to arrive at the marsh each morning do so within an hour of daybreak, and on most days several individuals remain until close to nightfall (Figure 6.5). Nevertheless, on any given day the number of birds feeding can fluctuate from less than a dozen to over 100 on almost an hourly basis.

Although most White Ibises catch between 1.5 and 2.0 fiddler crabs per minute, some individuals have caught as many as 29 crabs

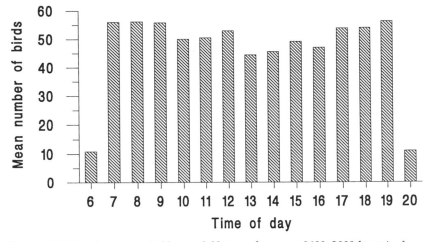

Figure 6.5. Hourly counts (6:00 A.M.–8:00 P.M., shown as 0600–2000 hours) of White Ibises on the Bly Creek drainage. Means are based on data collected from 1984 to 1989.

during a single 4-minute observation (i.e., more than 7 crabs per minute). Ibises walk at a brisk pace while searching the marsh for crabs, usually in excess of 10 meters per minute, or over 0.5 kilometer per hour. Nevertheless, since ibises rarely walk in a straight line for more than several paces, individuals often remain within several hundred meters of their starting points for hours. Ibises probe for crabs at a rate of just over 11 probes per minute, and they are successful about 14% of the time (Table 6.2). Individuals appear to be especially intent while searching for prey, and many forage for prolonged periods without interruption (Figure 6.6). When they do rest, few remain on the marsh for more than several minutes. Most fly to nearby roost trees, where they spend a considerable amount of time preening.

Table 6.2   Foraging rates of adult White Ibises on the Bly Creek drainage, Hobcaw Barony, 1982–90

Foraging rate	Mean ± standard deviation	
Steps per minute	38.5 ± 15.5	(779)
Probes per minute	11.1 ± 4.0	(779)
Captures per minute	2.02 ± 1.0	(779)
Probes per capture	6.91 ± 5.1	(777)

Note: Number of 4-minute observations is in parentheses.

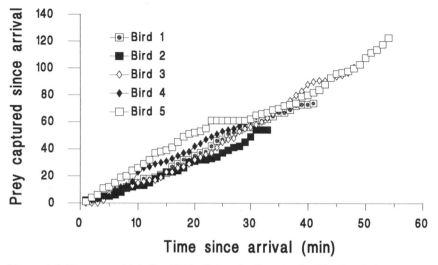

Figure 6.6. Rates at which five White Ibises feeding on the Bly Creek drainage in 1984 captured prey.

Flocking Behavior

Although some White Ibises feed alone, most feed in flocks, usually within several meters of each other, in groups that fluctuate between 2 and 75 individuals. Between 1982 and 1985, for example, more than 99% of the 13,814 ibises that we counted were feeding in flocks, and each flock averaged just over 17 birds in size (Figure 6.7). I considered ibises to be part of a flock if they were feeding within 50 meters of their nearest neighbor. Although this is a rather large distance, birds within this range did appear to be responding to each other's presence in ways that were not apparent in more distantly separated individuals. For example, birds that were within 50 meters of each other typically moved across the drainage in concert, and in most instances they departed the marsh at about the same time.

Flocks arrived and departed throughout the day. Most moved slowly up and down the marsh, with individual birds tending to move farther afield the longer a flock remained at the site. Even so, most of the birds we watched fed within 5 meters of each other (Figure 6.8).

Although it is not possible to know for certain, several lines of evidence suggest that White Ibises are more at ease when feeding together than when feeding alone. For example, on dozens of occasions I have watched single birds fly to the marsh from communal day roosts in the trees that surround the site, only to turn and stand looking back in the direction of the roost without feeding until one or more additional individuals joined them. In most instances, if additional ibises do not arrive within a minute or so, the singleton leaves the marsh without feeding and rejoins its roosting companions. Indeed, in many of these

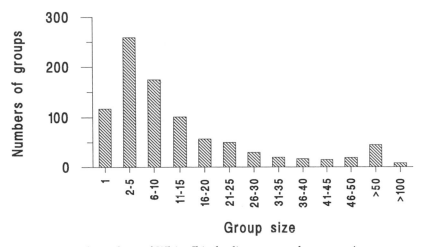

Figure 6.7. Total numbers of White Ibis feeding groups, by group size, observed on the Bly Creek drainage, 1982–85.

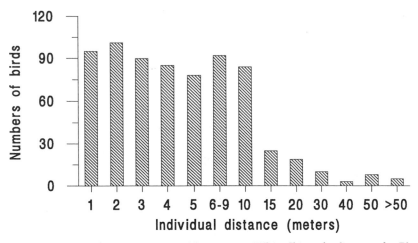

Figure 6.8. Distance to nearest neighbor among White Ibises feeding on the Bly Creek drainage in 1989.

episodes, lone birds departing from day roosts turn and look back toward the roost even while in flight, and many come about and withdraw without landing when other individuals fail to follow. In contrast, when groups of two or more birds arrive on the marsh, they typically begin feeding within several seconds of landing, and I have never seen individuals in flocks glancing back toward their day roosts.

Ornithologists have long assumed that, in addition to looking for mates, birds flock for one of two reasons: to reduce their risk of predation or to increase their foraging success. Flocking reduces the risk of predation in at least two ways. First, a flock has more eyes with which to detect predators than does a single bird (Pulliam 1973). Second, flocking offers safety in numbers because individuals crowding near the center of the flock are shielded from predation by those on its periphery, as well as because flocking makes singling out a target more difficult for attacking predators (Hamilton 1971, Page and Whitacre 1975, Kenward 1978, Caraco 1979). Likewise, flocking can enhance foraging success either by increasing the probability that birds will find and use food resources (because unknowing individuals can follow the knowledgeable ones to the best feeding sites) (Ward and Zahavi 1973) or by allowing individuals to copy the successful foraging techniques of their flock mates (Krebs et al. 1972). Of course, reducing the risk of predation and enhancing one's feeding rate are not mutually exclusive, and flocking may serve both purposes simultaneously (Abramson 1979).

We noticed early in our observations that White Ibises were extremely "jumpy" when they foraged on the marsh, perhaps because their continual probing forces them to look down for prolonged periods of time (Rudegeair 1975). Soaring predators, including Bald Eagles, Ospreys, Redtailed Hawks, and even scavenging Black and Turkey vultures (but not the similarly sized Great Blue Herons), frequently frightened entire flocks of ibises from the marsh. Even more surprising was the fact that fixed-wing aircraft, and even helicopters, did the same. Low-flying A-10 military aircraft on maneuvers from nearby Myrtle Beach Air Force Base appeared to be especially worrisome. I have watched ibises desert their feeding sites on overcast days when aircraft were well above the cloud layer, out of sight, and barely audible. The sound of the aircraft's jet engines was a Pavlovian bell of sorts, but, strangely, no ibises seemed conditioned to the fact that no problem follows. On the other hand, noisier boat engines caused little disturbance. Nor did potential ground threats such as humans and Raccoons walking across the marsh—both of which were often able to approach to within 25 meters of feeding ibises—seem to frighten the birds excessively.

Fear of predation also may have affected where the White Ibises fed on the marsh. Although feeding ibises usually spent less than 10% of their time looking toward the sky, presumably scanning for aerial predators, sometimes individuals spent as much as 90% of their time doing so. At least some of the variation in this behavior is linked to habitat. Elizabeth Henderson found that both juveniles and adults feeding in tall cordgrasses along the creek banks interrupted their feeding bouts twice as often as did those feeding in shorter vegetation elsewhere on the marsh, and that overall such birds spent almost twice as much time looking up as did birds in shorter vegetation. Elizabeth attributed these differences to increased vigilance (Henderson 1981). Although other factors may influence ibis use of such sites, the fact that areas of tall cordgrass are used decidedly less often than are other portions of the marsh suggests that individuals take their risk of predation into account when choosing where to feed in the drainage.

Nevertheless, after spending thousands of hours on the marsh watching feeding White Ibises, I have yet to see one even be attacked by a predator, let alone captured. Nor have any of my co-workers witnessed such an occurrence. Throughout our studies, we have found only one potentially "suspicious" carcass on the marsh. And even that bird, a recently fledged Tricolored Heron that was being fed upon by a Turkey Vulture, was not necessarily a victim of predation. Bald Eagles prey upon ibises elsewhere in their range, and it may be to that threat that Bly Creek's ibises are responding. Whatever the cause, the cost of this presumed antipredator behavior appears to be substantial, since on many days hundreds of birds are repeatedly flushed from the marsh as a result of overflying birds and aircraft. In 1981 and 1982, for example, feeding ibises responded to apparent aerial disturbances more than once every 2 hours (Bildstein 1983).

Discerning the Benefits of Flocking

Although the observations detailed above suggested that feeding ibises flocked in response to a perceived risk of predation, additional "controlled" observations were clearly in order. During the summer of 1984, former intern Dan Petit and I set out to collect such observations and to test the flocking-to-reduce-risk-of-predation hypothesis (Petit and Bildstein 1987). Dan and I recorded in detail the foraging behavior of ibises feeding alone (i.e., at least 50 meters from other ibises), in small flocks (less than 5 birds), and in large flocks (greater than 15 birds). For birds feeding in larger flocks, we also noted whether the observed individual was located centrally or peripherally within the flock. To focus on the effects of social grouping and minimize the effects of other factors, we were careful to pair each observation of a bird foraging within one social group with that of another (i.e., we collected couplets of 4-minute observations within several minutes of each other). Regardless of social grouping, most ibises foraged in the same general area of the marsh. During this aspect of our study, we studied only adult ibises, whose behavior differs significantly from that of younger individuals feeding at the site (as discussed later in this chapter).

We predicted that, if adult ibises were feeding in flocks to reduce their risk of predation, such behavior would have two effects on their foraging behavior. First, birds in large groups should exhibit significantly fewer scanning efforts than would those feeding in small flocks or as singletons. Birds in large groups should look up less often and for briefer periods because other flock members would be, in effect, sharing this responsibility. Second, birds feeding in large groups should forage more efficiently (i.e., capture prey more frequently and with fewer steps and probes) because they would be spending more time looking for prey and less time looking up for predators.

Throughout the summer of 1984, Dan and I recorded the behavior of almost 200 singleton and flocking White Ibises, which we followed during 97 pairs of 4-minute observations. As predicted by the first part of our hypothesis, ibises feeding alone, as well as those feeding in small groups or on the peripheries of large groups, looked up significantly more often, and for longer periods of time, than did ibises feeding in the centers of large flocks (Figure 6.9). Our data clearly suggested that ibises at the centers of large groups were spending less time searching for predators— and more time foraging—than were birds in other situations. We attributed this shift in behavior to what W. D. Hamilton (1971) has called the "selfish-herd effect": Individuals at the centers of flocks (in our case, ibises feeding in the centers of flocks of at least 15 birds) gain an advantage over those in other situations by being protected from intruding predators because they are surrounded by other birds, which approaching predators would presumably take first.

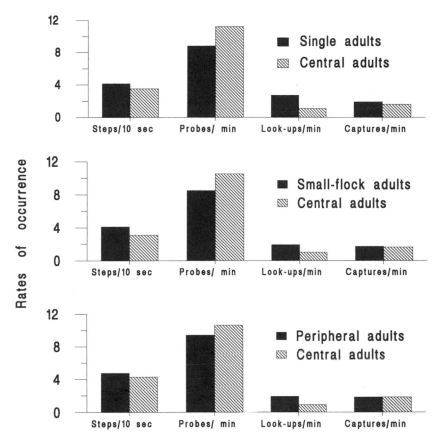

Figure 6.9. Behavior of White Ibis adults feeding alone, in small flocks (less than 6 birds), or in peripheral or central positions in large flocks (more than 14 birds) on the Bly Creek drainage in 1984.

But although our observations supported the first prediction associated with the hypothesis, they failed to support the second. Prey capture rate did not increase with size of the foraging group. Likewise, capture rate did not differ as a function of a bird's location within a flock (Figure 6.9). At first Dan and I were confused by these results. What were the central birds doing with their "extra" feeding time? Were the birds that hunted in the centers of large flocks at a disadvantage over other individuals? And if so, what might that disadvantage be?

We quickly rejected local prey depletion (Zwarts 1980) as a possible cause for the difference. The birds moved across the marsh too quickly and fiddler crab densities were too high for that to have been a factor. We also dismissed another potential disadvantage that is sometimes associated with flock feeding, that of fighting over food (see Goss-Custard 1977, Silliman et al. 1977). Ibises rarely fought among themselves for food. Only during a brief 2-week period in late July 1984 did we observe any interference or aggression, and even then, aggressive interactions occurred less than once every 2 hours, hardly enough to affect the intake rates of centrally foraging individuals.

An analysis of the accompanying data on stepping and probing rates was what finally led to an explanation. When Dan and I subtracted the time each bird spent looking up during our observations and recalculated the stepping and probing rates of all of the birds we had observed, we discovered that singletons and birds in small flocks stepped significantly more frequently, probed significantly less frequently, but captured prey at rates identical to their counterparts in the centers of large flocks (Figure 6.9). Peripheral individuals in large flocks also stepped more and probed less than did central individuals, but the differences were not quite statistically significant. Why would central birds probe more and step less than other birds? We believe that these differences reflect a reduction in available fiddler crabs in the centers of flocks.

Fiddler crabs feeding on the surface of the marsh must be retreating into their burrows in response to advancing flocks of ibises, thus depleting the area of its crabs, at least in appearance. That the crabs retreat in this manner is supported not only by our own experiences with fiddler crabs at the site, but also by our observations of interactions between ibises and crabs in captive situations (the details of which are provided later in this chapter). As a result, ibises feeding at the centers of large flocks are feeding in areas where most, if not all, of the crabs have already descended into their burrows. Because more crabs are in burrows than on the surface in such situations, central birds must depend more on tactile strategies such as burrow probing than on visual strategies such as chasing surface crabs. Thus, central ibises spend more of their time probing, and less of their time stepping, than do other ibises. And because many of the burrows into which central birds probe yield no crabs at all, central ibises will have a greater number of probes between captures than will their less central flock mates.

On the other hand, ibises on the peripheries of flocks, ibises in small flocks, and especially singletons, which are the first birds to reach undisturbed areas, will be in a better position to find and catch surface crabs. During our more lengthy observations, we found additional behavioral evidence to support the notion of the decreased availability of surface crabs in the centers of flocks. Ibises that changed positions within large flocks (i.e., birds that moved from peripheral to central locations and vice versa) switched from probing more and stepping less to probing less and stepping more.

That most White Ibises forage in flocks even though they receive no apparent benefit in terms of increased foraging efficiency strongly supports the notion that ibises, via the selfish-herd effect, flock mainly to reduce their risk of predation. Why then are some ibises content to forage on the edges of large flocks, in small flocks, and even alone, where they are presumably at greater risk of predation? Research suggests that dominance behavior often plays an important a role in determining where an individual forages (Morse 1970, Peters and Grubb 1983). In ibis flocks, subordinate individuals perhaps are forced, or they may actually choose, to feed alone or in peripheral positions.

In birds, as in mammals, larger individuals usually dominate smaller individuals. I have already noted that female White Ibises are smaller and have substantially shorter bills than the males (Figure 3.3). Either of these features might place any females that are feeding in the centers of large flocks at a decided disadvantage. Our observations, however, do not support such a case. Females did not appear to be more common on the edges of flocks, nor did they appear to feed alone more frequently than males. Individual ibises may simply differ in their abilities to socialize with other ibises, or especially hungry individuals may be willing to forgo the increased safety of large flocks and feed alone when their companions are not willing to do so. Studies involving individually marked birds may be the only way to address this issue.

Age-related Foraging Differences and Their Meaning

In an evolutionary sense, all White Ibises are the same. All are descended from a common ancestor, all share the same genetic heritage, and all belong to the species we call *Eudocimus ruber*. But I wanted to know whether the different "kinds" of White Ibises I was considering (i.e., adults versus juveniles, females versus males) were ecologically the same as well? On a theoretical level, if adults and juveniles—or females and males—were extracting fiddler crabs at decidedly different rates, I would need to account for these differences when modeling the species's overall impact in the marsh. On a more practical level, information on gender- and age-specific differences would also be important during the development of habitat management plans and other conservation strategies for ibises. For these reasons, I decided to study foraging behavior in greater detail.

How does the feeding behavior of adult and juvenile White Ibises compare? How long does an ibis take to develop the hunting skills of an adult? Do age-related differences in foraging behavior in any way explain why ibises wait until they are nearly 2 years old to begin breeding? I hoped to address these questions by comparing the feeding behavior of adult and juvenile ibises in much the same way that Dan and I had compared the feeding behavior of singleton and flocking ibises: by collecting paired 4-minute observations of adults and juveniles and examining these comparisons for evidence of age effects.

Most birds, especially small and short-lived species, breed as soon as it is "ecologically possible" (Lack 1968)—that is, as soon as weather and prey availability permit. Thus, species living outside the tropics often begin breeding at slightly less than 1 year of age. Species in less seasonal environments, such as Australian Zebra Finches, can begin breeding as early as 6 to 8 months of age (Campbell and Lack 1985). When birds are in captivity, even briefer generation times are possible. The current avian record for age at first breeding is held by a Coturnix Quail that began laying eggs 38 days after it hatched (Padgett and Ivey 1959). Still, many other birds, especially those belonging to both larger bodied and longer lived species, delay or defer breeding until they are older. The larger birds of prey and storks, for example, regularly begin breeding at 4 to 6 years of age, and the Royal Albatross breeds for the first time no earlier than at 8 years of age (Campbell and Lack 1985).

Although some researchers have suggested that such differences reflect variation in the amount of time birds of different sizes need to mature physically, David Lack (1968) gave a more convincing explanation: Some species of birds delay reproduction because any attempt by individuals to breed earlier would not be likely to succeed and, in fact, might be dangerous to the individual. Thus, Lack implied that younger birds are inadequately prepared for reproduction, and that they refrain from breeding because of the prohibitively high cost-to-benefit ratio of doing so.

As is true for many species of colonial waterbirds, White Ibises delay breeding until they are at least nearly 2 years of age (Beebe 1914,

Kushlan and Bildstein 1992). The delay does not appear to be influenced by local conditions. Even the ibises we had raised in captivity on ad libitum food waited until at least their second spring before beginning to court and mate. But why should ibises practice what has come to be called "deferred maturation"?

Since David Lack's classic paper on the subject (see Lack 1968), many researchers have linked deferred maturation to age-related inadequacies in foraging efficiency. Some have claimed that younger birds simply do not catch prey as fast as do older individuals, and hence lack the wherewithal to provide sufficient food for developing young. Data supporting this argument are known for several species of colonial waterbirds (Table 6.3), and both Rudegeair (1975) and Henderson (1981) had made observations that suggested the same might be true for White Ibises. With this in mind, I began to look for differences in the behavior of adult and recently fledged juvenile ibises feeding on the Bly Creek drainage during the summer of 1980. (For more detailed accounts of the results of these studies, see Bildstein 1983 and 1984.)

Recently fledged juvenile White Ibises begin to arrive on the feeding site in late June or early July each year, usually within days of the first sightings of fledglings leaving the Pumpkinseed Island colony site. Nevertheless, even in late summer, juveniles rarely constitute more than half of the birds feeding on the marsh, and in most years juveniles make up less than 10% of all birds observed on the drainage. Although there is no evidence suggesting that juveniles are fed by their parents after they leave the colony site, most of the juveniles that feed in the Bly Creek drainage stay with numerous adults in mixed-age feeding flocks. As a result, I have been able to collect more than 100 pairs of 4-minute observations of adults and juveniles feeding en masse at such times.

Two lines of evidence suggest that the observed juvenile White Ibises had followed adults onto and off the marsh. Ibises fly onto and off the Bly Creek drainage throughout the day, presumably to secure fresh water to dilute their salty prey (see Chapter 8) or to rest at the many roosting sites that surround the drainage. Most of these flights consist of a few birds (usually fewer than 10 individuals) arriving or departing in close synchrony. For the 3 years during which I monitored such flocks in detail, all-adult flocks averaged just under 3 individuals per flock, whereas those containing both adults and juveniles averaged nearly 4.5 individuals per flock. This difference in flock size suggested that mixed-age flocks might be formed when juveniles append themselves to existing adult

Table 6.3.   Species of colonial waterbirds for which age-related differences in foraging behavior have been reported

Order	Species
Sphenisciformes	Adelie Penguin
Pelecaniformes	Brown Pelican
	Olivaceous Cormorant
	Magnificent Frigatebird
Ciconiiformes	Grey Heron
	Great Blue Heron
	Eastern Reef Heron
	Little Blue Heron
	White Ibis
Charadriiformes	Eurasian Oystercatcher
	Black-necked Stilt
	Ruddy Turnstone
	Laughing Gull
	Ring-billed Gull
	Herring Gull
	Glaucous-winged Gull
	Caspian Tern
	Royal Tern
	Sandwich Tern

Note: As reviewed in Bildstein (1983).

flocks. To test this possibility, I subtracted from the mixed-age flocks the numbers of juveniles involved in each and compared the numbers of remaining adults in these flocks with the numbers of adults in all-adult flocks. I found that the average number of adults in the two types of flocks was nearly identical: 2.81 adults for mixed-aged flocks (based on a sample size of 92 flocks) and 2.82 for all-adult flocks (sample size of 319 flocks). Also, when I compared the ages of birds flying in the leading halves of such flocks with those traveling in the trailing halves (most of the birds flew in relatively linear skeins onto and off the site), I learned that, in approximately two-thirds of the flocks, the juveniles were following the adults rather than leading. These findings were as I had expected, and they confirmed that most of these mixed-aged flocks had in fact been adult groups to which juveniles had appended themselves.

The percentage of juveniles feeding in mixed-age flocks remained relatively constant regardless of the size of the flock. Also, early in the course of my studies I noticed that juveniles were inclined to feed not only in groups but also at the peripheries of such assemblages. One consequence of the nonrandom distribution of adults and juveniles was that more than twice as many juveniles as expected (61 versus 30%) had another juvenile as their nearest neighbor. Why juveniles tended to be found at the peripheries of flocks was unclear. Most juveniles stepped and probed at the same rates as did adult ibises feeding nearby. But, regardless of their position within the pack (i.e., next to an adult, next to a juvenile, central, or peripheral), juvenile ibises were decidedly less successful in capturing prey than were their adult counterparts. Those feeding in the company of other juveniles, in which cases they usually were located at the peripheries of flocks, caught prey at only 40% of the adult rate. Those foraging near adults and away from other juveniles, in which cases they were usually in the centers of flocks, caught prey at only 43% of the adult rate (Figure 6.10).

In addition, recently fledged juveniles that fed near adults may have paid a price for doing so. Many of these birds were chased by one or more adults during my observations, and one was robbed of its prey by its adult neighbor. However, I have also seen juveniles robbing each other of prey.

Why then, do juvenile White Ibises tend to follow adults onto the marsh? I believe juveniles do so because adults are more likely to know where the most profitable locations are on the marsh, and juveniles, by feeding in the same general vicinity, benefit from this knowledge. If this explanation is correct, then information about appropriate feeding sites may be passed from one generation to the next in much the same way that knowledge about appropriate breeding locations is passed along. I leave it to those who are more philosophical than I to conclude whether such information transfer, if it indeed occurs, signifies that ibises have culture. But at the very least, ibises appear to be somewhat constrained by tradition.

Even though most juvenile White Ibises fed in mixed-aged flocks, the spatial distributions of juveniles on the marsh differed consistently from the spatial distributions of the adults over the years. Although adult densities were invariably higher on the southeastern side of the creek than on the northwestern side, juvenile densities tended to be more equal on both sides of the creek (Figure 6.11). At first, I thought that this pattern might merely reflect differences in the habitat preferences of the two age-groups, but I was not sure how the habitats on the two sides of the creek differed. Another possibility was that the high densities of adult ibises southeast of the creek in some way limited juvenile densities there.

Adult Eurasian Oystercatchers, for example, limit densities of juveniles on preferred feeding sites (Goss-Custard et al. 1982), and the same appeared to be true of adult White Ibises. In oystercatchers, the juveniles are less aggressive, less successful in defending their prey, and more likely to avoid other birds than are the adults. At first, this scenario

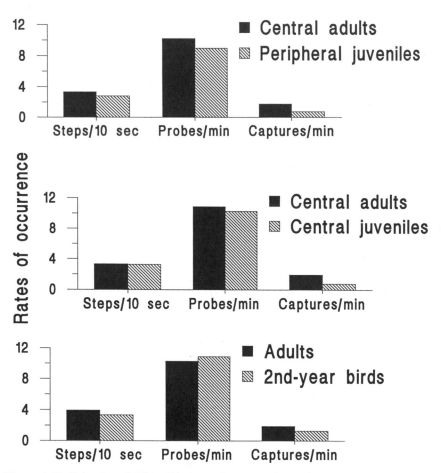

Figure 6.10. Behavior of White Ibis juveniles, second-year birds, and adults in central or peripheral positions in flocks feeding on the Bly Creek drainage. Rates of occurrence are means based on data collected from 1980 to 1983. Modification of a figure in Bildstein (1983). Reproduced by permission of the Colonial Waterbird Society.

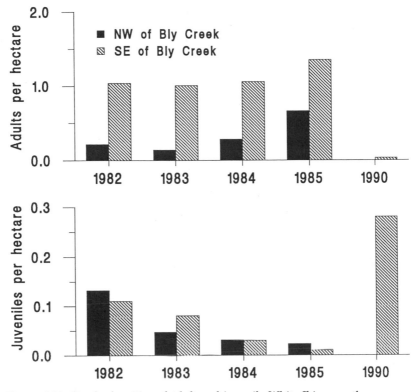

Figure 6.11. Yearly densities of adult and juvenile White Ibises on the northwestern and southeastern sides of Bly Creek, 1982–85 and 1990.

seemed unlikely for ibises, since I have only detected relatively low levels of aggression among foraging birds. Data collected during the summer of 1990 after the passage of Hurricane Hugo, however, have forced me to reevaluate the possibility that aggression influences the distribution of juvenile ibises on the Bly Creek drainage.

Not only did White Ibises fail to breed on Pumpkinseed Island in 1990 (see Chapter 11), but also they failed to return in their usual numbers to Bly Creek. Indeed, numbers of ibises on the drainage dropped to about 5% of what they had been during each of the previous 8 years. But more importantly, for the first time ever, the juvenile ibises feeding on the marsh greatly outnumbered the adults. In most years juveniles made up fewer than 10% of all foraging individuals. In 1990 they constituted 90%. Juveniles began arriving in late June, probably from successful colony

sites in North Carolina, Florida, or Georgia. Stripped of the usual comple-
ment of adult ibises, these juveniles used the drainage differently than
had their predecessors.

In 1990, all juvenile White Ibises foraged on the southeastern side
of the creek (Figure 6.11). The situation appeared to fit the old adage "When
the cat's away the mice will play." In addition to foraging on the side of the
creek generally preferred by adult ibises, on many days juvenile ibises also
favored the same quarter-hectare plots that adults had favored in previous
years. Although these observations do not demonstrate unequivocally that
adults had previously kept many juveniles from using these areas—after
all, Hurricane Hugo might have differentially affected the marshes on either
side of the creek—they certainly support this hypothesis. I hope to resolve
this issue in the not-too-distant future by documenting where juveniles
feed when adult ibises return to the drainage.

What about the question of deferred maturity? Although the observations described above demonstrate that White Ibises are not born with
fully developed hunting skills, they do not directly address the question of
whether or not birds returning to the site 1 year later still lack those foraging
skills. To answer this question I needed to compare the foraging efficiencies
of second-year birds with those of older individuals. (Ornithologists and
bird banders use the term *second-year bird* to indicate individuals in their
second calendar year, even when the bird in question is not yet 2 years
old. For example, an individual that hatched in June of one year would be
considered a second-year bird from 1 January through 31 December of the
next, in much the same way that a thoroughbred horse born in one calendar
year is considered to be a 2-year-old throughout the next.)

Before I could compare the foraging efficiencies of second-year
and older White Ibises, I needed to locate sufficient numbers of each.
Finding large numbers of older individuals presented little problem. Each
spring and summer, dozens of these birds, if not more, frequently fed
near the base of my observation tower at the edge of the drainage. Locating
adequate numbers of second-year birds was another situation entirely.
Between 1979 and 1982, few of the ibises at the site were individuals
that had been born during the previous breeding season. Apparently,
members of this cohort summer elsewhere. However, in March and April
of 1983, many second-year birds arrived at the site along with the annual
influx of older individuals. Although none of these second-year birds bred
at the Pumpkinseed Island colony site (indeed, none ever developed the
scarlet fleshy areas typical of courting adults), many fed together with

older individuals in mixed-aged flocks. These younger birds frequently made up more than 10% of a flock, and most lingered in the area at least through early August. As a result, during the summer of 1983, I was able to compare the foraging efficiencies of these birds with those of the numerous older breeding-age individuals with which they fed, many of which were raising young (Bildstein 1984).

I failed to detect any differences between second-year and older ibises in their stepping, probing, or looking rates. However, on a per-probe basis, second-year birds were only half as successful at securing prey as were older birds, and, more importantly, the younger birds caught prey only 67% as frequently as did the older birds with which they were feeding.

These observations suggest that the foraging efficiency of second-year birds, although considerably greater than that of recently fledged birds, is still far short of that of breeding adults. Several species of gulls show similar improvements in foraging skills with age (Burger and Gochfeld 1983, Greig et al. 1983, MacLean 1986).

As a result of their inferior foraging skills, second-year White Ibises, if they were to breed, would need to allocate approximately 50% more of their time for feeding than would older individuals. Since raising juvenile ibises appears to be a rather trying experience even for the more proficient adult parents, my observations of foraging inadequacies in second-year ibises support Lack's explanation for deferred breeding. In White Ibises, at least, parenting requires a degree of maturity not yet achieved by second-year birds.

Although some researchers have suggested that selective mortality of the most inept individuals may be responsible for some of this apparent "improvement" (i.e., as incompetent individuals die off, the average for an age-group improves accordingly; see Recher and Recher 1969), all of the individually marked captive ibises we raised substantially improved their foraging skills after prolonged exposure to live fiddler crabs, and I believe that most of the differences I observed in the foraging efficiencies of fledgling and second-year ibises represents actual improvement on the part of individual birds, rather than the selective mortality of genetic "losers." Nevertheless, about the only way to test the extent to which both of these possibilities influenced my observations would be to observe the foraging behavior of individually marked free-ranging ibises from fledging through their first attempt at breeding.

The plumage of third-year White Ibises is indistinguishable from that of older individuals. Thus, I have been unable to look for differences between the foraging efficiency of this age class and that of older ibises. It is possible that even third-year birds are not as proficient as older individuals, and that the foraging efficiency of individual birds improves throughout their lifetime.

Gender-related Foraging Differences

Having established that a White Ibis's age affects its foraging behavior, I next focused on whether or not gender had an effect. I did so for several reasons. Male ibises are substantially heavier than females, and they have longer legs and wings and, perhaps most importantly, significantly longer bills than do their female counterparts (Kushlan 1977d, Bildstein 1987) (Figure 3.3). I assumed that these differences might affect the ways male and female ibises hunted for their prey. But, although the larger body and longer bill of the male ibis appear to be beneficial during courtship and mating, their impact on foraging behavior had not been examined in detail.

To explore the potential effects of what ornithologists refer to as *sexual size dimorphism* on feeding behavior, I collected a series of 4-minute paired observations of adult male and female White Ibises feeding side by side on the Bly Creek drainage during the summers of 1985 and 1986. As I had done in my earlier observations, I controlled for a "flock effect" on feeding behavior by analyzing pairs of birds feeding at the peripheries of larger flocks or in small flocks separately from those feeding in the centers of large flocks, and I controlled for a "habitat effect" by limiting my observations to birds feeding in relatively short vegetation and away from the creek banks.

Although I failed to determine the relative numbers of males and females feeding on the marsh, the ratio appeared to be close to 1:1 (males : females) overall. Likewise, the sexes were present in roughly equal numbers in large and small feeding flocks, and in the centers and peripheries of larger feeding flocks. Overall, male ibises feeding at the peripheries of large flocks and in small flocks caught prey at only 87% of the rate of their female counterparts. Males feeding in the centers of large flocks caught prey at only 90% of the rate of females feeding by their sides. However, neither of these rate differences was close to being statistically significant. There were no significant gender-related differences in any of the other aspects of the foraging behavior that I measured. Nor did males and females exhibit any differences in the amount of time spent looking up, presumably in search of aerial predators. (Additional details of this study can be found in Bildstein 1987.)

These observations suggest that gender had little, if any, effect on the feeding rates of White Ibises searching for fiddler crabs on the Bly Creek drainage. Even so, since male ibises are significantly larger than females, males should require more prey to maintain energetic equilibrium. Thus, males should need to feed for longer periods of time each day. But how much longer?

To investigate the impact of sexual size dimorphism on this aspect of ibis feeding ecology, I constructed a simple mathematical model that estimated how feeding behavior and morphology combined to affect the amount of time males and females would need to spend feeding each day to remain in energetic equilibrium. The model I used merged the feeding-rate data I had just collected at the site with previously published information on the masses of adult male and female White Ibises, a time–activity budget for adults, and the standard metabolic equations for birds of the sizes of male and female ibises (Bildstein 1987).

With the capture rates I had observed, the model suggests that nonparental male White Ibises would need to spend approximately 3.5 hours feeding on the marsh each day, whereas females would need to spend only about 2.5 hours each day. Parental males and females would, of course, need to spend additional time securing prey for their nestlings. Despite considerable uncertainty in my calculations of daily energy requirements, these data, together with those collected on ibis courtship and mating (Rudegeair 1975, Frederick 1985b), suggest that the large body size of males, which may be advantageous at the Pumpkinseed Island colony site, is not without cost on the Bly Creek drainage feeding site. I use the word "suggest," rather than a more definitive term, on purpose. Although the data reported above had initially led me to believe that males "paid" for their larger size by feeding for longer periods each day, results of more recent investigations with captive ibises have forced me to reevaluate the validity of this conclusion.

Feeding Experiments with Captive White Ibises

During the summer of 1987, Susan McDowell and I decided to use the captive flock of White Ibises that we were maintaining at the Savannah

River Ecology Laboratory to explore several questions concerning the feeding behavior of ibises. With the captive birds, we could conduct experiments under more controlled circumstances than would be possible in the field. First we needed to make to make certain that the behavior of captively reared birds was similar to that of free-ranging individuals and not an artifact of their captive lifestyle. To do this, we had to capture thousands of fiddler crabs at the coast each week during May and June and transport them 240 kilometers (150 miles) to the Savannah River Ecology Laboratory, where we offered them to our captive birds.

There is no easy way to catch large numbers of fiddler crabs. A crab-catcher simply must grab a small bucket, march out onto an exposed creek bed at low tide, and begin chasing crabs across the marsh surface. The crabs will, in turn, retreat hastily to the nearest available burrows. Since individual ibises can consume over 300 crabs per day, three to five crab-catchers were required to catch the thousands of crabs we needed each week. Once caught, the crabs were rinsed free of mud, placed in "crabberies" (45-liter insulated picnic coolers) and sent 240 kilometers inland to the aviary near Aiken, South Carolina.

By late June, our captive birds were handling fiddler crabs like pros, and Susan and I decided to initiate our first experiment. Our initial efforts involved offering the White Ibises an opportunity to search for fiddler crabs in artificial burrows of known length. Our burrows consisted of 70-, 110-, and 130-millimeter lengths of vinyl tubing that were 20 millimeters in diameter and had been plugged at the bottom with a cork. (The dimensions of all of our artificial burrows were well within the range of natural burrows actually excavated by fiddler crabs at our Bly Creek study site [Frix et al. 1991].) Each of the 18 burrows we used extended vertically below an elevated plywood feeding bench. Before these experiments and immediately before we had started giving the birds the live fiddler crab prey, which we had been releasing on the ground inside the aviary, Susan had been feeding the birds literally out of her hands. Consequently, many of them were initially reluctant to feed on the feeding bench. However, once they learned that food was available only there, and that the food often consisted of live fiddler crabs, all of the birds quickly adapted to this new cafeteria-style dining, and we had little trouble convincing them to probe the artificial burrows during our experiments. In fact, we frequently had trouble keeping the ibises off the bench while we restocked the burrows.

Because ibises typically forage in groups for fiddler crabs, we allowed all of our birds simultaneous access to the bench during each experiment (Figure 6.12). We each concentrated our observation efforts on one ibis during individual runs. Although allowing the birds to feed as a group meant that the bench was rather rapidly depleted of prey, often within half a minute, we felt that flocking was necessary to ensure typical feeding behavior.

Before each experiment, Susan and I randomly assigned burrows of different lengths to the 18 burrow locations available on the table (Figure 6.13). We then placed an individual male or female fiddler crab in each burrow, carefully making certain that the major claw of each male was flexed and faced toward the burrow opening. In most cases, the crabs immediately retreated to the bottom of their burrows. Crabs that the White Ibises had removed and dropped before consumption quickly retreated back into a burrow, and we believe that the way the crabs responded to their artificial burrows closely resembled that of free-ranging crabs fleeing in advance of ibises feeding on the Bly Creek drainage. After filling each burrow with one crab, we sat down within a meter of the bench and recorded the probing success of our individually marked birds (Figure 6.14). Most of our experiments were run with alternating batches of approximately 80 male or female crabs, which we restocked whenever all

Figure 6.12. Captive White Ibises feeding cafeteria-style on fiddler crabs.

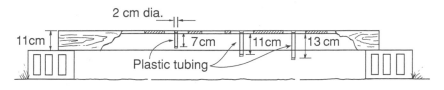

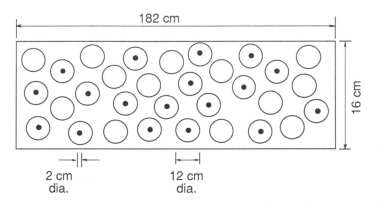

Figure 6.13. Design of the ibis cafeteria. *Top:* Side view, showing burrows made of plastic tubing of different lengths. *Bottom:* View from above, showing the 18 randomly assigned burrow locations.

Figure 6.14. Susan McDowell recording the feeding behavior of captive White Ibises.

but 2 or 3 crabs had been removed from their burrows (Bildstein et al. 1989).

Our experimental results were surprisingly consistent. When probing into burrows for male and female fiddler crabs, all seven captive birds rejected male crabs almost twice as often as they rejected female crabs. The preference for female crabs was even more obvious when crabs were offered outside their burrows. To simulate the contact a noncaptive ibis would have with exposed surface crabs, Susan and I offered the captive birds a simultaneous choice between same-sized male and female crabs in a small white porcelain tray (Figure 6.15). All of our ibises chose female crabs more than four times as frequently as they chose male crabs.

Field data support the gender-related prey selections that Susan and I documented in our "cafeteria" experiments. Surveys of fiddler crabs on the Bly Creek drainage indicate that the ratio of male to female crabs shifts in favor of males as crab size increases (from 55:45 [males : females] for crabs less than 2.5 centimeters long to 74:26 for crabs longer than 2.5 centimeters). Thus, male crabs appear to survive better than females. This

Figure 6.15. An adult male White Ibis selecting a fiddler crab from a porcelain tray.

pattern is exactly what would be expected if ibises preyed on female crabs more than on male crabs. My own anecdotal observations of free-ranging White Ibises at the Bly Creek drainage, as well as others' observations of ibises elsewhere (see, for example, Christy 1980), suggest that free-ranging ibises do indeed prefer to eat female crabs.

To see if differences in the behavior of male and female crabs, rather than the presence or absence of the enlarged major claw, were responsible for the definite differences we observed, we surgically removed the major claw from several male crabs and simultaneously offered pairs of declawed and "intact" males to our captive ibises. Once again ibises selected crabs without major claws by more than a 4:1 ratio.

These results demonstrate that the absence of a large claw increases a fiddler crab's vulnerability to ibis predation. Most of the male crabs we used in our experiments possessed major claws that were about 3 centimeters long or more, and in many males the major claws appeared to represent more than one-third of their total body mass. Claws of this size are apparently effective deterrents for White Ibises, whose long, decurved bills are tactilely sensitive (Kushlan 1978). Although many male crabs were consumed by our ibises, often a male crab that an ibis was pursuing retaliated by grasping either the upper or lower mandible of the ibis with his major claw (Figure 6.16). In such a situation, the ibis usually remained perfectly motionless, sometimes for as long as 30 seconds, after which either the crab would release its grip and retreat unharmed or the ibis would shake it vigorously from its bill. On several occasions, the crab *autotomized* (i.e., self-amputated or dropped off) its claw, leaving the jettisoned appendage clinging to a confused ibis while the rest of the crab made a hurried retreat. Autotomy appears to be an effective diversionary tactic. Dismembered claws often continue to grasp ibises for 10 seconds or more, providing ample time for the crabs to withdraw into a nearby burrow. Such behavior, although energetically costly—the regeneration of a new major claw typically requires several molts—is clearly the lesser of two evils. A similar tactic is commonly used by geckos and other lizards retreating in the face of almost certain predation, except that reptiles leave a writhing tail rather than a pinching claw to confuse their predators (Edmunds 1974).

Captive White Ibises that did consume male fiddler crabs almost always induced the crab to autotomize its claw by holding the crab at or near the base of its claw while shaking it frantically. And as a rule, ibises appear to be especially wary of swallowing the greatly enlarged major

Figure 6.16. A male fiddler crab clinging to the bill of a White Ibis. Drawing by M. Davis.

claws of male crabs. Free-ranging individuals behaved similarly. Most of the ibises that we watched prepared their prey carefully before consuming it, usually by "mandibulating" the crab up and down their partially closed bills, taking ample time to crush the crustacean's bulky carapace and to remove most of its walking legs.

Sometimes White Ibises forgo such table manners. Individuals feeding close together in dense flocks frequently down their prey immediately upon capture, presumably to reduce the risk of piracy on the part of associates feeding nearby. Although such hasty consumption typically proceeds without interruption, problems can arise. In July of 1984, for example, I watched an adult male ibis that was feeding in a dense flock capture and, without delay, swallow an especially large male crab—major claw and all—only to have the crab crawl back up its throat five times before finally being swallowed for good. The bizarre struggle, which lasted for more than half a minute, drew the attention of several of the bird's nearest neighbors, who suspended their feeding activities and watched the contest. The ibis involved spent only a few minutes recovering before continuing to search for additional prey.

Although I have not yet studied the behavior of free-ranging ibises feeding upon crayfishes, Susan and I have watched hand-reared birds feed on this important dietary component. Whereas small crayfish (i.e., those less than 30 millimeters) are usually consumed in their entirety, larger individuals are often broken in two before their fleshy parts are extracted from the eventually discarded exoskeleton. I suspect similar preparatory procedures are used for other large prey as well.

Fiddler crabs were not the only animals that exhibited gender-related differences during our feeding experiments. Male and female White Ibises also differed in their behavior during these interactions. Although ibises of both sexes extracted burrowing female crabs more often than they extracted burrowing male crabs, female ibises were overall decidedly less successful with their extractions than were their male counterparts. Although this difference appeared to be greatest in trials involving our longest (130-millimeter-long) artificial burrows, small differences were also evident during several trials involving substantially shorter (70- and 110-millimeter-long) burrows (Figure 6.17). Although none of our captive female ibises exhibited significant differences in their ability to extract crabs from 70- versus 110-millimeter-long burrows, all had considerably more difficulty removing crabs from 130-millimeter-long burrows than from 110-millimeter-long burrows. These findings suggest that as a burrow's length extends beyond the length of an ibis's bill (a female's bill averages 112 millimeters in length, and a male's averages 142 millimeters) crab vulnerability to extraction declines accordingly.

Seemingly in contrast to these results, my study of free-ranging White Ibises suggested that males and females do not differ in their ability to capture fiddler crabs. Does this mean that one or both of the studies was flawed? Not necessarily. The captive male and female ibises Susan and I studied were feeding only on burrowing crabs, whereas the free-ranging birds I had watched earlier were taking both burrowing and surface crabs. Furthermore, all 13 of the captive ibises used in our aviary experiments were second-year birds at the time of our observations, whereas all of the free-ranging birds were adults (i.e., at least third-year birds). Either of these differences could easily explain the apparently conflicting results we observed. Although a cynic might consider such seemingly conflicting results reason to dismiss both studies, I believe such results to be an acceptable risk associated with conducting a multifaceted study. In my mind, such inconsistencies are intriguing enigmas awaiting further study.

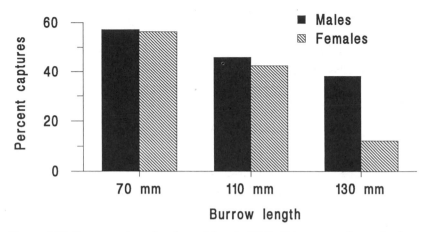

Figure 6.17. Success rates of male and female White Ibises extracting crabs from artificial burrows of different lengths.

Form and Function of Decurved Bills

Birds use their bills to secure and process food. As such, a bird's bill typically reflects its diet. For this particular trophic appendage, the fit between form and function is usually so tight that, in most instances, an ornithologist can tell what a bird eats, or at least how it acquires its prey, simply by looking at its bill. Seedeaters—Northern Cardinals, for example—characteristically possess stout, conical bills, which are useful for cracking seeds. Many excavating species, including most woodpeckers, possess chisellike bills, which they use to uncover and remove bark-dwelling insects. Flesh-eaters, such as hawks, eagles, and falcons, are often equipped with powerful hooked bills for subduing and dismembering their prey. Piscivorous wading birds, such as herons, egrets, and bitterns, typically possess daggerlike bills.

Downwardly curving or decurved bills are relatively uncommon. Although all species of ibises possess a characteristically decurved bill, this apparent adaptation is otherwise restricted mostly to kiwis, flamingos, curlews, bee-eaters, sunbirds, and several species of hummingbirds. Although birds with decurved bills presumably use their unusual trophic appendage to secure their prey more efficiently, the functional significance of this feature in ibises remained something of a mystery. After watching White Ibises feed on fiddler crabs for several weeks, I was certain I had discovered why their bills are decurved. Many burrows of fiddler crabs are angled affairs whose curvature bears an uncanny resemblance to that of an ibis's bill (Figure 6.18). Might it be that this was more than a coincidence, that decurved bills of ibises enable them to extract crabs more efficiently from their burrows?

Although I had first thought of this possibility in 1980, not until

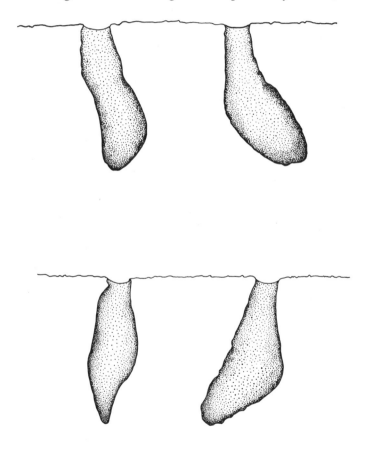

$\vdash--\dashv$
20mm

Figure 6.18. Shapes of fiddler crab burrows on the Bly Creek drainage. Sketches were made from fiberglass casts of individual burrows. Drawing by P. Cowart-Rickman.

the summer of 1988 did I have the opportunity to test it. Susan and I modified the ibis cafeteria table to accommodate angled burrows ranging in length from 70 to 130 millimeters. We then observed the capture rates and probing directions (Figure 6.19) of White Ibises feeding on crabs located therein. The burrows used in this experiment descended, not 90° from the horizontal as they had in our earlier studies, but at either a 45° or a 60° angle. The results of these experiments surprised us. Although fiddler crabs were more vulnerable in shorter burrows than in longer ones, and although female crabs continued to be more vulnerable overall than were the male crabs, we were unable to detect any suggestion of an "angle effect" during our trials. The birds were equally able to extract crabs from their burrows without regard to their angle of descent. Although the ibises tended to avoid probing angled burrows frontally, a posture that required a distinctively awkward stance, they were equally likely to probe angled burrows sideways and from between the legs (Figure 6.19). These results, together with observations from the field that indicate that ibises rarely reposition themselves once they have started probing a burrow, suggest that these birds do not align their decurved bills with a burrow's angle of descent. Nor is there any indication that decurved bills permit the more efficient extraction of crabs from angled burrows.

Although decurved bills do not appear to help ibises capture their prey, might they be useful in some other aspect of feeding behavior? Perhaps this bill design enhances an ibis's ability to handle prey after capture but before swallowing? A little geometry is in order here. As a result of nearly parallel curvature, the distance between the upper and lower mandibles of a partially opened decurved bill varies less over the length of the bill than it would in straightened bills of the same length: A long straightened bill would open relatively more near the tip of the bill and less near the base than does the decurved version. For example, flamingos, which filter-feed in much the same fashion as baleen whales (i.e., by alternately gulping food-laden water and pumping it from their mouths through sieve-like teeth), are able to do so effectively because strongly decurved bills enable them to space their upper and lower mandibles equally along most of the gape.

Although ibises feed on decidedly different prey and in a decidedly different manner than do flamingos, they too appear to benefit from the geometry of curvature. White Ibises customarily mandibulate and eventually crush their hard-shelled crustacean prey by running each item back and forth between the tip and base of the bill several times before swallowing it. Presumably, this routine reduces the risk of ingesting live prey and speeds the digestive process. Decurved bills enhance this predigestive activity by providing ibises with greater control over their prey. Because of the directions of the forces involved, straightened bills tend to direct hard prey toward the tip as they are closed, whereas curved bills tend to trap and crush the prey. This trapping effect is accentuated in White Ibises by a slight but distinctive gap between the upper and lower mandibles near the center of the bill (Kushlan and Bildstein 1992). The effect of this gap is evident in the bird depicted in Figure 6.20, in which the gap between the partially opened upper and lower mandibles remains constant over approximately 20% of the bill's length.

Nevertheless, although ibises' long, decurved bills enable them to extract prey from burrows, crevices, and flooded areas they would not otherwise be able to access, possessing this protruding appendage does incur a cost. I know of several instances in which captive White Ibises have lost a portion of their upper or lower mandible. In these cases, the birds appeared to have collided with the walls of their cages. In most instances, the birds were unable to secure sufficient prey as a result of the accident. On at least three occasions, reattaching the severed portion of

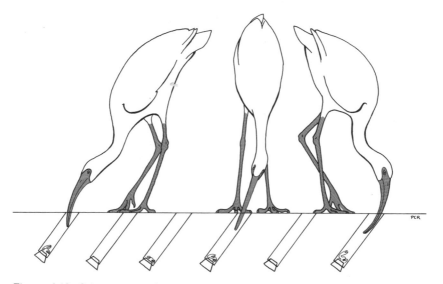

Figure 6.19. Orientations of White Ibises probing in artificial burrows set at angles. Drawing by P. Cowart-Rickman.

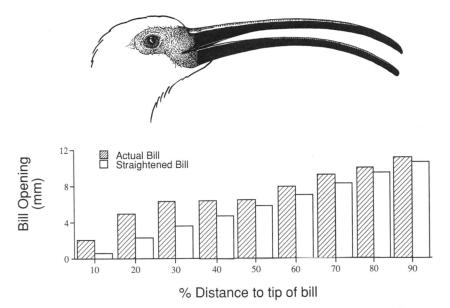

Figure 6.20. Actual distances between the upper and lower mandibles of the ibis illustrated above compared with distances in a hypothetical straightened bill of the same length when opened the same amount at the tip. Drawing by P. Cowart-Rickman.

the bill with dental acrylic, or attaching a specially constructed acrylic prosthesis, enabled the birds to continue to feed without difficulty.

The extent to which such accidents occur in the wild is unknown. An adult White Ibis whose upper and lower mandibles were severed at midlength was sighted flying over the marsh less than a week after Hurricane Hugo had passed through the area in the fall of 1989 (D. Allen, personal communication). Based on what we know about captive birds, the prognosis for such an individual is poor.

7 Inland Habitat Use

> ... to do the science of geographical ecology is to search for
> patterns of plant and animal life that can be put on a map.
>
> Robert H. MacArthur, 1972

Each year, the White Ibises that breed at the Pumpkinseed Island colony
site spend a considerable amount of time searching for fiddler crabs in
salt marshes lying directly north of the colony. And each year my students
and I spend a considerable amount of time documenting the feeding
ecology of these birds. But Pumpkinseed's White Ibises do not feed on
fiddler crabs only, and they do not feed on the North Inlet Marsh only.
Most parental ibises spend a considerable amount of time feeding at
freshwater sites that are farther inland. Although we have had little opportunity to actually watch birds feeding at these inland sites, we have spent
a considerable amount of time monitoring their use of such areas. Here
I describe those studies and the intriguing patterns they have revealed.

Ornithologists usually assume that the birds they are studying
are behaving in the best interests of their individual genes. Such an
approach is rooted in the Darwinian notion that, in general, animals act
selfishly to increase their own individual reproductive success rather than
to increase that of the species. Thus, in relation to feeding habitats, birds
are generally assumed to distribute themselves in an adaptive or self-
serving manner. In light of this assumption, I began to wonder why,
during each breeding season, many of Pumpkinseed Island's White Ibises
were flying directly over the nearby North Inlet Marsh—and its readily
abundant fiddler crabs—en route to more distant feeding sites inland.

In 1981, Bobbie McCutchen and I spent some time trying to find the White Ibises we had watched flying north over North Inlet. Although we had read about parent ibises flying considerable distances to secure prey for their nestlings, both of us were surprised to discover that many of Pumpkinseed Island's birds were regularly flying between 20 and 40 kilometers inland to feed in the region's many freshwater marshes and bottomland hardwood swamps. (The current distance record for ibises is a whopping 110 kilometers [one way] and is held by a coastal North Carolina colony of ibises, as Walker Golder and Jim Parnell have reported.) Subsequent studies of nestling regurgitant collected at our colony site (the details of which are presented in Chapter 5) revealed that the birds were ferrying freshwater crayfishes back to their young from such sites. But why?

More specifically, why were only some of the birds feeding as close to the colony as possible? Was something wrong with the North Inlet Marsh? Perhaps it was too crowded or lacked sufficient amounts of fiddler crabs. Or perhaps parental White Ibises needed to feed crayfishes rather than fiddler crabs to their young. Whatever the reason, Pumpkinseed Island's ibises were expending a considerable amount of additional time and effort ferrying food back to their young. The question of why some ibises fed on brackish-water fiddler crabs in nearby salt marshes while others fed on freshwater crayfishes in the more distant inland swamps was on my mind throughout the early 1980s. However, I did not decide to address this issue in detail until 1984.

Population Studies

Bobbie and I first decided to determine whether or not White Ibises used the two habitats differently over the course of the breeding season. Seasonal differences might help explain why the birds were behaving as they were. We felt that there was a pattern. Although both of us recalled seeing many ibises flying over the marsh to inland feeding sites in early May through early July each year, neither of us could recall seeing such flights much earlier or much later in the season. To test this hypothesis, Dan Petit and I began to take counts of the ibises feeding on the North Inlet Marsh and of those flying inland over it.

Our sampling techniques were simple enough. First, we laid out a 66-hectare study grid in an area approximately 6 kilometers north of Pumpkinseed Island on the Bly Creek drainage basin near the base of our observation tower, and we began to count the White Ibises using this site. The birds were counted at hourly intervals during weekly dawn-to-dusk (15-hour) observation marathons. We also located another observation point approximately 4 kilometers farther north. The second site was along the Barony's North Boundary Road, near the center of the birds' inland flyway. Dan and I took turns counting ibises flying over the salt marsh to and from inland feeding sites.

Counting birds at North Boundary Road was a bit more taxing than counting them on the marsh. It proved impossible, even for two observers working in shifts, to maintain sufficient mental concentration over the course of a whole day to count all of the birds flying to and fro over the road. Therefore, we decided to shorten the observation periods and to group the data according to "composite days." Each composite day consisted of several 2- to 4-hour nonoverlapping watches that were conducted over the course of a week and that, when considered together, spanned from dawn to dusk (Bildstein et al. 1990).

Even though we had managed to collect only half a season's worth of data in 1984, the results of this effort confirmed what Bobbie and I had suspected. Many more White Ibises flew inland in June and early July than later in the season, and in general, the numbers of birds feeding on the marsh increased when the numbers of birds flying inland decreased. The two of us felt that our observations provided an accurate index of how ibises were dividing their time between the two habitats. By this time I had seen enough to convince me that inland feeding sites were essential for successful breeding in our population of ibises, and I wanted to learn more about how the birds used them on an annual basis. Although collecting each data point required at least 14 hours in the field, I decided to continue to collect the Bly Creek and North Boundary Road population data for several additional years.

Beginning in March of 1985, and every year since, my students and I have carefully documented seasonal fluctuations in the numbers of ibises using freshwater and brackish feeding sites. Although the same general pattern has held each year (i.e., a simultaneous decrease in the use of the more distant freshwater sites over the course of the breeding season, coupled with an increase in the numbers of ibises using the salt marsh), comparisons among years have revealed several intriguing correlations. These discoveries have helped explain why ibises expend so much energy flying inland to feed. But before explaining this dependency, I first need to describe the region's rather variable rainfall pattern.

Local Rainfall and Breeding

Coastal South Carolina has two wet seasons. The first occurs between November and April, the second between June and September (Barry 1980). As a result of the first rainy season each year, coastal waterways ordinarily overflow their banks in the spring, extensively flooding adjacent bottomland hardwood forests. At least these are the occurrences in an *average* year. But as any ecologist worthy of the title is quick to point out, nature rarely provides an average year.

The U.S. Weather Service lists 50 centimeters as the 30-year average rainfall for the winter-to-spring wet season for nearby Georgetown, South Carolina; the actual amounts of rain that fell between 1979 and 1991 ranged from 29 to 86 centimeters. Only twice during this time was the amount of rainfall within 10% of the 30-year mean (i.e., 45 to 55 centimeters). The other 11 years were off by an average of plus or minus 35%. During relatively wet years, the winter-to-spring rains cause considerable flooding of the area's lowlands. However, in drier years relatively little flooding occurs, and most, if not all, of the rivers are well within their banks by the time White Ibises have started to raise their young. Because of these effects, the winter-to-spring rainfall plays a major role in determining the success or failure of each year's breeding season.

Seasonally inundated lowland forests are ideal feeding sites for White Ibises. In wet years, freshwater crayfishes tend to concentrate in these areas, especially along the water's rising and falling edge, gorging themselves on a transitory banquet of decaying leaves from the previous autumn. Ibises, in turn, make short work of the invertebrates at such times. However, in drought years, when few lowland areas are flooded, crayfishes typically retire to estivate in deep burrows earlier in the spring (Pollard et al. 1982). As a result, they are no longer readily available to parental ibises. The extent to which rainfall affects this relationship is best seen by comparing the use of inland feeding sites in several wet and dry years.

Between 1984 and 1987, rainfall ranged from lows of 29 and 59 centimeters in 1985 and 1986, respectively, to highs of 80 centimeters in 1984 and 1987. White Ibises responded to the different hydrological conditions by switching from feeding in inland freshwater sites to feeding in the salt marsh considerably earlier during the 2 dry years than they did during the 2 wet years (Figure 7.1). As a result, the diets of developing nestlings remained relatively rich in crayfishes well into the wet breeding seasons of both 1984 and 1987. In 1985 and 1986 (the drier years) parental

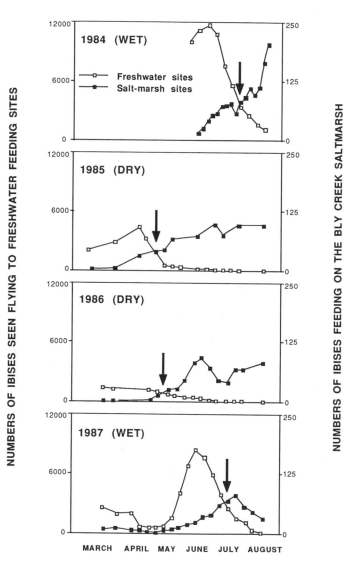

Figure 7.1. Three-week running means of the numbers of White Ibises seen flying back and forth over North Boundary Road between the Pumpkinseed Island colony site and freshwater wetlands further inland, compared with the numbers of adult ibises feeding on a 66-hectare portion of the North Inlet salt marsh. Arrows indicate when numbers of birds using the salt-marsh feeding site first exceed those seen flying inland to freshwater sites. Note that in wet years (1984 and 1987) this crossover occurs several months later than in dry years (1985 and 1986). Modification of a figure in Bildstein et al. (1990). Reprinted with permission of the Wilson Ornithological Society.

ibises were forced to turn to alternative sources of prey for their developing young. In 1985 most parents switched to feeding fiddler crabs to their young, whereas in 1986 most switched to fishes (Figure 7.2). Crayfishes appear to be a necessary ingredient for successful breeding in Pumpkinseed Island's White Ibises, and any declines that occur in crayfish populations before ibises fledge their young can have dire consequences (see Chapter 8 for details). Amazingly, ibises seem to be able to anticipate such events. Several lines of evidence soon brought us to this conclusion.

The number of White Ibises breeding on Pumpkinseed Island has fluctuated considerably over the years. Superficially at least, the vacillations appeared to be patternless (Figure 3.1); the number of ibises breeding in any one year provided little indication of what was likely to happen the next year. Mathematically, the fluctuations did not appear to be haphazard or random events. If each bird was merely randomly deciding whether or not to breed each year, the law of averages suggested that the proportions of breeders and nonbreeders should remain somewhat consistent from year to year. But the magnitude of the fluctuations suggested that this simply was not the case. Many of the birds seemed to be deciding whether or not to breed in concert, so perhaps something in the environment was simultaneously cuing them. But what was the cue, and why were they responding to it?

The answer became apparent in late 1986, when I used a statistical technique known as correlation analysis to compare the number of breeding ibises each year with the amount of rain that had fallen during the preceding winter-to-spring wet season. The results of this analysis indicated that, in general, the wetter the winter-to-spring wet season, the larger the number of breeding White Ibises. This trend continued throughout the decade (Figure 7.3).

That the correlation between rainfall and breeding effort was adaptive was revealed in a second analysis performed at the end of 1989. By that time Toni De Santo, Jim Johnston, and I had managed to collect 5 years of nestling survivorship data at the colony. Comparing those numbers with the numbers of nesting adults revealed another significant correlation: More White Ibis chicks were likely to survive to fledging when many ibises bred than when only a few birds decided to put forth the effort (Figure 7.4).

Together, the two correlations suggested that many White Ibises were deciding not to breed at all in the years when their chances of success were low. But how did the birds decide? Because the ibises often made

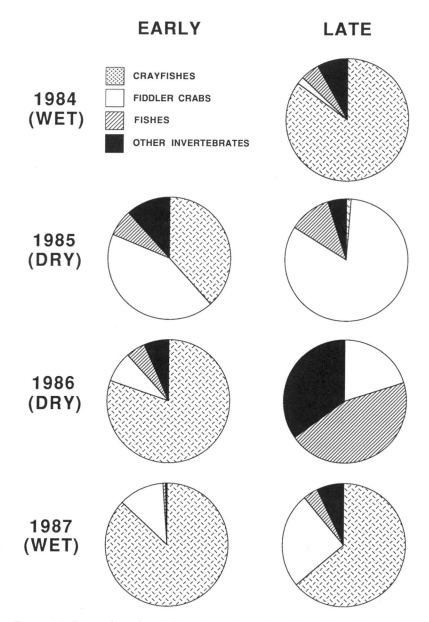

EARLY

LATE

1984 (WET)

1985 (DRY)

1986 (DRY)

1987 (WET)

CRAYFISHES

FIDDLER CRABS

FISHES

OTHER INVERTEBRATES

Figure 7.2. Diets of nestling White Ibises during the 1984, 1985, 1986, and 1987 breeding seasons. *Early* indicates May and early June each year; *late* indicates late June and early July.

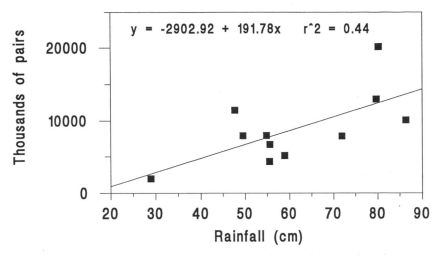

Figure 7.3. Relationship between the numbers of White Ibis pairs breeding on Pumpkinseed Island and the amount of rainfall during the preceding winter-to-spring wet season, 1979–89. (The relationship is significant at $P < 0.05$.) Modification of a figure in Bildstein et al. (1990). Reprinted with permission of the Wilson Ornithological Society.

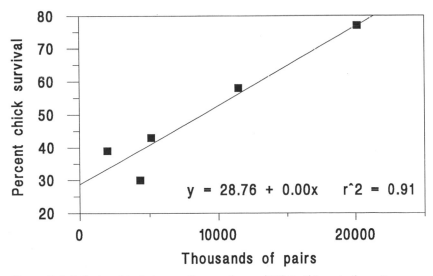

Figure 7.4. Relationship between the numbers of White Ibis pairs breeding on Pumpkinseed Island and nestling survivorship through 2 weeks after hatching, 1985–89. (The relationship is significant at $P < 0.05$.)

their decisions about breeding as early as late March or early April, they certainly were not basing this decision on the number of crayfishes available. Even in drought years crayfishes were readily available in large numbers well into April, several weeks *after* most of the birds had decided whether or not to breed. Perhaps the birds were using the weather, or more specifically, the amount of spring rainfall and bottomland flooding, to forecast the crayfish availability weeks in advance of when the indispensable item was needed as food for their developing young. That March thunderstorms commonly trigger courtship flights in White Ibises (see Chapter 3 for details) makes perfect sense in light of this notion.

Habitat Studies of Individual White Ibises

By the mid 1980s, it became obvious that, on average, White Ibises prefer to feed crayfishes to their nestlings and that, in general, parental birds go to great lengths to do so. But what about individual ibises? Do all parental birds routinely fly inland to secure freshwater crayfishes for their young? Are some ibises more skillful than others in securing this essential resource? Do the same birds return repeatedly to certain feeding sites, or are individuals constantly sampling different sites throughout the area? Finally, do parental birds wait until after their young hatch to search for crayfish prey, or do they begin the search before their chicks hatch, in anticipation of this need? Having grown tired of our ignorance in this area, Toni, Jim, and I decided in the fall of 1986 that we needed to address these issues. Little did we realize what we were getting into. Tracking the behavior of individual ibises proved to be even more difficult than the plenty-difficult task of tracking an entire population of ibises.

Our studies required radiotelemetry: placing tiny signaling devices on the backs of individual ibises and using radio receivers to follow their movements for weeks and even months. Our plan was to capture several dozen parental adults, equip each of them with radio transmitter, and follow their movements, both from the ground and from fixed-wing aircraft, as they raised their young over the course of the breeding season. We would repeat these procedures during three breeding seasons. Having laid out a strategy we set about achieving our goal, which was to describe in detail the daily activities of individual breeding White Ibises.

Our first task consisted of purchasing the necessary supplies. In addition to transmitters and receivers, we needed to procure an assortment of antennas, cables, headsets, null-peak boxes, mounting brackets for the aircraft, and other tools of the telemetry trade. After poring over several equipment catalogs, we came to realize that all of these were expensive and fragile pieces of field equipment. To many researchers, sophisticated electronic gadgets are seductive toys, playthings to challenge one's ingenuity. However, to a closet Luddite such as myself, nothing is so sure of failure in the field as a piece of field equipment powered by a battery. I began to have second thoughts. Perhaps the three of us were getting in over our heads. Before I had the chance to change my mind, David Mech, U.S. Fish and Wildlife Service biologist and telemetry freak extraordinaire visited the area to give a talk about his work with wolves. The two of us discussed at length the whys and wherefores of radiotelemetry. David convinced me that even three neophytes could manage to pull off what we had planned. In less than a week, Jim, Toni, and I spent thousands of dollars on telemetry equipment.

Choosing a receiver was relatively straightforward. There are a limited number of buyers of this highly specialized equipment and, consequently, few sellers. We decided to go with the most reputable—that is to say the most expensive—radio receiver available. It cost considerably more than the others, but it was the only one for which a plastic, watertight case was available (guaranteed by the manufacturer to float for 30 minutes). Since we planned to ferry the receiver out to Pumpkinseed Island over brackish water on a regular basis, we decided that peace of mind was worth the extra cost.

Purchasing transmitters proved to be more complex. Transmitters are tailor-made to fit the needs of both the project and the study species in question. Radio transmitters almost always affect the behavior of the birds to which they are attached, and the weight of the unit and the manner in which it is affixed play major roles in determining how much a bird is hampered by the device (Kenward 1987). Although smaller transmitters that are affixed in an aerodynamically benign positions produce the best results, they also produce weaker signals, especially when equipped with shorter, drag-free antennas. Thus, we were faced deciding how best to balance transmitter side effects with signal strength. Because we planned to follow our birds for less than 3 months, the batteries that powered our transmitters could be quite small. The manufacturer that we chose constructed transmitters that were smaller than a book of matches and that weighed less than 3% of the weight of the birds we tracked, but whose signals could be detected for several miles (Figure 7.5). We tested the units, which were harnessed to the birds as backpacks, on several captive individuals before using them at the Pumpkinseed site.

Our equipment in hand, we next needed to learn how to use it. We did so during several trips to the coast in early spring of 1987, when each of us took turns playing signaling ibis and receiving scientist. Radiotelemetry is as much of an art as it is a science, and although both Toni and Jim mastered the discipline in several weeks, an embarrassing lack of talent on my part slowed my progress considerably. It was just as well that I had this setback, since Jim's and Toni's stomachs proved to be considerably more capable than mine in reconciling the contorted flight patterns our pilot used while tracking the birds.

The next step was to trap several parental ibises and harness them. We began to do so in May of 1987. All of the birds we used were trapped at their nest sites by a highly effective self-tripping cylindrical wire trap with an open bottom. Peter Frederick (1986) had devised this trap while working on the island in the early 1980s. Whenever we wanted to capture a bird, we simply waited until it left, placed one of Peter's contraptions over its nest, opened the trap door, set the trip wire, and retreated to the nearest cover. The nest's contents, which typically consisted of one or more nestlings younger than 1 week old, served as "bait." If all went well, we were back at the trap in less than 15 minutes, removing a snared parent. Less than half an hour later, we were radio-tracking a telemetered ibis.

During the three breeding seasons of 1987–89, we managed to trap and subsequently monitor the movements and the behavior of 15 parental White Ibises (6 males and 9 females), all of which provided considerable insight into the day-to-day life of breeding White Ibises. Although trapping and monitoring additional birds would have been easy, at $250 per radio transmitter and $75 per hour in the airplane, we simply did not have the funds to do so.

The essence of our telemetry efforts was the plotting of the activities of each individual. What we learned about one bird monitored in 1988, whom we designated female 5, serves as an example:

Female 5 was radio-tagged at 11:30 A.M. on 9 June, when her nest contained one 2-day-old chick and two unhatched eggs. Upon release, she immediately returned to the nest, where she remained for the rest of the afternoon. Female 5 tended her nest for 1- to 3-hour intervals until her nestlings were 2 weeks old. She continued with her visits, although

Figure 7.5. Breeding adult White Ibis being fitted with a radio-transmitter backpack.

they were considerably abbreviated, until the chicks had fledged 7 weeks later.

While her nestlings were less than 3 weeks old, female 5 was located 11 times on Hobcaw Barony, 4 times on the salt marsh, once at a brackish-water pond several kilometers north of Pumpkinseed Island, and 10 times at one of two freshwater swamps. However, once her chicks were 3 weeks old, female 5 began visiting more distant feeding areas south and west of the colony site. On 4 consecutive days, for example, she was found feeding in freshwater swamps and impoundments on Cat Island, 7 kilometers south of her nest, and immediately thereafter in another impoundment in the Santee Delta, more than 15 kilometers south of the colony. Subsequent "sightings" during this period placed this female far to the south of the colony, generally in freshwater habitats (Map 7.1). Throughout this stage of the breeding cycle, female 5 returned to the colony three or four times a day, presumably to feed her young.

Once her young were ready to fledge, female 5 began frequenting a brackish-water pond 5 kilometers north of the colony site, as well as the surrounding salt marshes, and was never again found in freshwater habitats (Map 7.1). Her last recorded visit to Pumpkinseed Island was during the second week of August, when her youngest offspring would

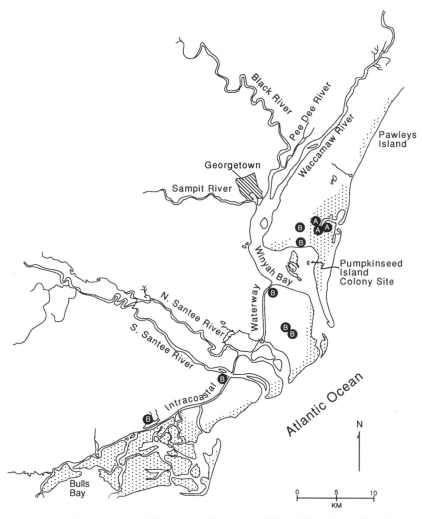

Map 7.1. Feeding sites used by two radio-tracked White Ibis adults, female 3 in 1987 and female 5 in 1988, before *(B)* and after *(A)* their young fledged. Stippled areas are coastal salt marshes.

have been 9 weeks old. She was last recorded on a salt marsh 5 kilometers north of the colony 2 weeks later.

Each of the 15 White Ibises we followed behaved uniquely. Nevertheless, when we considered our observations in their entirety, several consistent patterns emerged. First, while caring for nestlings that were less than 3 weeks old, all but four of the birds fed exclusively in freshwater wetlands, usually in the numerous abandoned rice fields, impounded marshes, and bottomland swamps associated with the region's four major rivers. Most returned to their nests with crayfishes or other species of freshwater prey.

Second, in all 3 years, parental White Ibises traveled considerable distances to find such prey. In 1987, for example, three of the four radio-tagged birds traveled 21 to 31 kilometers from the colony site to feed on crayfishes during this period of their nesting cycles. This phenomenon was repeated in 1988 and in 1989.

Third, most of the birds we tracked displayed considerable site fidelity during this period: Most returned repeatedly to two to four feeding locales during the course of several weeks of observation. Darrel Bateman, who, while a doctoral candidate at Auburn University in the 1960s, had radio-tagged and tracked seven breeding ibises at inland colony sites along the Alabama–Florida border, also reported a high degree of site tenacity among individual birds (Bateman 1970). This agreement of results suggests that such behavior is typical of White Ibises. Unfortunately, although Bateman also reported that the birds he watched were flying long distances to secure prey for their young, he was unable to follow any of his birds for more than a few weeks, and their behavior after their young had fledged remains a mystery.

Fourth, in addition to using freshwater feeding sites, two of the four birds we had tracked in 1988 routinely visited nearby salt marshes during the times they were still providing food to their young. However, in almost all of these instances, the visits occurred either late in the day or en route to other feeding sites. Only rarely did these birds return directly to the colony after such visits. These observations, together with the fact that simultaneous collections of regurgitant and fecal samples taken from the nestlings of these birds contained only fishes and cray-fishes, suggest that these two individuals were collecting food for their own use at such times.

Fifth, once parents were freed from the responsibility of caring for their young, either because their nestlings had fledged or because their nests had failed, all 15 individuals invariably shifted, usually within a day or so, from feeding in the more distant freshwater habitats to feeding much closer to Pumpkinseed Island, in salt marshes and other brackish-water wetlands. In 1987, for example, adults were never found more than 14 kilometers from the colony site after their young had fledged, and in 1988, none were recorded more than 5 kilometers from the site. In both years, radio-tagged ibises located during this period of their nesting cycle were feeding almost exclusively in salt marshes and brackish-water ponds. We failed to collect data during this period in 1989, however.

The $64,000 Question

Our population survey and our telemetry data confirmed what Bobbie McCutchen and I had suspected earlier. Parental White Ibises were flying long distances to freshwater feeding sites to secure crayfish for their young. A lack of fiddler crabs certainly was not the motivating factor. Our observations demonstrated that ibises captured fiddler crabs at similar rates throughout the breeding season (McCraith 1992), before, during, and after the time that they were raising nestlings.

Long-term observations of adult feeding rates, along with the known energetic value of the crabs and the metabolic requirements of adults and developing young (Bildstein 1987, Bildstein et al. 1992), suggest that a typical pair of parental White Ibises would have been able to secure enough fiddler crabs in 8 to 10 hours of combined hunting each day to provide more than enough food for themselves and their young. Yet they were not concentrating their efforts on this food source, at least not as long as crayfishes were available. And this choice meant spending an additional 3 hours in flight daily, which boosted their metabolic requirements by as much as 25% (Pennycuick and De Santo 1989, Bildstein et al. 1992).

Initially, the solution to this mystery seemed to lie in one of three areas: (1) fiddler crabs were inappropriate food for nestling White Ibises (even though they seemed to be perfectly adequate for free-ranging adult and recently fledged ibises), (2) crayfishes were providing an essential dietary component for nestling ibises that was unavailable in fiddler crabs, or (3) parental ibises simply were not behaving adaptively. Taken as a whole, the data presented in Figures 7.1 to 7.4 eliminated the third possibility. Parental ibises were behaving adaptively. Securing freshwater crayfish for their developing young was necessary. The next step was to find out why.

8 Salt Stress and Prey Choice

Water, water every where,
Nor any drop to drink.

Samuel Taylor Coleridge, 1798

Life originated in the sea. But although most of us recognize water as life's universal solvent, few accord the same recognition to its universal solute, salt. In fact, the extracellular fluid flowing through our bodies, as well as that coursing through the bodies of all White Ibises, is quite salty, although not so much as full-strength seawater. But salt is something of an incongruous biological commodity: essential at low levels, lethal in excess. Understanding its impact requires a knowledge of its chemical and physical effects on the body.

Salt's Paradoxical Nature

Chemically, salts are neutral compounds in which elements or radicals have replaced hydrogen in an acid. As solids (dry table salt, for example) they exist as lattices of positively and negatively charged ions. In aqueous solutions such as seawater, the lattice breaks down as the ions dissolve into solution. Most metabolic processes, both in and out of cells, take place in saline solutions. But not all of them are as concentrated as those of seawater, nor do all of them contain the same ratios of ions. The actions of the vertebrate nervous system, for example, rely on ionic concentrations of sodium and potassium differing considerably inside of its cells. The maintenance of these differences, which occurs at considerable metabolic cost, is essential for nerve cell transmissions and muscle cell contractions.

Molecules dissolved in liquids tend to spread out, or diffuse, from areas of high concentration into areas of lower concentration. The end point of this process is an equal concentration of the dissolved material, or solute, throughout the solvent. When salt dissolves inside an animal's body, its ions immediately begin to diffuse into the surrounding environment. But salt can diffuse only so far in multicelled organisms, because the selective permeability of cell membranes impedes such movements. Water molecules, however, are free to move across such barriers and readily do so. This process, which is called *osmosis*, is often responsible for salt's negative impact on organisms.

As water moves across cell membranes to reduce the concentrations of saline solutions, its physical bulk produces osmotic pressures capable of bursting fragile cell membranes and destroying cell function. This is the dark side of the salt crystal, the side linked to hypertension in humans and salt stress in marine and desert animals.

Human attitudes toward salt reflect its paradoxical nature. Although salt is valuable enough as a preservative and seasoning to have been the cause of numerous bloody confrontations among 16th-century European powers vying for control of important New World sources, nutritionists warn that, in excess, salt poses a significant threat to human health. Even so, many mammals and birds possess what nutritionists refer to as a "specific hunger" or "drive" for the substance. North American Porcupines, for example, have been known to rasp sodium-rich paint from metal trail markers in an attempt to satisfy their requirements for this essential nutrient (Roze 1989). On his second voyage to the New World in 1494, Columbus reported seeing "birds like cranes but bright red" (i.e., American Flamingos) that the natives raised on cassava bread and salt water (Morison 1942). More recently, zookeepers have reported similar salt requirements in penguins and other marine species.

On the other hand, too much salt, especially in combination with insufficient fresh water, is thought to limit the distributions of many species of animals. And, as this front-page report from the 21 January 1988 edition of the *Charlotte Observer* indicates, excessive salt can have devastating consequences for birds:

SALT KILLS 50,000 CHICKENS

Feed-mix Mistake Hits Perdue Farms Inc.

By Gene Stowe

Fifty thousand Perdue Farms Inc. chickens died of diarrhea after operators put too much salt in the chicken feed at a state-of-the-art feed mill in Montgomery County [North Carolina] . . .

Perdue feed is about one-quarter of 1% salt, but some at the Candor mill got 1% to 2½% salt by accident. The computer system at the month-old plant failed, and workers operating the mixing equipment manually caused the error . . .

Anyone who has watched a shipwreck movie knows that humans are unable to drink full-strength seawater. Not only does seawater taste horrible, it also contains measurable quantities of magnesium sulfate, an all-too-effective diarrhetic. Most vertebrates, including humans and birds, maintain the overall concentrations of dissolved salts in their blood and body fluids within a relatively narrow range about one-fourth the concentration of seawater. Should they fail to do so, water in the surrounding body tissue would automatically diffuse out of that tissue into the blood in an ill-fated attempt to reduce the body's circulating levels of salt. The cost of this action is a collection of dehydrated tissues, all of which have lost the capacity to function normally—hence salt's toxic effect.

Avian Salt Glands and Maintenance of the Balance

The simple solution to this problem would be to have the body excrete the excess salt. However, the human kidney is, at best, able to secrete a 2% salt solution, but seawater has a salt content of approximately 3.5%. The only way to get rid of the excess salt that one would imbibe when drinking seawater is to use up water within the body to do so (Schmidt-Nielsen 1959, 1983). The kidneys of birds are even less efficient than kidneys of mammals at excreting excess salt. Yet many marine birds are capable of ingesting salt water. How, then, do coastal and marine birds manage to thrive in salty ecosystems? How do they avoid the problem of excess salt?

Birds have several ways of ridding their bodies of excess salt. One relatively unimportant route is through the reabsorption of water from fecal material in their cloacae before defecation. A far more important route involves the use of so-called salt glands, extremely efficient secretory devices situated in the heads of many marine, coastal, and desert-dwelling birds. Salt glands are capable of excreting salt against a prevailing concentration gradient. They are paired organs that vary considerably in size among species and are usually located in distinctive depressions in the skull, just above the bird's eyes. Such glands are unknown in mammals. Human tears, which are not especially salty, function primarily to wash dust and other debris from the surfaces of the eyes and to express emotions, not to reduce salt load.

Although salt glands were first described at an anatomists' convention in 1665, they were initially referred to as merely nasal glands, and not until 1958 was their role in salt regulation made clear (Schmidt-Nielsen et al. 1958). Until then, biologists had assumed that the glands functioned to clear the nasal mucosa of potentially damaging salt water (Technau 1936). The glands concentrate salt in much the same way that kidneys concentrate nitrogenous wastes. Microscopically, salt glands consist of many parallel lobes branching from a central duct. Numerous capillaries carrying blood in parallel but opposite directions establish a countercurrent flow that, with an accompanying ionic pump, enables the glands to concentrate and eliminate salt in much the same manner that kitchen refrigerators concentrate and eliminate the heat content of indoor air (Scholander 1957, Raven and Johnson 1989). Concentrations of the solutions secreted from salt glands, although relatively constant within species, vary considerably among different species of birds. Such concentrations are strongly correlated, as might be expected, to the degree of each species's dependence upon marine environments (Staaland 1967). For example, birds living in environments where fresh water is not limited rarely possess the glands.

Salt gland secretions, which are almost twice as concentrated as normal seawater, are induced whenever osmoreceptors located in the heart transmit the appropriate signal (Peaker and Linzell 1975). Dumping salt at this rate enables many birds to evacuate quickly the salt that accumulates as a result of ingesting seawater. In fact, the salt glands of many species of marine birds are capable of secreting half their weight in salt solution each minute. (A comparison with human excretory abilities is humbling: Our kidneys, at best, take 10 times as long to produce half their weight in urine.) Many bird species are capable of eliminating fluids equal to 15% or more of their body weight each day (Shoemaker 1972, Schmidt-Nielsen 1983), a human equivalent of several gallons of salt water.

Salt glands, then, are what allow many seabirds to maintain themselves on diets of marine prey and seawater, far from any source of fresh water. But functional salt glands also occur in many coastal species, including numerous wading birds, and anyone who has watched White Ibises for any length of time cannot help but notice that they too produce a clear fluid that trickles from their nostrils, along their upper mandibles, and off the tips of their bills. Do ibises have truly functional salt glands, and if so, why are parental ibises that nest on Pumpkinseed Island so reluctant to feed fiddler crabs to their young? In 1985 Jim Johnston and I decided to examine these questions in detail.

Salt's Effects on Nestling White Ibises

Jim Kushlan had earlier suggested that the significantly smaller clutches he found in coastal versus inland colonies of White Ibises may have resulted from increased physiological stress associated with marine eco-systems (Kushlan 1977c). Hence, I could not help wondering whether parental ibises were avoiding feeding brackish-water fiddler crabs to their young because of a "salt problem."

Fiddler crabs were suspect because they, like most marine crusta-ceans, are *osmoconformers*, species that respond to differences in the salt content of their environments by adjusting their internal concentrations to loosely reflect external environmental conditions. (In contrast, White Ibises are *osmoregulators* and maintain internal concentrations at a constant value, regardless of external conditions.) Fiddler crabs benefit from this strategy by avoiding the energy expenditure of maintaining a steep os-motic gradient within their relatively leaky exoskeletons. They are more than twice as salty as freshwater crayfishes, and, perhaps most impor-tantly, more than three times as salty as nestling ibises (Figure 8.1).

Parental White Ibises were avoiding feeding salty prey to their young but eating it themselves. Many parental birds raise their young on diets that differ from what they themselves eat (O'Connor 1984). Some do so because their rapidly growing young require diets that are richer in protein and calcium or that are calorically more dense; others are accommodating their nestlings' smaller gapes (Kahl 1962, Snow 1974, Best 1977, Raven 1986). Diets are also known to differ in species whose

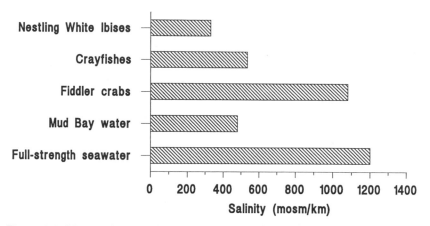

Figure 8.1. Mean salinities of full-strength seawater, brackish water typical of the North Inlet Estuary, and the body fluids of fiddler crabs, crayfishes, and nestling White Ibises.

nestlings face a greater risk of water stress because of their smaller size, higher water turnover rates, and inability to fly to supplemental fresh-water drinking sites (see Dawson et al. 1984). Storks regurgitate water directly to their young (Thomas 1984), Egyptian Plovers and several species of African sandgrouse transport it on soaked belly feathers (Cade and MacLean 1967, Howell 1979, MacLean 1983), and Brewer's Blackbirds dunk their prey in fresh water before feeding it to their young (Koenig 1985). Parental penguins, petrels, albatrosses, and flamingos solve the problem of salty prey by feeding semiprocessed, desalted food to their young, or by producing food from their own low-salt tissue and body fluids (O'Connor 1984). Many heron and egret species raise their nestlings on a diet of osmoregulating fishes, and other bird species provide low-salt crustaceans and gastropods to their young, specifically avoiding salt-ladened bivalves during the breeding season.

In 1985 Jim and I examined the possibility that Pumpkinseed Island's White Ibises were flying long distances to secure freshwater prey because their nestlings were unable to develop normally on the more locally available fiddler crabs. For this experiment, the two of us hand-reared 28 nestlings on one of three diets: (1) low-salt crayfishes, similar to what parental ibises feed their young at the colony site, (2) high-salt fiddler crabs, which are consumed by adult ibises at the site but are rarely fed to the young, and (3) high-salt crayfishes (i.e., crayfishes whose salt content we had boosted to the salt level of fiddler crabs by soaking them in aquarium salt for several hours). The high-salt crayfishes were used to control for the differences between fiddler crabs and crayfishes other than their respective salt contents (Johnston and Bildstein 1990).

After arranging to have three industrious interns assist us in our work, Jim and I scheduled the experiment to begin in May of 1985, nestling availability permitting. Before we collected any nestling White Ibises, we needed to know how we were going to feed the little beggars. We knew that developing ibises grew at phenomenal rates. Indeed, we could expect to see our nestlings increase in mass more than 15-fold in less than 2 months (Kushlan 1977a). The food requirements of three or four nestlings are often more than enough to keep a pair of experienced adult ibises busily searching for sufficient prey, and here we were, without any experience, planning to raise 10 times that many nestlings.

We realized the need for a major food campaign. Freshwater crayfishes were easy to secure. The local fish market would provide all we wanted at $1.98 per pound, and we eventually purchased 300 pounds (136 kilograms). Fiddler crabs were not so easily obtained. Because they were not on any of the menus of the area's seafood houses, their only reliable sources were biological supply houses, and they wanted $1.25 per crab, or perhaps $1.10, if we promised to buy in bulk. We estimated that we would need 50,000 to 60,000 crabs to complete our experiments. Buying crabs was out of the question. We would have to catch them ourselves.

Fiddler crabs are easily the most abundant macroinvertebrates at the North Inlet Marsh, and we felt that the solution to our crab problem was well within our grasp. At first we considered, but then rejected, laying out baited box traps. Although the technique works well for the larger Blue Crab, we needed too many crabs too quickly. Unless we were willing to build hundreds of traps, we needed to look elsewhere for a solution. We ultimately settled on the same technique that White Ibises use: looking for fiddler crab assemblages in areas with little cover and few burrows, and running the crabs down before they have a chance to retreat.

However, although we considered ourselves to be the crab's mental superiors, we ran headlong into what Richard Dawkins (1982) refers to as the *life–dinner principle*, an evolutionary asymmetry that takes its name from an Aesop's fable. As paraphrased by Dawkins (1982, 65): "The rabbit runs faster than the fox, because the rabbit is running for his *life* while the fox is only running for his *dinner*." Despite my series of pep talks, the likes of which would have made Knute Rockne proud, the fiddler crabs were always more motivated than we were, and on a one-on-one basis they almost always won.

Our assaults were restricted to the several hours on either side of low tide, when thousands of fiddler crabs predictably crawled from the safety of their burrows higher on the marsh to feed in exposed locations along the creek bank. At such times two to six crab-catchers, buckets in hand and spaced at 5-meter intervals, quickly descended upon the crabs, which immediately scattered in the most inappropriate directions. The technique consisted of controlled pandemonium.

Fiddler crabs are capable of fleeing at a remarkable pace when faced with an approaching predator. Many found refuge among the razor-sharp clusters of American Oysters that fringed the creek. Others possessed the unerring ability to lure pursuers onto seemingly supportive stretches of pluff mud—the local equivalent of quicksand. This inconceivably treacherous material, although capable of supporting an army of 1-gram crabs, willingly sucks researchers up to their armpits. Extracting oneself from such a quagmire is a decidedly singular affair, since anyone attempting to help quickly becomes equally engulfed. The only way out of the predicament involves swimming and crawling through the sulfurous morass to the nearest solid marsh.

Nevertheless, many crabs invariably retreated in what was for them the wrong direction, and thus fell easy prey to our groping hands. Others, especially the larger males, often stood their ground and challenged our predatory advances by waving their major chelipeds, a defiant gesture that all but sealed their fate. Somewhat startling at first, the pincherlike defensive actions of such individuals are relatively painless, except for the occasional well-placed nip at the tender fold of skin at the base of the human finger. Even so, hundreds of pinches can have a cumulative effect. Several weeks into the experiment, the tips of Jim's fingers were so sore that he had trouble performing even the most essential manual tasks, including zipping his trousers.

On any one tide, most of the crabs that could be caught were usually gathered within the first 15 minutes. Once we had collected the day's crabs we regrouped and compared our hauls before returning to the lab's all-important water spigot. Rinsing the crabs, as well as ourselves, we carefully processed as many as 5,000 crabs, packed them into small plastic bags, and placed them in deep freeze.

Once we were convinced that we had enough fiddler crabs to begin the experiment, we began gathering our experimental nestlings. To avoid having to hand-feed all of our nestlings—a tedious and time-consuming affair—we had decided to individually color-mark birds upon hatching and wait until they were 21 days old and capable of feeding on their own before taking them into the lab. Each of the 28 nestlings used in our experiment was the older of two siblings and was taken from two-chick clutches at the colony site.

Throughout the experiment, all of our nestlings were maintained outdoors in shaded cages. Each cage was lined with polyethylene sheeting to enable us to collect feces and any uneaten food that the nestlings knocked from their food cups (Figure 8.2). Nestlings were randomly assigned to one of our three experimental diets: fiddler crabs, unaltered crayfishes, or crayfishes whose salt content had been boosted to that of fiddler crabs (Table 8.1). Nestlings were offered weighed portions of crabs or crayfishes in small cups three times a day, a schedule resembling that of parental feedings at the colony site. All of the chicks were maintained on ad libitum diets, and we cleared away the food and considered a meal ended when a chick had not fed for at least 10 minutes. Initially, we also provided the nestlings with a constant supply of brackish bay water, which would have been available to them had we not removed them from the colony. Nestlings were weighed and measured when first brought in from the field and every other day of the experiment thereafter.

In addition to monitoring the impact of each of the three diets on nestling growth and development, Jim and I also measured the effects of these diets on the metabolism of each of our birds. The easiest way to measure metabolic expenditure is to use the so-called energy-in-minus-energy-out technique. Doing so required estimating the amount of food entering each bird and then subtracting it from an estimate of how much of that material was passing, unused, through each bird. The first part was easy. We simply weighed the food before feeding, and subtracted that weight from the amount that remained uneaten.

The methods required to measure the energy-out component did little for our popularity at the lab. Not only did obtaining this information involve the onerous task of carefully scraping and bagging fecal material from each bird's cage every 48 hours, it also required drying this material in one of the field lab's ovens. Performing these tasks on a regular basis made about as much sense to the other members of the lab as releasing mosquitoes indoors. For about a month of the summer of 1985, we bird people were most definitely persona non grata. Unfortunately, drying fecal material was a necessary step in preparing it for the bomb calorimeter, the sophisticated furnace Jim was using to determine the caloric content of each substance, and we had little choice in the matter.

The impact of the high-salt diets was evident almost immediately. While White Ibis nestlings feeding on the unaltered, low-salt crayfish diet quickly began gaining weight, those feeding on high-salt fiddler crabs or salt-loaded crayfishes began to lose weight. Indeed, birds on the low-salt diet grew at approximately the same rate as parent-reared nestlings on Pumpkinseed Island, whereas at 1 week into the experiment nestlings on either of the high-salt diets weighed approximately 25% less than they had at the beginning of the experiment (Figure 8.3). The bills and wings of nestlings on the low-salt diet were also increasing at significantly faster, and more typical, rates.

The reasons for these differences were clear. Although all of the birds had been allowed to feed to satiation, nestlings on the fiddler crab diet had consumed 50% less food, and those on the salt-loaded crayfish diet had consumed 30% less food, than had birds on the low-salt (unaltered) crayfish diet, despite the availability of equal amounts of food to all. The difference between birds on high-salt fiddler crab diets and those on low-salt crayfish diets is even more impressive when one considers that the caloric content of fiddler crabs is significantly lower than that of

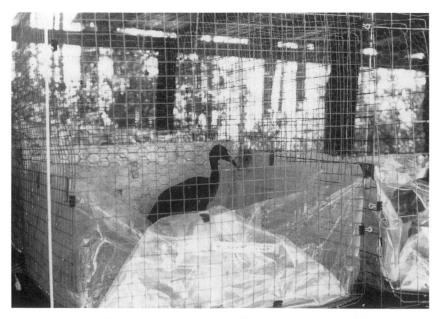

Figure 8.2. A nestling White Ibis and its outdoor cage used in our feeding experiment.

Table 8.1   Analysis of diets provided to nestling White Ibises reared in captivity

Prey item	N	Osmotic content (mosmol/kg)	Caloric content (kcal/g)	Protein content (%)	Water content (%)
Unaltered crayfish	10	535 ± 12	4.36 ± 0.15	12.7 ± 0.7	74.2 ± 2
Salt-loaded crayfish	10	1,090 ± 23	4.32 ± 0.15	12.3 ± 0.7	74.3 ± 3
Fiddler crabs	10	1,080 ± 20	2.23 ± 0.10	10.2 ± 0.8	62.4 ± 3

Note: Summarized from Table 1 in Johnston and Bildstein (1990). Data are given as means ± standard error.

crayfishes (Table 8.1). Consequently, nestlings on high-salt crab diets were consuming only one-third as many calories as were those feeding on low-salt crayfish diets. Not surprisingly, whereas birds on the low-salt diet appeared healthy and vigorous 5 days into the experiment, most of those on high-salt diets were sickly and lethargic. Apparently, young White Ibises dislike salty food, even to the point of self-starvation.

Additional evidence that salt itself was responsible for the differences we observed came from the birds' blood chemistry. Our analysis of the blood of nestlings on the low-salt diet indicated no signs of abnormalities. However, in nestlings on the high-salt diets, the hematocrits (the ratio of the volume of packed red blood cells to the total volume of the blood, including plasma) and ionic concentrations of sodium, potassium, and chloride were significantly elevated, clearly signaling salt toxicity. Further evidence for the role of salt toxicity came during the second week of our investigation.

By the end of the first week of our experiment, it had become obvious that nestling White Ibises found high-salt diets intolerable, and we decided to modify our protocol. On day 8 we substituted fresh tap water for the brackish bay water in the diets of birds on either of the high-salt diets. On the other hand, nestlings on the low-salt diet continued to receive only bay water throughout the experiment. Although we never quantified the amounts of water consumed by each of the birds, it was readily apparent that all 10 of the birds on the high-salt diets substantially increased their water consumption as soon as fresh water was made available to them, and all 10 began to increase their food consumption shortly thereafter. Indeed, in stark contrast to what had happened during week 1 of the experiment, birds on all three diets consumed nearly equal amounts of food during weeks 2 and 3, and every one of the birds on

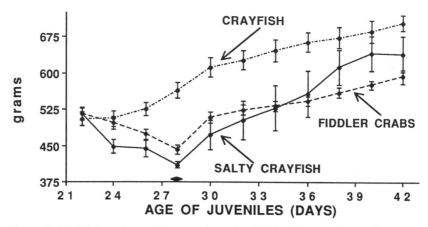

BODY MASS

Figure 8.3. Weight gains and losses of nestling White Ibises on low-salt crayfish, high-salt crayfish, and high-salt fiddler crab diets. Fresh water was substituted for brackish water at 28 days of age for birds on the two high-salt diets. From Johnston and Bildstein (1990). Copyright by The University of Chicago Press. All rights reserved.

high-salt diets reversed the pattern of weight loss they had established initially (Figure 8.3). Also, blood samples taken from the birds revealed that, at the end of the experiment, the hematocrit and salt concentrations of birds on the high-salt diets had returned to normal.

The results of this effort and of subsequent field studies clarified why parental White Ibises regularly fly long distances to secure freshwater crayfish prey: Nestling White Ibises are unable to develop normally on locally available brackish-water fiddler crab prey. That this effect is caused by differences in the salt contents of these two food sources, rather than by differences in their caloric contents, is evidenced by two aspects of our study: (1) the response of nestlings maintained on crayfish prey whose salt content had been altered to that of fiddler crab prey, and (2) the reversal of this response by adding freshwater ad libitum during the second week of the experiment.

Subsequent studies at the colony site provided field results that corroborated our laboratory results. Between 1985 and 1989 Toni De Santo, Jim, and I monitored the growth, development, and survival of parentally reared White Ibis nestlings, and we simultaneously collected regurgitant for osmotic analysis. During all 5 years of this study, we carefully limited the growth studies to the oldest nestling at each nest. To avoid affecting the growth of these birds, we collected regurgitant only from their younger sibs and from birds in nearby nests. As can be seen in Figure 8.4, annual fluctuations in nestling growth closely parallel fluctuations in the salt content of prey being delivered to the nests.

The actions of both parental and nestling White Ibises during the breeding-season drought of 1985 are especially telling. In that year, many birds at Pumpkinseed Island failed to breed, and most of those that did breed attempted to raise their nestlings on fiddler crabs rather than on crayfishes (Bildstein et al. 1990). Almost all of these nestlings were lethargic, and even moribund, and many were decidedly lighter than normal for their age. By June of 1985, there were signs that parental care at the colony site was waning, even while many prefledged young remained in their nests. Many of the nestlings whose development we followed that year ultimately starved to death.

At the same time, a different but no less tragic series of events was unfolding some 90 kilometers down the coast, at Drum Island. By mid-June of 1985 a colleague of ours, Will Post, was reporting that parental ibises at Drum Island were also deserting listless young. But unlike the situation at Pumpkinseed Island, where unattended nestlings simply wasted away, the enormous population of Fish Crows inhabiting Charleston Harbor was making short work of this newfound source of nourishment.

But what about salt glands? A quick examination of several salvaged carcasses of adult White Ibises revealed tell-tale depressions in the skull above the orbit of each eye, as well as remnants of what appeared to be glandular material that was associated with paired ducts leading to the birds' nostrils. With this information in hand, we decided to see whether or not nestlings possess salt glands and, furthermore, whether the salt content of the diets of our experimental nestlings had affected the development of these glands.

Nestling White Ibises do possess salt glands (Figure 8.5), and the salt glands of nestlings on high-salt fiddler crab diets were considerably larger than those of nestlings on low-salt crayfish diets. Indeed, after only 1 week of captivity, the salt glands of nestlings feeding on fiddler crabs were more than one-third larger than those of nestlings feeding on crayfishes, and after 3 weeks they were more than two-thirds larger (Figure 8.6). However, although nestling ibises apparently respond to salt stress by increasing the development of their salt glands, they are unable to circumvent the problem of salt stress entirely.

Numerous researchers have conducted careful studies of the secretory capacities of salt glands in nestlings developing in marine environments. As might be expected, most of these studies suggest that nestlings of many species increase their ability to secrete salt as they develop (Schmidt-Nielsen and Kim 1964, Ensor and Phillips 1972, Hughes 1984).

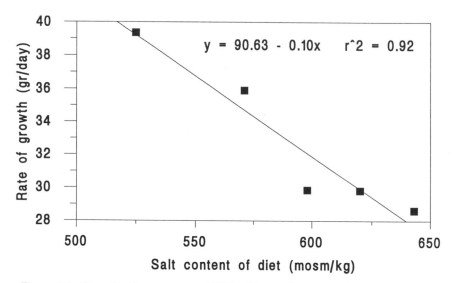

Figure 8.4. Growth of parent-reared White Ibis nestlings, as a function of the salt content of their diets.

Figure 8.5. The salt gland of a 6-week-old White Ibis nestling that was hand-reared on a high-salt fiddler crab diet. The gland is located above and to the right of the bird's eye. Drawing by M. Davis.

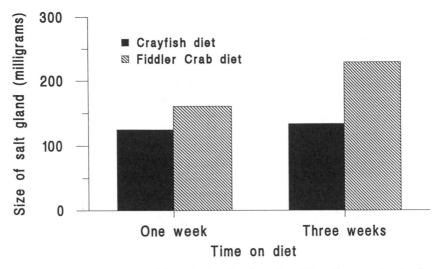

Figure 8.6. Relative sizes of the salt glands of nestling White Ibises maintained on low-salt crayfish and high-salt fiddler crab diets for 1 or 3 weeks.

On the other hand, several studies reveal a decrease in salt-secreting ability with age (Hughes 1968, Zucker et al. 1979), and there is even evidence of salt secretions from pipping young in both gulls and penguins (Douglas 1968, Hughes 1984), presumably the result of long-term adaptation to especially stressful saline environments.

In White Ibises, however, younger nestlings are more limited in their salt-excreting abilities than are older nestlings. Although the ducts that eventually drain the salt glands of embryonic ibises are visible in histological sections as early as 10 days into incubation, or more than a week and a half before hatching, our investigations suggest that the salt glands of hatchling ibises are not well developed. After 7 years of looking for evidence of salt secretions in parentally reared young on Pumpkinseed Island, we have yet to see them in nestlings younger than 5 days of age. The results of several field experiments bolster the validity of these anecdotal observations. The first of these experiments involved salt-loading several nestlings at the colony site during the summer of 1986. During May and June of that year, Jim Johnston carefully infused a small dose of seawater-strength saline solution through a stomach tube into the digestive tracts of 1- to 9-day-old ibis nestlings. He then collected salt gland secretions resulting from this load by placing a thin tube into the gland's ducts. No bird less than 6 days of age produced any salt secretions, and none of the older chicks secreted more than 1% of the load during the subsequent 90-minute period. When tested 2 to 4 days later, several individuals managed to secrete as much as 2% of the ingested salt load.

Both our controlled experiments and our field studies suggested that the availability of fresh water enabled normal growth. Unfortunately, except for rainwater that sometimes collects in shallow puddles on Pumpkinseed Island, fresh water is not available to nestlings. Nor do the nestlings appear to consume any vegetation on the island, a tactic employed by several other species of birds to increase the amount of water in their diet (Ensor and Phillips 1972).

Nestling White Ibises are not alone in their intolerance of high-salt prey. Although experiments such as ours have yet to be performed on most species of coastal birds, similar responses to salt stress—depressed growth, retarded development, diarrhea, and lethargy—have been reported in many of the species that have been tested. Although the relative toxicities of the various ionic components of naturally occurring saline waters have yet to be resolved, magnesium salts, and particularly magnesium sulfate, appear to be especially problematic (Mitcham and Wobeser 1988a, 1988b).

Why, then, are the adults not providing fresh water to their young? Parental White Ibises, which feed on fiddler crabs throughout the summer, regularly interrupt their feeding bouts to drink at nearby freshwater ponds. My calculations (see Chapter 7) reveal that a pair of adults could easily secure enough crabs both for themselves and for their young. The only explanation I can suggest is that, although the digestive tract of adult ibises enables them to regurgitate recently ingested semisolid food, it does not allow the birds to ferry and subsequently regurgitate liquids such as water. Apparently, liquids are far more difficult to retain in the esophageal region that acts as a storage place for regurgitated food.

Parental individuals in some species of birds are able to circumvent this problem by soaking their belly feathers and bringing fresh water to their nestlings that way. I have never seen White Ibises attempt to use this tactic. Although one of my graduate students has reported seeing Glossy Ibises soak their belly feathers before returning to their nests, the birds were doing so with the brackish, not fresh, waters of Mud Bay. Such behavior probably functions to cool nestlings rather than to provide them with a drink. Even in drought years when crayfish and alternative freshwater prey are not available and parental White Ibises can only supply fiddler crabs (which they give in toxic doses) to their young, they fail to provide accompanying fresh water. The failure to do so cannot be understated: It literally determines the distribution and abundance of breeding populations of this species.

9   Ibises in Ecosystems

> . . . it seems unlikely that birds exert any major influence on ecosystem structure, functional properties, or dynamics through their direct effects on either the flux or storage of energy or nutrients. . . . their role instead might be as governors or controllers . . .
>
> J. A. Wiens, 1973

Ecology is a relatively young science. In 1866, when Ernst Haeckel first defined the discipline as the "science of the relationship of the organism to the environment" (Haeckel 1866), ecologists were "naturalists" who spent most of their time simply mapping the distributions and abundances of the organisms they encountered. Times have changed. Today, the field of ecology—at least relative to Haeckel's definition of it—has grown considerably, and many of its current practitioners bear little resemblance to their 19th-century counterparts. Although my colleagues in the discipline each view it in a personalized way—much as the fabled five blind men viewed the elephant—modern ecology, in general, is peopled by two kinds of scientists: autecologists and synecologists.

Autecologists are the more traditional of the two; most study the environment or "ecosystem" from the organism's point of view, typically focusing their efforts on describing how different environments affect those organisms. *Synecologists,* on the other hand, study the entire ecosystem, often focusing on the antithetical question of how organisms affect the systems in which they live. (Figure 9.1 graphically depicts the areas of interest to the two subdisciplines.) The term *ecosystem*, which is intu-

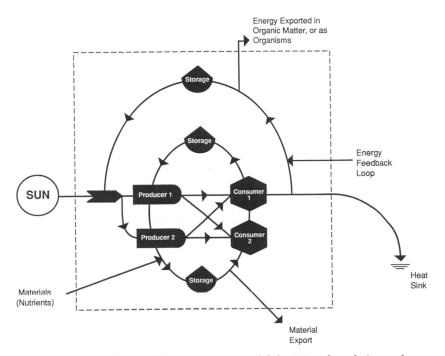

Figure 9.1. A greatly simplified ecosystem model depicting the relative realms of autecology and synecology. Autecologists spend most of their time describing the ecology of organisms *within* the model's "black boxes" (labeled *producers* and *consumers*). Synecologists spend most of their time studying interactions *among* the black boxes. Modification of Figure 2 in Odum (1989). Reprinted with permission of Sinauer Associates, Inc.

itively alluring, has proved to be a rather elusive concept about which ecologists have yet to reach a consensus. *Webster's Ninth New Collegiate Dictionary* defines *system* as "a regularly interacting or interdependent group of items forming a unified whole." Many autecologists define *ecosystem* as a community of organisms, its physical environment, and the interactions occurring therein, but most synecologists consider ecosystems to be far more organized than that. To them, ecosystems are "superorganisms" or complex cybernetic, self-controlling, self-organizing, and self-maintaining ecological units, capable of sustaining life in isolation from all but their atmospheric surroundings (O'Neill et al. 1986).

Most of my fieldwork—indeed, most of the efforts described in this book—clearly define me as an autecologist. I have, however, dabbled in the subdiscipline of synecology. What follows is a summary of these efforts.

Birds' Relative Importance to Their Ecosystems

White Ibises are one of the more conspicuous components of the salt-marsh ecosystem. But are they truly part of the interacting system? Do their activities significantly modify the wetlands they inhabit? Or are they insignificant ecological "frills" (as defined by Wiens 1973), birds whose presence or absence has little bearing on the way that coastal ecosystems function? My initial studies of avian-induced energy flow, briefly outlined in Chapter 2, suggested an affirmative answer to the latter question. At North Inlet, the entire avian community, including all of its White Ibises, appeared to play a rather minor role in ecosystem function, in terms of both energy flux and material transport (Christy et al. 1981, Dame et al. 1986). Studies of avian communities in other habitats, including temperate forests (Holmes and Sturges 1973, Weiner and Glowackinski 1975), prairies (Risser 1972, Wiens 1973), and offshore waters (Evans 1973) also suggest that birds play minor roles in those habitats. Indeed, most attempts to address this issue indicate that the amount of energy flowing through avian communities typically represents considerably less than 1% of the total amount of energy being photosynthesized by the ecosystem's plants. White Ibises appear to be relatively unimportant ecological entities, at least at the ecosystem level. Or are they?

Although available evidence suggests that birds do not significantly affect nutrient processing and energy flow *within* ecosystems, research suggests that birds may be important processors of nutrients *between* ecosystems, principally because of their ability to extract (by feeding), transport (by flying), and deposit (by defecating) nutrients and other materials over long distances across the ecological landscape. The effects of such transport are especially apparent in the immediate vicinity of large roosting and breeding assemblages, where feces are often deposited in massive amounts (Hutchinson 1950, Zelickman and Golovkin 1972, McColl and Burger 1976, Onuf et al. 1977). Perhaps the best example of the phenomenon comes from the historical accounts of 18th- and 19th-century European travelers visiting coastal Peru. One 18th-century account describes overwhelming quantities of birds and the inevitable result:

> The lands in the jurisdiction of Chancay [Peru] are manured with the dung of certain seabirds, which abound here in a very extraordinary manner. These they call Guanoes, and the dung

Guano, the indian name for excrement in general. These birds, after spending the whole day catching fish at sea, repair at night to rest on the islands near the coast . . . their numbers being so great as entirely to cover the ground, they leave a proportionable quantity of excrement or dung. (Juan and de Ulloa 1748, as cited on pp. 286–87 in Murphy 1936)

The next century held much of the same in this region, so people apparently started dealing with it:

The quantity of this manure is enormous. . . . Several small vessels are constantly employed to carry it off; some of the cuts, where embarkation is convenient, are from forty to fifty feet deep, and their bottom is yet considerably above the level of the sea. (Stevenson 1825, as cited on p. 287 in Murphy 1936)

What on the surface might seem to be a problem was turned into profit. The economic value of these accumulations was soon discovered:

Guano owes its value to the peculiar manner in which its components are united, by the alchemy of the bird's intestinal tract, into a compound more easily absorbed by plants from the soil to which it is applied than any fertilizer synthetically composed. To put the matter as simply and forcibly as possible, it may be said that, if the value of fertilizer be calculated according to nitrogen content, the best Peruvian guano is more than thirty-three times as effective as farmyard manure. (Murphy 1925, as cited on p. 289 in Murphy 1936)

The commercial utility of this natural fertilizer was such that, by the mid-1850s, North American ports were handling about 200,000 tons (180,000 tonnes) annually. By 1857, Peruvian guano sales, then valued at over $5 million annually, were responsible for more than 60% of the country's public revenues (Murphy 1936).

Hutchinson (1950) suggested that erosional losses of guano into surrounding oceanic waters act to increase the primary productivity and fish production of nearby coastal zones to such an extent that larger bird colonies, rather than reducing commercial catches of fish through competition, might in fact increase catches as a result of biochemical concentration.

Although the enormity of South America's guano deposits is unmatched anywhere, lesser concentrations of nutrient-rich avian fecal material occur wherever birds congregate in large numbers, including Pumpkinseed Island. After slipping and sliding through such accumulations for more than half a dozen years, Peter Frederick and I decided to join forces with Baruch Institute geochemist Liz Blood to assess the potential role of White Ibises as "biotic vectors" of nutrients in the North Inlet Estuary ecosystem (Bildstein et al. 1992).

One of the many benefits of working at an active field station such as the Baruch Institute is that of an expanded information base, since your colleagues are often studying other aspects of the local environment. Thus, in 1987 when Liz Blood told me that she had been collecting data on the extent to which rainfall and upland stream flow were contributing nutrients to the North Inlet Marsh, Peter and I saw an opportunity to collaborate with her on a study comparing the relative importance of birds and rainfall as nutrient transporters at the site.

Estuarine ecologists have known for some time that nutrient availability, especially nitrogen, affects the primary productivity and species composition of coastal salt marshes (Valiela et al. 1975). Furthermore, nutrients are believed to be especially limiting during spring and summer, when rapidly growing plants quickly drain nutrients from salt-marsh sediments (Bedard et al. 1980). But, although nutrient processing at Hobcaw Barony had been studied in considerable detail (Dame et al. 1986), the relative importance of birds in modifying such processes was largely unknown.

The three of us hoped to resolve this unknown by determining the amount of nutrients White Ibises deposited at Pumpkinseed Island each year and comparing these figures with those that Liz had accumulated for rainfall and stream flow. We decided to focus our attention on 1984 and 1985: 1984 had been a relatively wet year with many ibises successfully breeding at the colony site, whereas 1985 had been a dry year with few breeding ibises. A comparison of these years promised to be enlightening.

Since we already had field data for these years, we envisioned a short project, resulting in a manuscript for publication within 2 or 3 months. After all, we only needed to construct the two models simulating nutrient input from rainfall and from White Ibises. Nothing in science is ever as simple as it first appears, and modeling nutrient flow proved more complicated than we had ever expected. We did finally complete both models, but the project took several years.

Modeling Nutrient Flow at North Inlet

Nutrient Inputs of Rainfall and Stream Flow

In many ecosystems weather provides an important source of nutrients (Likens et al. 1977). In much the same way as precipitation becomes acidified while falling through polluted air, it is capable of becoming nutrified as well. The extent to which the atmosphere fertilizes an ecosystem depends upon three factors: the amount of nutrients in the air, the prevailing wind direction, and the amount and periodicity of local precipitation (Blood et al. 1989). After examining such conditions along the eastern seaboard of the United States, Reimold and Daiber (1967) suggested that the combination of westerly winds and fertilizer-enriched dust from spring plowing in inland agricultural areas caused an increase in phosphorus levels in the region's coastal bays and marshes each spring and summer.

The atmosphere is not the only potential source of nutrients in the rainwater that finds it way into the North Inlet Estuary. Once rain has begun to pass through the forested canopy of the upland watershed, additional modifications of its nutrient content can occur. Nutrient enhancement results both from passive washing of nutrient-enriched materials from plant surfaces and from active leaching from plant tissues. Nutrient depletion results as nutrients are adsorbed by plant tissues or are sequestered by microbes living in the canopy (Blood et al. 1989). Similar enrichments and depletions continue to occur after the water has reached the forest floor and begins to drain in rivulets toward the marsh.

To account for all of this, Liz was forced to assess the nutrient content of the rainwater falling directly over the marsh, as well as the stream flow draining into it. Rainwater was collected from numerous gauges throughout the property, while stream water was collected in a single representative watershed. After each storm and major rainfall, Liz estimated the volume of rainwater falling over the 3,200-hectare estuary, as well as the volume of stream flow for the 990 hectares of forested uplands that drain directly into the estuary. She used these two volumes, and their calculated nutrient densities, to model nutrient input into the marsh via rainfall and stream flow.

Nutrient Inputs of White Ibises

As I have already described, many of Pumpkinseed Island's White Ibises feed on fiddler crabs from the North Inlet Estuary. But during chick rearing, most parental White Ibises also feed on crayfishes in bottomland forests farther inland. Later in the season, parental ibises return to feeding on fiddler crabs within the estuary, this time with their fledged young. By late August, most of the population has departed for the wintering grounds (Christy et al. 1981, Bildstein 1983).

Because of the enormous size of Pumpkinseed Island's breeding population, White Ibises customarily constitute more than one-sixth of the entire avian biomass in the estuary (Bildstein et al. 1982). That ibis concentrations can act as significant conveyers of nutrients across the ecological landscape is supported by the results of a study conducted in the Okefenokee Swamp in southern Georgia. In that investigation, University of Georgia doctoral candidate Deborah Stinner (1983) simulated nutrient input at a White Ibis colony and convincingly argued that the birds were importing more than 10 times as much calcium and phosphorus into the system as were rainfall and stream flow.

Peter, Liz, and I used a similar procedure to assess the extent of nutrient transport induced by White Ibises at the North Inlet Estuary. The model we used consisted of two parts: a nutrient input submodel that estimated nutrient input by ibises on a per-pair basis, and a population submodel that estimated the numbers of ibises at the colony site. The two submodels simulated how much prey was needed by the colony on a seasonal basis, what the nutrient content of that prey was, how much of that prey came from outside the estuary and how much from inside, and what proportion of that prey passed through the birds unused. And finally, these submodels simulated what the nutrient content of White Ibises was, and how many nestlings died (and at what age) and were themselves deposited at the site over the course of the breeding season. Although much of the information needed to run the model was already in our field notes, a good portion of it had to be mined from rather obscure sources in the published literature.

For example, to determine the amount of food required for each pair of breeding adults, we first had to determine the daily caloric food requirements of individuals of different sizes and different levels of activity (which we did from published information as well as from our data), combine them with the digestive efficiencies of the birds (from published information and our data), and then determine the caloric contents of fiddler crab and crayfish prey (from our data). These calculations gave us an estimate of the amount of food being used by each pair. But we also needed to know what proportion of the nutrient content of that food was passing through the digestive tracts of the birds and being deposited at the colony site. To estimate this input variable, we fed several captive White Ibises either fiddler crabs or crayfishes for several days, collected all of their fecal material, and analyzed it for its nutrient content.

Then, to assess the fecal output being deposited into the system, we needed to estimate how much time each bird spent at the colony site each day. For nestlings, the amount was obviously 100% of their time. For adults, the answer was less obvious. Peter's doctoral dissertation provided our answer. More than 4,000 hours of observing parental White Ibises and carefully recording their comings and goings throughout the breeding season (see Frederick 1985b) had finally paid off. But these data were only half of the story. We also needed to estimate the size of the breeding population, and nesting success each year. Fortunately, this proved to be a notably easier task.

The numbers of pairs of ibises breeding on Pumpkinseed Island had already been determined from aerial photographs. We assumed that each pair hatched two nestlings, and that mortality in the nest occurred entirely within the first 2 weeks of life. These assumptions resulted in an arguably simplified version of what actually occurred and probably a slightly conservative estimate of the numbers of nestlings on the island. We then counted the numbers of birds feeding on a representative portion of the estuary, and used that number to estimate how many birds were feeding on the entire estuary. By process of elimination, we were then able to estimate how many birds were feeding elsewhere.

Finally, because Pumpkinseed Island is at the southern edge of the estuary and some of the fecal material deposited on it was regularly washed from the island and into Winyah Bay, we assumed that only one-fourth of the nutrients deposited on the island were eventually transported to the marsh by tidal activity. With this information in hand, we calculated the nutrient input of Pumpkinseed's White Ibises and compared it with the nutrient inputs of rainfall and stream flow.

Table 9.1   Annual nutrient transport to the North Inlet Marsh by rainfall, stream flow, and White Ibises, 1984–85

Nutrient	Imported by rainfall and stream flow (kg)		Imported by White Ibises (kg)	
	1984	1985	1984	1985
Nitrogen	6,210	23,300	640	60
Phosphorus	470	680	230	20
Calcium	360,000	260,000	1,290	120
Potassium	13,900	16,300	47	4

Note: Modified from Bildstein et al. (1992).

Comparing Nutrient Inputs

Annual precipitation at Hobcaw Barony averages 130 centimeters (approximately 50 inches) per year, and most annual variation results from occasional tropical storms and hurricanes (NOAA 1985). Summer and fall are usually the wettest times of the year. The intermittent stream that Liz was using to monitor the amount of nutrient input draining from the watershed flows only between November and May in most years, and overall runoff to the marsh usually averages about 40% of the rainfall input. In 1984, rainfall was below normal, but runoff was above normal. In 1985, both were below normal. However, because nutrient concentrations of both rainwater and stream flow were strikingly higher in 1985 than in 1984 (Bildstein et al. 1992), the two atmospheric sources imported substantially more total nitrogen, phosphorus, and potassium into the estuary in 1985 than they had 1984 (Table 9.1). How do these nutrient amounts compare with those imported by ibises?

The numbers of White Ibises breeding at the site dropped by 85% between 1984 and 1985 (i.e., from just under 13,000 breeding pairs in 1984 to just under 2,000 pairs in 1985), presumably because of the concurrent decline in freshwater crayfishes in the area. This decline, together with substantial reductions in both nestling survivorship and off-site feeding in 1985, meant that ibises imported less than one-tenth as many nutrients to Pumpkinseed Island in 1985 as they had in 1984 (Table 9.1). This abrupt decline, together with the notable increase in nutrient input from both rainfall and stream flow in 1985, produced a significant shift in the relative importance of these transport mechanisms during the years of our study (Figure 9.2).

Our results suggest that rainfall and stream flow are considerably more important transport mechanisms, especially with regard to calcium and potassium, than are White Ibises. On the other hand, ibises contributed substantial amounts of both nitrogen and phosphorus to the marsh in 1984. Furthermore, because ibises import all of their nutrients in spring and summer, at the peak of the growing season for cordgrasses, their impact on this event probably is disproportionately more important than their annual input suggests.

Winyah Bay, which lies several kilometers south of the Pumpkinseed Island colony site and the North Inlet Estuary, drains an immense four-river watershed of over 47,000 square kilometers, much of which is agricultural land. Because much of this land is intensively farmed and heavily fertilized, the waters of Winyah Bay are often heavily ladened with nutrients, especially when compared with those of the estuary. Although most of the fresh water flowing through the bay appears to bypass the estuary, occasionally some of it does enter the estuary, especially during wind-driven intrusions (Kjerfve and Proehl 1979). As a result, as much as 25% of the water exchange in the estuary may actually be between the estuary and Winyah Bay, rather than between the estuary and the ocean (Bildstein et al. 1992). If substantial amounts of the bay's nutrients enter the estuary, they would further reduce the importance of any role played by White Ibises in this regard.

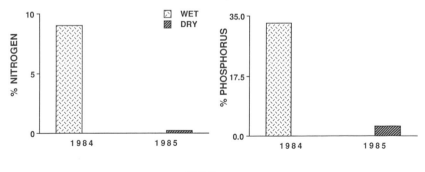

Figure 9.2. Nitrogen and phosphorus input of nesting White Ibises, expressed as a function of input by rainfall and stream flow, into the North Inlet Estuary, 1984 and 1985.

Speculations about White Ibises' Ecological Importance

Do our results signify that White Ibises are merely window dressings in the salt-marsh ecosystem? I would say no. Although their activities may be insignificant with regard to any *direct* impact on energy and material fluxes in ecosystems, ibises actually have an important *indirect* role in affecting these processes. Consider, for example, the predator–prey relationship between ibises and fiddler crabs. Fiddler crabs, because of their burrowing activities, are believed to be important agents in sediment bioturbation, mineralization, and oxygenation, all of which could increase the primary productivity of the salt marsh (Montague 1980). The degree to which crabs' burrowing activities affect local primary productivity of a salt marsh has been examined experimentally by Bertness (1985), who removed crabs from portions of the marsh and measured shifts in primary productivity. In some areas, removing crabs reduced productivity by more than 40%, and this result shows that crabs are truly important ecological agents. Although ibises rarely totally eliminate crabs from portions of the marsh, when considered over the course of an entire breeding season, their activities almost certainly affect the distribution and abundance of crabs in areas of highest use. Thus, through such activities, ibises undoubtedly affect the productivity of the marsh.

Another intriguing possibility is that the actual mechanics of ibis predation (i.e., ibis probing behavior) may also affect salt-marsh productivity. Barbara McCraith, one of my graduate students, conducted a preliminary examination of this possibility by using decurved bills recovered from the carcasses of deceased ibises and repeatedly probing several experimental plots on the site. Her preliminary results suggest that ibises too may serve as important agents of bioturbation, and that bill probing too may affect salt-marsh productivity.

In addition, White Ibises, by acting as predators, have played an evolutionary role—and perhaps a significant one, although it is impossible to measure—in fashioning the burrowing behavior of their fiddler crab prey. Although most crustacean biologists would probably agree that fiddler crabs excavate and use burrows for numerous reasons in addition to predator avoidance—courtship and mating, for example (Crane 1975)— the necessity of avoiding predators has almost certainly affected the extent to which the crabs burrow on the marsh. Thus, even if today's White Ibises are no longer playing a significant role as regulators of the influential estuarine phenomenon of burrowing, the ancestors of these birds, acting through the "ghost of predation past" (as defined by Connell 1980), are certainly having an important effect.

What does all of this mean? To me it means that ecologists still know very little about how ibises function in ecosystems. If my journey into synecology and ecological modeling has taught me anything, it is that ecosystems are incredibly complex, multidimensional historical entities whose secret codes are difficult to decipher. Although the ecosystem concept has been around for more than 50 years, its boundaries remain largely unknown, as does almost all of what lies within. So should we give up and stop asking whether or not birds are important in ecosystems? Surely not. Sooner or later autecologists and synecologists will learn enough about organisms and their ecosystems to answer such complex questions. Until then, we will have to be content with the answers to simpler questions.

10 Trouble in Paradise

The Plight of Trinidad's Scarlet Ibises

O parakeets & avocets, O immortelles
& ibis, scarlet under the stunning sun,
deliciously & tired I come
toward you in orbit, Trinidad!

John Berryman, 1972

One of the nicest things about being a college professor is taking a sabbatical, or furlough from teaching, every seven years. When mine came due in 1989, I decided to head for Trinidad. Having studied the ecology of White Ibises at Hobcaw Barony for more than a decade, I planned to spend six weeks studying the behavior and ecology of their tropical color-morph cousins, Scarlet Ibises. I was especially interested in answering a question that had been bothering me for some time: Why did Scarlet Ibises no longer breed in that country?

Scarlet Ibises have long been associated with Trinidad, and there is ample evidence that Scarlet Ibises have been regular, if not common, inhabitants of the island for at least 150 years (Joseph 1838, Leotaud 1866, Belcher and Smooker 1934). (White Ibises, by comparison, are rare visitors to the island [ffrench 1991].) The Scarlet Ibis is Trinidad and Tobago's national bird, and its image appears prominently both on the country's coat of arms and on its one-dollar bill (Figure 10.1). But although Scarlet Ibises formerly bred in the Caroni Swamp in northwestern Trinidad, none has done so since 1970. Today, most of that country's ibises leave the island each spring to nest on the South American mainland. Fortunately for the tourists, several thousand nonbreeding ibises continue to feed and roost in the Caroni Swamp, just south of the capital city of Port-of-Spain

Figure 10.1. Scarlet Ibises on the one-dollar bill of Trinidad and Tobago.

(Map 10.1, Figure 10.2) (Hislop and James 1990). Their presence, however, offers small comfort to the Trinidadians who want to reestablish the breeding populations of their national bird.

I met Carol James, the head of Trinidad's Wildlife Section, in March of 1988 at a Scarlet Ibis workshop in Venezuela, where I was presenting a paper on Pumpkinseed Island's White Ibises. Carol found our studies of nestling salt stress intriguing. Might it be possible, she asked, that Scarlet Ibises no longer bred in Trinidad because of decreases in the availability of freshwater prey? Within minutes, the two of us were discussing the possibility of my studying Trinidadian Scarlet Ibises. Three months later, I received a letter from the Trinidad Wildlife Section inviting me to visit the island, look over the situation, and offer suggestions.

The prospect of working with Scarlet Ibises in a tropical paradise was too much to pass up, and less than a year later, I was stepping off a Boeing 727 at Trinidad's Piarco Airport.

"Dr. Bildstein, I presume?" the khaki-clad young man with an East Indian accent asked while pushing his way through the muddle of cab drivers and relatives waiting outside the airport.

I was impressed. I had been on the island for less than 30 minutes, my baggage, including several potentially suspicious pieces of laboratory paraphernalia, had just passed through customs—"Have a pleasant holiday in Trinidad, sir," the customs officers had said—and Carol James, my Trinidadian host, had followed through on her promise of having someone meet my midnight flight.

"My name is Roopnarine Singh—you may call me Singh—and Carol James has asked me to take you to the rest house where you will be staying during your visit. We can pick up your rental car on the way to the swamp tomorrow morning when things open up."

"Yes," I interrupted, "I am Keith Bildstein, and I am glad to meet you, Mr. Singh. But how did you manage to pick me out of the crowd?" Hundreds of people were leaving the airport and my thoughts raced ahead to conjecture Singh's most likely response: "You look like a field biologist, Dr. Bildstein."

But what he said was "I spotted you while you were waiting in line at the customs desk. Dr. James told me to look for a balding, middle-aged North American, and you were the only one in line."

"Well, thank you very much, Mr. Singh. How do we get to the rest house?" I replied. "So much for my image," I thought.

Map 10.1. Trinidad and its wetlands of interest. Dashed line indicates the Caroni River catchment basin. Thick solid line represents the Uriah Butler Highway.

Figure 10.2. Trinidad's Caroni Swamp, with the Northern Range in the background and the Gulf of Paria in the foreground.

Singh and I traveled to the rest house in a well-seasoned Land Cruiser. As the vehicle twisted and turned along the narrow pavement, I sensed the country's gently rolling terrain. Although the rest house was less than 20 kilometers away, the trip took almost an hour, the result of a washed-out bridge along a more direct route. By the time we arrived I was too tired to do anything but unpack my bedding and fall asleep.

I woke the next morning in the Caribbean equivalent of a Wild West bunkhouse, a massive cinder-block structure situated at the edge of the Arena rain forest and outfitted with its own cook. Since I was the rest house's only regular inhabitant during my six-week stay, I had the chance to sample whatever cuisine I wanted, as long as it was Trinidadian. After a quick shower and even quicker meal, I was off to the Caroni Swamp with Singh for a planning session and initial tour. Along the way we stopped to pick up Jerry Farrier, another biologist for Trinidad's Wildlife Section, who, along with Singh and two considerably more massive game wardens, had been assigned to my project.

My first trip to the swamp offered a taste of what lay in store for me for the next month and a half. The rest house was situated on the eastern edge of Port-of-Spain's suburbs, whereas the Caroni Swamp was located much closer to the capital's center. The rush-hour traffic I weathered during my first morning on the island proved to be typical. Twenty kilometers and 60 minutes after leaving the rest house, we arrived at the Caroni Swamp headquarters.

The Caroni Swamp

On my map, the 5,000-hectare Caroni Swamp looked like a rather simple affair. From the ground, it was a different matter entirely. Unlike South Carolina's coastal salt marshes, the Caroni Swamp offered little in the way of expansive vistas. Indeed, the swamp's impenetrable tangle of mangrove trunks and prop roots seemed to swallow us as we entered (Figure 10.3).

The Caroni Swamp, located near the center of Trinidad's growing population of over 1.3 million people, is the country's largest intact mangrove-dominated wetland, a wildland oasis surrounded by tropical suburbia (Figure 10.2, Pannier and Dickinson 1989). Although most of the swamp was declared a national park in the late 1970s, in practice most of this mangrove forest remains largely unprotected.

Many tropical coastlines, especially in the Indo-Pacific region, support up to 40 species of mangroves. Trinidad's coast supports just 7 species, commonly grouped as Red, Black, White, and Yellow (or Button) mangroves. Plant ecologists classify mangroves as halophytic, or salt-loving, plants. Although all of them do not actually require salt to survive, their ability to tolerate salinities far higher than those tolerated by most other plants provides them with a competitive edge in tidal habitats. Mangroves are also somewhat unique in their development of two types of aboveground roots: pneumatophores and prop roots. Pneumatophores, which jut up to 20 centimeters from the water-logged sediments where mangroves are often found, increase the amount of oxygen available to the plants. Prop roots, which arise from nodes on aboveground branches, help to buttress and mechanically support the trees, many of which grow in shifting soils.

Most of the seaward half of the Caroni Swamp consists of a dense tangle of Red Mangroves, the most salt-tolerant member of the group. Black Mangroves, the second most abundant species at the site, are typically found farther inland, usually in dense, monospecific stands away

Figure 10.3. The seemingly impenetrable interior of the Caroni Swamp's Red Mangrove forest.

from open water, on higher, firmer soils. White and Yellow mangroves occur farther inland still, chiefly in nontidal areas.

The Caroni Swamp is bordered to the west by the Gulf of Paria, to the north by the Caroni River, to the south by the Madame Espagnol River, and to the east by the Uriah Butler Highway (Map 10.2). Most fresh water enters the swamp from the Caroni River, whose catchment basin constitutes 15% of the island's land mass. At least 40% of Trinidad's 400 species of birds inhabit the swamp, including all but 4 of the country's 22 species of wading birds (ffrench 1978, James et al. 1984). Photographs taken earlier in this century suggest that the eastern third of the swamp, then known as "The Reeds," was once a herbaceous freshwater marsh. Today most of this part of the swamp is dominated by mangroves and other halophytes.

Humans have been modifying the Caroni Swamp for at least 300 years. In the 1920s, proponents of the so-called Cipriani Scheme had attempted to reclaim approximately 900 hectares along the landward edge of the swamp for rice cultivation. As part of the elaborate program, nine drainage canals were constructed from the Caroni River in the north to the Madame Espagnol in the south, and the north–south drain was built

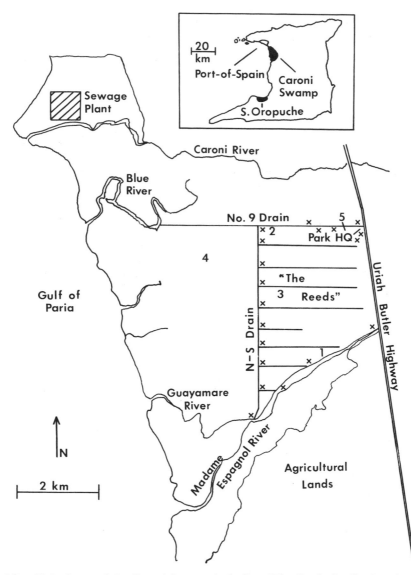

Map 10.2. Areas of the Caroni Swamp, including "The Reeds," collection sites for water samples (marked by x) and for samples of Scarlet Ibises' prey (marked by 1–5), and human-made structures mentioned in the text. Reprinted from Bildstein (1990) with permission of Elsevier Applied Science Publishers, Ltd.

to receive water from these canals. A pump station was constructed where the north–south drain met the Caroni River and sluice gates were built at both the northern and southern ends of the drain. Peat-filled mangrove embankments were constructed to manage the waters that flooded the areas. As a result of these modifications, aquatic life flourished in the area and numerous species of birds, including Scarlet Ibises, began to inhabit the swamp in increasing numbers. However, as time passed, the swamp's peaty soil, external economic forces, and inconsistent management practices conspired to doom the scheme, which was officially abandoned in 1954. Within a few years, the entire system of canals and drains was in disrepair. Today, remnants of these canals scar the Caroni landscape, which is currently open to tidal flow (Figures 10.4, Map 10.2).

The consequences of this derelict scheme were obvious as I toured the swamp in January of 1989. All but a small portion of the site was dominated by salt-tolerant herbaceous vegetation and mangrove forest.

We first saw some Scarlet Ibises—a flock of 15 adults and young-of-the-year flying over Drainage 9—less than 5 minutes into our trip. Locating feeding flocks on the ground proved to be a bit more difficult. Although we frequently caught glimpses of ibises feeding in the shadows at the bases of both Red and Black mangroves, whenever we attempted to maneuver our boat for a closer look, the birds disappeared into the impenetrable tangle.

Because we had been scheduled to tour almost all of the swamp, I had decided to take my refractometer along and record salinities. The first reading I took was at dead low tide in Drainage 4, several hundred meters landward of its confluence with the north–south canal; the refractometer registered at 1.4%, slightly less than half the salinity of full-strength seawater. My second and third readings, which were taken along the Guayamare River at the southern edge of the swamp, were similar. Five hours and 15 readings later, a pattern emerged. On 25 January 1989, at least, the Caroni Swamp appeared to be a mainly brackish-water estuary, with little in the way of freshwater habitat.

Studying Caroni Swamp Scarlet Ibises

Having spent a day sizing up the situation, I decided to map out my plan of attack. If I wanted to test the hypothesis that Scarlet Ibises have stopped

Figure 10.4. Looking for Caroni Swamp Scarlet Ibises along the north–south drainage.

breeding in the Caroni Swamp because recent saltwater intrusion had reduced or eliminated populations of essential freshwater prey, I needed to answer five questions. First, where were ibises feeding in the swamp, and what were they feeding on? Second, were ibises leaving the swamp to feed elsewhere and, if so, where were they going? Third, how salty was the Caroni Swamp? Fourth, how salty was the prey that ibises were feeding on? And fifth, did historic changes in the salinity of the swamp correlate with changes in breeding activity?

Monitoring ibises in Trinidad was more difficult than in South Carolina. The mangrove vegetation was too thick, and my boat-level vantage point was too low, to permit the kind of detailed observations I had managed to collect from the 18-meter tower at Hobcaw Barony. The best I could do was document, in general, where Scarlet Ibises were feeding in the swamp. Determining whether individuals were leaving the area on a daily basis to feed elsewhere could be accomplished by counting ibises at several points along the perimeter of the site as they returned to their traditional roost sites each evening.

Collecting information on the birds' feeding behavior was also difficult. Although I might have been able to watch birds feeding in some of the swamp's more open habitats, watching them in the mangrove forest was out of the question. I settled on a two-pronged approach. First, I carefully recorded the behavior of Scarlet Ibises feeding in more open habitats. And second, whenever I encountered ibises in mangroves, I determined whether or not they were feeding at the site, and if they were, my companions and I would get out of the boat, collection bags in hand, and gather potential prey.

Determining the degree of saltwater intrusion was easy. Whenever we went into the Caroni Swamp looking for Scarlet Ibises, we took refractometer readings at each of the 19 sampling sites throughout the swamp (Map 10.2), and at most of the spots where we located feeding ibises. Determining the salinity of ibises' prey was a bit more challenging. Collecting prey from within the Red Mangrove forest, where most birds fed within the site, frequently meant climbing through a tightly woven jungle of slippery prop roots. Collecting prey in the more open sites meant wading through Trinidad's equivalent of pluff mud (Figure 10.5). Neither was fun. We soon found that Scarlet Ibises fed principally upon several species of fiddler crabs, as well as on Blue Crabs, Mangrove Land Crabs, Mangrove Tree Crabs, and Large Sandworms (Bildstein 1990). The pinching actions of Trinidad's fiddlers, especially those of the Scissor-clawed

White Ibis

Fiddler Crab, seemed to be more powerful than those of their cousins in South Carolina—but maybe the heat was just getting to me.

Why Trinidad's National Bird No Longer Breeds in the Caroni Swamp

As is true of Scarlet Ibises elsewhere, those that nested in the Caroni Swamp typically did so in large, multithousand bird colonies, usually in Red Mangroves and often in association with other wading birds (ffrench 1984). Between 1953, when the species's activities first began to be monitored in detail, and 1970, when the bird last nested on the island, thousands of ibises bred in the Caroni Swamp on a regular basis (Hislop and James 1990). Many ibises still inhabit the swamp, especially in fall and early winter, when their abundance peaks at approximately 10,000 birds. Unfortunately, by late spring, which should be the species's breeding season in Trinidad, most birds have left the island, presumably to breed in nearby South America (Spaans 1975).

When Scarlet Ibises did breed in the Caroni Swamp, most switched from feeding in brackish areas of the swamp to foraging in "freshwater marshes, rice fields, and flooded savannas" during the breeding season (ffrench and Haverschmidt 1970). Today, most if not all ibises apparently feed in brackish-water habitats year-round. On three evenings my companions and I counted several hundred, mostly juvenile, ibises flying north at the wetland's southernmost point on their way back to roosting sites within the swamp. Most of the birds we saw each evening appeared to be returning from coastal areas south of the swamp, in the direction of the South Oropuche (Map 10.1). Subsequent trips to that swamp confirmed that ibises fed there regularly (Bildstein 1990).

I also counted, or I should say attempted to count, the Scarlet Ibises returning from historic freshwater feeding areas directly east of the swamp (ffrench and Haverschmidt 1970). On the three evening watches, I failed to see a single individual. Nor did I see any ibises in areas directly east of the swamp during more than a dozen roadside surveys this region. Thus, most of the ibises appeared to be feeding within the Caroni Swamp, and those that were not feeding there must have been feeding in other coastal sites farther south.

The lack of inland feeding was not surprising. Little undisturbed

Figure 10.5. Collecting the prey of Scarlet Ibises in the Caroni Swamp.

freshwater wetland habitat remains in the 675-square-kilometer Caroni River basin. Since the 1960s, development has claimed most of the floodplain. Portions of the once-mighty Caroni River have been channelized and diked, and the rainy season waters that once flooded the drainage's lowlands now stay well within the river's banks, traveling directly to the Gulf of Paria with minimal circulation through the swamp. Where freshwater swamps and marshes once thrived, housing developments, sugarcane, and rice now dominate the landscape. This was certainly not the kind of habitat that Scarlet Ibises would choose, so their absence did not surprise me.

The automobile has also played a role in changing Caroni Swamp hydrology. Although relatively timely and inexpensive public buses and maxi taxis run to all but the most remote portions of the island, most Trinidadians use cars to commute to work. Given a population density of almost 270 people per square kilometer (700 people per square mile)—the United States, by comparison, has a population density that is one-tenth that of Trinidad's—many Trinidadians spend a considerable amount of time each day in rush-hour traffic. In an attempt to relieve some of this congestion, the government of Trinidad constructed a freeway between the country's two largest cities, Port-of-Spain in the northwest corner of the island and San Fernando in the southwest.

The Uriah Butler Highway was completed in the early 1970s. The pride and joy of Trinidad's Department of Transportation, this four-lane interstate-grade road forms the eastern boundary of Caroni Swamp (Map 10.2). Before the highway was built, each wet season a considerable amount of rainwater flowed directly into the swamp across a broad front. Today, the highway's elevated, flood-resistant roadbed effectively dikes and diverts this freshwater input around the swamp.

The extent to which river channelization and diking, together with highway construction, had altered the region's hydrology was reflected in the salinity readings I had gathered in the swamp. The readings demonstrated conclusively significant salt-water intrusion to within several hundred meters of the highway, well within the swamp's former freshwater zone. In most locations, salinity readings were over 50% the strength of seawater, and the only truly low readings I recorded (i.e., salinity less than 5% full-strength seawater) were taken at a small 20-hectare freshwater marsh located directly south of park headquarters (Bildstein 1990). In fact, my readings, almost all of which were taken *landward* of the north–south canal (Map 10.2), were similar to those recorded during the late 1960s for several areas *seaward* of the canal (Bacon 1970).

The Scarlet Ibises I watched feeding within the swamp fed exclusively upon osmoconforming invertebrates, all of which were quite salty (Bildstein 1990). Indeed, all of the prey being taken by ibises in the Caroni

Swamp were far too salty to serve as acceptable dietary components for nestling White Ibises (see Johnston and Bildstein 1990). The Scarlet Ibises that were feeding in the South Oropuche were also seen taking salty fiddler crab prey. Thus, most, if not all, of Trinidad's ibises apparently were feeding on prey that would be unacceptable to breeding ibises in South Carolina.

I felt that I had found the "smoking gun." Scarlet Ibises were no longer breeding in the Caroni Swamp because the swamp had lost its ability to provide the freshwater prey necessary to support ibis nestlings, and because there were no longer any freshwater wetlands inland of the Caroni Swamp to provide such prey. Although the swamp itself still seemed to be capable of providing a necessary bedroom for breeding ibises, the kitchen was gone, and without it, successful breeding could not occur.

I could not help wondering what noted ornithologist Richard ffrench would think of my study. ffrench, a schoolteacher who had come to the West Indies in 1955 and had fallen in love with the island's avifauna, literally wrote the book on Trinidad's birds (ffrench 1991). His studies of Scarlet Ibises had spanned more than a quarter of a century (see ffrench 1966, 1978, 1984, 1985; ffrench and Haverschmidt 1970). When the birds stopped breeding in the early 1970s, ffrench suggested that poaching might be responsible (ffrench 1984). But a prescient statement in his first publication on the subject kept ringing in my ears: "What is the future of the Scarlet Ibis in Trinidad? I see no reason to be pessimistic, provided no one decides to drain all of the swamps" (ffrench 1966).

Well, someone has drained all of the swamps, and the Scarlet Ibis responded as ffrench suggested it would.

Poaching and Other Concerns

Unfortunately, adequate feeding habitat alone will not ensure the return of Trinidad's breeding Scarlet Ibises. Water pollution, poaching, and disturbance by both tourists and anglers must also be addressed. Port-of-Prince's secondary wastewater treatment facility is both overloaded and in poor repair (Map 10.2). As a result, raw sewage is regularly dumped into the Caroni Swamp. Considerable agricultural and industrial effluent also flows into the swamp. Organochlorine pesticides have been detected in the swamp's food chain. Poaching especially threatens Scarlet Ibises, even the current nonbreeding population.

Although Scarlet Ibises were considered game birds in Trinidad up until 1985, the current law fully protects, at least in theory, this species on the island. Nevertheless, the Scarlet Ibis is still poached in the Caroni Swamp area. Luthin (1985), for example, witnessed shooting at a supposedly protected roost site near the center of the park in 1983. And BBC cameraman Michael Richards, who spent several days filming in the swamp during my visit, also reported an attempt. The incident occurred at a mangrove hammock well within the park's boundaries. As darkness fell, a small boat approached a roost where hundreds of ibises had just settled for the evening. Richards watched and listened in horror as several shots rang out and the birds scattered into the night. A return visit three days later indicated that the ibises had abandoned this traditional roosting site.

I, too, witnessed poaching in the swamp. The first incident occurred near the southern edge of Caroni Swamp. Three men, one of whom was carrying a rifle and a partially filled pillowcase, approached our group. When we asked them what they were up to, the three responded that they had been collecting bait for use on a family fishing trip. The bait turned out to be three Cattle Egrets, all of which had been shot in the park. My companions confiscated the birds and the rifle and ferried the elderly gentleman who was carrying them back to park headquarters for a quick trip to the Chaguanas Police Station. All was proceeding rather smoothly until the alleged poacher tried to bribe everyone in the boat into releasing him. I never found out what happened to him after we deposited him at the police station.

In my second encounter with a poacher, Scarlet Ibises were the target. The event occurred in broad daylight, less than 100 meters from park headquarters. My companions and I had spent most of the morning on a refractometer run through the swamp, and we had just finished lunch, when we decided to take a brief hike along Drainage 9. Less than a minute later we heard something fall into the canal behind us. Turning to see what had happened, we spotted an ibis thrashing about in the canal. Several seconds later we noticed a young man with a sling shot descending the bank of the canal and heading toward the bird. Jerry Farrier, the biologist who was with me at the time, ordered the poacher to halt, and, surprisingly enough, he did. While I attempted to stare him down from across the canal, thus encouraging him to stay put, Jerry raced back to headquarters, jumped into a vehicle, and shortly thereafter appeared with two wardens on the opposite side of the canal. They took the fellow into custody, gathered the injured bird, and confiscated a dead one. After measuring and photographing the two birds, both of which became evidence, the five of us crammed into a Land Cruiser and were on our way to the Chaguanas police station to hand the poacher over to the local authorities. A hearing was set for the following day.

The man, who was dressed in rags when apprehended, turned out to be an illegal alien from Guyana. His defense seemed altogether plausible. The ibises, he explained to the magistrate, which were the first he had ever killed in Trinidad, were food for his family. In his native Guyana he had killed many ibises, as had many of his friends, and no one had ever been punished for doing so. He had no idea the birds were protected in Trinidad. Why else would he have been willing to kill several of them in the middle of the day within view of the park's headquarters? After being sternly admonished for his actions, and after having promised never again to commit such a crime, the young man somehow managed to pay what, for him, must have been an incredibly stiff fine (equivalent to $160 in U.S. currency) and was released. During my stay, he was not seen again.

My Report to Trinidad's Division of Forestry

In my report to the Division of Forestry, I needed to not only explain why Scarlet Ibises no longer bred in the Caroni Swamp, but also provide a solution to the problem. Had poaching been the only problem that ibises faced in Trinidad, I would have simply advised Carol James to hire more wardens and to lobby for higher fines and jail sentences. Habitat destruction was more difficult to handle. My observations of Scarlet Ibises in Trinidad and my studies of White Ibises in coastal South Carolina suggested that coastal populations of Scarlet Ibises required a source of freshwater prey for their young and that, in most instances, seasonally flooded riparian areas adjacent to isolated estuarine colony sites were an essential ingredient for successful nesting.

Regrettably, the financially strapped Trinidadian government is in no position to return low-lying areas adjacent to the Caroni Swamp to their former status as seasonally inundated freshwater wetlands. Thus it appears that the solution to the problem must rely on habitat changes within the Caroni Swamp itself. One strategy would be to return the eastern portion of the park to its former status as a freshwater herbaceous marsh. Doing so would require refurbishing the derelict dikes, canals, and sluices that already exist in the area, as well as rediverting some Caroni River flow into the area to compensate for the losses brought about by the construction of the Uriah Butler Highway. The proposal is *physically* feasible. Indeed, most of it is simply a reestablishment of the already-built, but ill-maintained, canal system from the Cipriani Scheme. However, for such a program to be *politically* feasible, the plan would need to incorporate financial incentives beyond those associated with any potential increases in tourism.

One approach would be to develop the site for aquaculture. Although the potentially thorny issue of wading-bird predation at such sites would need to be addressed, where this phenomenon has been studied in detail, wading birds appear to have a minimal effect on the size of commercial harvests (Martin and Hamilton 1985). This approach is consistent with a management plan previously laid out for the Forestry Division, a plan that called for "protection of the ecosystem, environmental education, research, facilitation of recreation and tourism, and accommodation of traditional and productive uses such as fishing and oystering" (Forestry Division 1979).

Because of the poaching I had seen, I also recommended in my report to the Wildlife Section a prompt increase in efforts aimed at protecting Scarlet Ibises throughout the park. I stressed the need for consistent sentencing of poachers, something that did not appear to be happening at that time.

In addition, I suggested that Trinidad become a contracting party to the RAMSAR Convention, an international group bound by a treaty whose objective is "to stem the progressive encroachment on and loss of wetlands, now and in the future" (Lyster 1985). I noted that the amount of sewage and industrial effluent pouring into the swamp must be reduced and that, given the recent history of oil spills in the area, contingency plans should be developed to reduce the potentially significant biological impacts of additional spills in the Gulf of Paria. Finally, I suggested that commercial tours of the swamp should be revamped to maximize their educational value and to ensure minimal disturbance to roosting birds.

To my knowledge, as of late 1992, not one these recommendations had been acted upon.

The Bigger Picture

Although Scarlet Ibises no longer breed in Trinidad, the species does not appear to be undergoing large-scale contractions in other portions of its range. The world population of Scarlet Ibises is currently estimated to be in excess of 35,000 breeding pairs (see Spaans 1990). Thus, on the surface at least, the species does not appear to be in immediate danger. Even so, the numbers of Scarlet Ibises breeding in any one year, as well as their breeding locations, fluctuate dramatically, especially in coastal areas (Spaans 1990). This color morph of the White Ibis may be more prone to extinction than its numbers indicate.

Recent history suggests that colonial birds, including most species of ibises, are rather vulnerable to extinction because of their gregariousness, especially when such coloniality is combined with nomadic behavior. The story of the Passenger Pigeon, a colonial and highly nomadic species serves as an example.

The Passenger Pigeon was once ranked as the most abundant bird species in all of North America. Greenway (1958, 305) describes the magnitude of their abundance:

> That flocks of Passenger Pigeons "darkened the sky," and that the "weight of their numbers broke great branches from trees" in tracts of uncut forest of hundreds of square miles during the first half of the nineteenth century cannot be doubted. . . . Wilson (about 1810) estimated over two billion birds in a single flock, and Schorger conjectured that there were probably as many as 136,000,000 birds in a concentrated Wisconsin nesting area, comprising 850 square miles [about 2,200 square kilometers].

Having eliminated or fragmented much of the pigeon's forested habitat, 19th-century farmers in eastern North America were frequently plagued by massive migratory swarms of the Passenger Pigeons, many of which are estimated to have exceeded several millions of birds. Enter the market hunters, gun- and dynamite-wielding entrepreneurs who, because the species traveled in enormous flocks, were able to eliminate all but a few isolated populations of the birds in less than 100 years. Harassed almost until the end, the last representative of this once-magnificent aerial armada, an individual named Martha, died at the Cincinnati Zoo on 1 September 1914.

Similar fates befell two of North America's other colonial-nesting birds: the brilliantly plumed, dove-sized Carolina Parakeet, which once ranged throughout much of the eastern seaboard of the United States; and the more than 60-centimeter-tall, penguinlike Great Auk, which once inhabited several islands off the North American coast. Although all three species were hunted for slightly different reasons—auks for meat and oil, pigeons for meat and pest control, and parrots for pest control and feathers—in all three species, their social nature apparently facilitated their demise. (Greenway [1958] offers readable accounts, although somewhat dated, of the extinction of these and other vanished forms. Enrique Bucher's [1992] more recent account of the demise of the Passenger Pigeon is especially intriguing.)

But what about Scarlet Ibises? They too are targets of considerable human predation both within and outside of Trinidad, and their social nature also facilitates such activity. Nevertheless, it appears unlikely that humanity will do to the Scarlet Ibis what it has already done to the Passenger Pigeon, Carolina Parakeet, and Great Auk, at least not in such a direct manner. Although direct assault on isolated populations continues to be of concern, especially on the South American mainland—where subsistence hunting persists—the greatest threat to this and other wetland species of birds is the indirect assault of habitat loss.

Development pressures in coastal-zone wetland habitats, both in Latin America in general, and in the Caribbean Basin in particular, are increasing noticeably almost daily (Pannier and Dickinson 1989). Although both inland and coastal wetlands are at risk, many of the region's problems are exacerbated along each country's narrow coastal zone, where the human population is most concentrated and where the need for goods and services is most acute. Coastal Venezuela, the supposed nesting locale for many of Trinidad's Scarlet Ibises, faces incredible development pressures, not only for agricultural and industrial purposes but also for high-density tourism. When I visited that country in 1988 and again in 1989, I was struck by how closely development in the region resembled what I remembered occurring in New Jersey in the 1950s, when I was growing up there.

Conservation efforts in the face of this onslaught are, by necessity, different from efforts made when hunting and poaching are the only pressures. Chapter 12 addresses these differences and the importance of the conservation issue.

11　What a Difference a Day Makes

Hurricane Hugo and the Catastrophe
of 22 September 1989

In 1989, there were over 11,000 pairs of White Ibises on Pumpkin-seed Island. In 1990, there were none. Something obviously had happened during this time, and that something was Hurricane Hugo.

Because they are decidedly *episodic* events, most individuals think of hurricanes as being *atypical*. They are not. Although hurricanes are certainly not as predictable as each day's sunrise and sunset, they are every bit as inevitable. Cyclonic gales frequent most of the world's equatorial waters, including the Caribbean Sea, the source of coastal South Carolina's tropical storms. Southernmost Florida, for example, has been buffeted by more than 200,000 hurricanes during the past 2 million years (Ball et al. 1967). In this century such storms have struck the South Carolina coast about once every 2.5 years (Gentry 1971). Before Hurricane Hugo, the South Carolina coast had been struck by several catastrophic storms within the past 100 years: Hurricane David in 1979 (15 deaths, $2 billion in damage), Hurricane Hazel in 1954 (95 deaths, $27 million in damage), and an unnamed storm in 1893 (2,000 deaths, $10 million in damage). Hurricanes of lesser magnitude have also hit the area in this century.

Hurricanes are tropical storms characterized by extremely low central barometric pressures, sustained high winds, and storm surges. Such storms have long been known for their ability to demolish human settlements. Less widely recognized is their destabilizing effect on natural environments. Aside from actual destruction, accompanying high winds and waters can accelerate coastal geologic processes and ecological succession (Tanner 1961, Hayes 1978, Lugo et al. 1983). Hurricanes play an

Map 11.1. Satellite photo of Hurricane Hugo as it struck the South Carolina coast on the morning of 22 September 1989. Photograph courtesy of the National Oceanographic and Atmospheric Administration.

integral role in the coastal ecology of the southeastern United States, including South Carolina.

Hugo made landfall just north of Charleston, South Carolina, at 12:01 A.M. eastern daylight time on 22 September 1989, well after that year's relatively successful White Ibis breeding season (Map 11.1). The hurricane, which has been characterized as the most destructive tropical storm to have hit the South Carolina coast in recorded times, started out innocently enough almost 2 weeks earlier as a tropical wave off the coast of West Africa. The storm built up strength as it crossed the Atlantic Ocean. By 15 September, when it earned the title of "Hurricane," Hugo was packing surface winds in excess of 255 kilometers (about 160 miles) per hour. It battered the Leeward Islands while entering the Caribbean Basin. Hugo then struck Guadeloupe and Puerto Rico on 17 and 18 September, when it was classified as an extremely dangerous "category 4 storm" (on the 1-to-5 Saffir–Simpson hurricane-intensity index; see Gray 1990). After crossing the northeastern corner of Puerto Rico, the storm began an accelerating northwesterly course toward the North American mainland, initially traveling at the rate of about 27 kilometers per hour.

The eye of the hurricane reached the coast shortly after midnight on the morning of 22 September, more than a month after we had left the field site at the end of the 1989 breeding season. The storm made landfall about 80 kilometers southwest of Pumpkinseed Island (Map 11.2). Unlike many of the state's earlier hurricanes, which typically had hugged the coast after making landfall, Hugo's trajectory remained unchanged, and 6 hours later—while still packing hurricane-strength winds in excess of 130 kilometers (81 miles) per hour—the eye of the storm passed over my house more than 260 kilometers inland in Rock Hill, South Carolina. On 23 September, a much-weakened Hugo passed through eastern Ohio before entering Canada. It moved back out over the Atlantic 2 days later.

At historic Fort Sumter in Charleston Harbor, several miles south of the storm's path, a tide gauge recorded an accompanying storm surge of 5.5 meters, approximately 18 feet above the mean high-tide mark (Ludlum 1989). The magnitude of the storm surge was exacerbated by coincidence with a nocturnal high tide. At Hobcaw Barony, approximately 90 kilome-

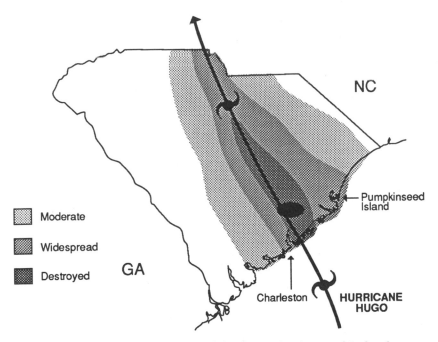

Map 11.2. Path of Hurricane Hugo and the destruction it caused in South Carolina. For comparison, the extent of tree-fall created by the eruption of the Mount St. Helens volcano is depicted as a black oval.

ters farther up the coast, abraded bark and cordgrass debris were left clinging to the branches of trees. Given the tenacious layer of sulfurous mud that coated much of the interior of our devastated lab, my colleagues and I figured that the surge that barreled over nearby Pumpkinseed Island had crested at some 2 to 3 meters above mean high tide. The region's gently sloping coastal terrain enabled surging salt water in excess of 2% salinity to penetrate up to 5 kilometers inland (Blood et al. 1991, Gardner et al. 1991a). Rainfall was remarkably light for a storm of this amplitude, with records of 2.1 centimeters (less than 1 inch) near Charleston, and 6.5 centimeters (about 2.5 inches) at Hobcaw Barony. Heavier rains would have resulted in even greater flooding.

Damage from the storm was both intensive and extensive. Hurricane Hugo downed more timber in South Carolina alone than had been downed by Hurricanes Frederick and Camille, the Mount St. Helens volcanic eruption, and the Yellowstone National Park fires of 1988 combined. At the time, Hugo was believed to have been the most economically destructive cyclonic storm in U.S. history. Immediately after the storm, there was no electrical power east of Interstate Highway 95 in South Carolina (Badolato et al. 1990), a region constituting more than one-quarter of the state's land area. Even in Rock Hill, more than 260 kilometers inland, my house remained without electricity for nearly 2 weeks. Damage from Hurricane Hugo has been estimated at over $10 billion, with destruction in South Carolina alone totaling more than $6 billion (Badolato et al. 1990).

Pre-storm preparedness in the state was high. Two days before Hugo struck, Governor Carroll Campbell's office authorized activation of coastal National Guard units. On the evening of 20 September, more than 24 hours before Hugo's landfall, state officials ordered the mandatory evacuation of Charleston and surrounding low-country communities. Southbound traffic flow was reversed on the interstate highway that normally leads into the region to hasten the unparalleled withdrawal of more than 150,000 of the state's residents living in the storm's projected path.

As a consequence of these actions, loss of life was lower than the storm's ferocity might suggest. Even so, Hurricane Hugo caused at least 35 deaths in South Carolina alone. Over half of the deaths occurred after the storm's passage, resulting mainly from house fires caused by using candles for light, and from electrocutions from downed wires and portable generators (Badolato et al. 1990).

Aside from its impact on humans, the storm also affected the region's bird life. A population of the Red-cockaded Woodpecker—a federally listed endangered species—in the Francis Marion National Forest north of Charleston was significantly affected when high winds damaged cavity trees at almost all 470 of the population's colony sites. Preliminary estimates indicate that up to 60% of the forest's population of this species may have been lost during the storm (LeGrand 1990b). Hurricane Hugo also destroyed nests at 25 of the state's 54 Bald Eagle breeding sites and killed at least 8 Wood Storks, both of which are endangered species. Two White Ibis carcasses were recovered 5 days after the storm from detrital wrack along a single kilometer of coastal beachfront near the center of impact (W. Post, personal communication). Almost certainly, smaller and less conspicuous species were also killed in significant numbers.

Most of the region's birding community was involved in rescue and repair efforts in the wake of the storm, and many local birding haunts were inaccessible for some time after the hurricane because of downed timber, washed-out roads, and sunken boats. As a result, sightings of unusual pelagic and tropical species of birds, which typically occur in the aftermath of such events, are lacking (LeGrand 1990a).

Despite its destructive nature, the hurricane had only a modest impact on the geomorphology of Hobcaw Barony's salt-marsh ecosystem (Gardner et al. 1991b). Pumpkinseed Island, for example, was little damaged by the event. Erosion on the island appeared to be no greater than that resulting from winter storms that annually buffet this portion of the coast. Such was not the case for the area's maritime forests and freshwater impoundments, where intruding salt water severely disrupted ecological processes in numerous freshwater habitats (Gardner et al. 1991a).

Pumpkinseed Island did not escape unscathed, however. When I was finally able to visit the site in mid-November, 7 weeks after the storm, a thick detrital mat, which in many places was more than 40 centimeters deep, was smothering much of the island's remaining Marsh Elder. About one-third of this brushy vegetation had simply disappeared, having been sheared from its roots and swept off the island by the debris-laden storm surge (Figure 11.1). In addition, much of the ornithogenic peat that had been accumulating on the island under this vegetation had been shoved and piled 5 to 10 meters to the west. Structures fabricated by humans fared even worse. The 3-meter metal observation tower at the north end of the island was a tangled heap. On the other hand, Pumpkinseed's herbaceous vegetation exhibited little evidence of distur-

Figure 11.1. Marsh Elder vegetation on Pumpkinseed Island: *top*, 7 weeks after the passage of Hurricane Hugo (fall 1989); *bottom*, 1 year later, after considerable resprouting.

bance. Expansive stands of Black Needlerush, Smooth Cordgrass, and Saltmarsh Bulrush were flourishing, as were towering culms of Giant Cordgrass—mute testimony to the adaptable nature of these species.

What about the birds? Since most wading birds would have already left the island by late September, there seemed to be little reason to fear for the safety of the bulk of the island's breeding inhabitants. Even so, a number of late nesters and reluctant migrants, possibly totaling as many as 500 or even 1,000 birds, were likely still on the island at the fateful time on 22 September 1989. All of these must have suffered incalculably. Had Hugo struck 6 to 12 hours earlier—before darkness had fallen—most of the wading birds in the area would have been active, and most probably would have been blown inland as the storm's intensity built over the course of the day. However, because the storm's winds increased to hurricane strength only after nightfall, most or all of the site's wading-bird inhabitants would have already been roosting, and most would have attempted to ride out the storm in place. Little could they have realized what lay in store for them.

Many of these birds apparently perished. At Hobcaw Barony, dozens of wading-bird carcasses could be seen protruding from the storm's detrital meander, a seemingly endless windrow extending well into the forested lowlands that border the eastern edges of Mud Bay and the North Inlet Marsh. Additional unseen bodies almost certainly lurked below. Others, such as the White Ibis mentioned in Chapter 6, whose bill was broken during the storm, probably survived the hurricane only to die of starvation later. Farther south along the coast, and closer to the storm track, observers reported similar scenes. Even so, Will Post, Curator of Birds at the Charleston Museum and the most likely recipient of such information, received no reports of thousands, or even hundreds, of wading-bird carcasses in the rubble left by the storm. Nor did Post himself see any evidence of wading-bird mortality on a large scale. Thus, there is no indication that a substantial portion of Pumpkinseed Island's breeding population perished during Hurricane Hugo's passage. What about the hurricane's long-term effects?

The Breeding Sabbatical of 1990

An ugly thought kept running through my head during the winter that followed. What if the storm changed the region's coastal habitats so much that White Ibises no longer found Pumpkinseed Island to be a suitable breeding site? Up until the fall of 1989 I had managed to convince myself that White Ibises would always return to Pumpkinseed Island, and that any annual variation in ibis abundance would still leave me with plenty of birds to study. After all, even during the drought of 1984, when rainfall in the area was more than 40% below normal, more than 1,900 pairs of birds had decided to breed at the site (Bildstein et al. 1990). But 1990 might be different. The previous fall's storm surge and associated saltwater intrusion had substantially disrupted many freshwater habitats that ibises had used as traditional feeding sites. Would the loss of these habitats be enough to forestall breeding in 1990? I could not do much for the situation except wait and hope for rain, which I thought might neutralize some of the storm's effects.

By late March, it became apparent that the 1990 breeding season was not going to be preceded by a wet winter and spring. The rainfall from November 1989 through April 1990, which eventually amounted to 39.9 centimeters, was the second lowest recorded during our 12-year study. I could only hope that tradition would win out and that some of the birds that had bred on Pumpkinseed Island in previous years would return to try again, regardless of any changes wrought by the hurricane.

My initial trip to the colony in early March of 1990 was reassuring. About 75 pairs of Great Egrets were building nests at the island's north-eastern corner—right on schedule—in a small stand of Marsh Elder that had managed to weather the storm. Although no White Ibises were on the island, it was still early in the season. Moreover, the next day, while replacing markers in the Bly Creek drainage that had been washed away by the storm, I noticed two flocks of approximately 15 ibises flying north overhead, exactly as expected for that time of year.

My second trip to the island, in mid-March, was decidedly less sanguine. Still there were no ibises. Even more ominously, the Great Egrets I had seen nesting nearly 2 weeks earlier had deserted. All that remained were a few broken eggs. The lack of egrets was especially troubling. I have long held that Great Egrets are something of a keystone species. As the first species to breed each year, Great Egrets, when they nest, seem to trigger nesting activities of other wading birds. Their absence from the site in mid-March was unparalleled. Would any wading birds breed? Later in the day, when I spotted a flock of 85 White Ibises flying north over the Bly Creek feeding site, I began to think that I was worrying about nothing.

One week later, Toni De Santo visited Pumpkinseed Island and also found no White Ibises. However, about 300 Great Egrets and half as many Snowy Egrets were once again building nests in and around the island's Marsh Elder, and Tricolored Herons, Black-crowned Night-Herons, and Glossy Ibises were courting at the site, although none had apparently begun to build nests. Two weeks later, the Great Egrets had completed their clutches and were incubating, while Snowy Egrets were beginning to lay their eggs. More importantly, by this time a flock of 150 White Ibises was roosting in a stand of matted-down Giant Cordgrass near the nesting egrets.

When Toni and I returned to the site on 20 April, we hoped that the breeding season would be in full swing and that courting, if not nesting, White Ibises would be in abundance. While the breeding activities of Great and Snowy egrets, Black-crowned Night-Herons, and Glossy Ibises all seemed to be under way, the 50 White Ibises that we saw exhibited little courtship color. Also, there was no indication whatsoever that any White Ibises were building nests.

My next visit to Pumpkinseed Island on 8 May was also disappointing. Only four White Ibises were on the entire island, and three of those were second-year birds. The probability of a year without breeding White Ibises began to take hold. The trend continued for the remainder of the season: One day we might see several hundred White Ibises roosting on the island, and the next day we would find none at all. None of the White Ibises that we saw during the spring and summer in 1990 ever assumed courtship colors, and at no time did we see any signs of White Ibises courting on the island. My worst fear was realized.

Such was certainly not the case for the four other common species of wading birds that typically nested on Pumpkinseed Island. Although the number of Great Egrets nesting at the site had dropped by more than 40%, and Tricolored Heron numbers were down by almost 20%, the numbers of Snowy Egrets were up 36% and Glossy Ibises were up 4% (Shepherd et al. 1991). Only White Ibises seemed to be having a problem. I felt certain that I knew what that problem was.

Although Hurricane Hugo had caused little damage to the colony's nesting vegetation, it had considerable impact on freshwater feeding sites in the area. Many of the region's freshwater impoundments (Le-Grand 1990b), as well as portions of the area's natural floodplain forests (Gardner et al. 1991a), had suffered substantial saltwater flooding during the storm. Damage to these feeding sites was almost certainly the reason for the breeding debacle of 1990.

Several lines of evidence support this hypothesis. The first is the relative availability, or rather the definite unavailability, of crayfish during the spring and summer of 1990. Toni and I had predicted that storm-surge overflow, coupled with crayfish intolerance of highly saline waters (Loyacano 1967), would substantially reduce local populations of this important prey item. And indeed, the numbers of crayfishes we captured at the Boardwalk Swamp, a freshwater feeding site about 4 kilometers northeast of Pumpkinseed Island, plummeted during the breeding season of 1990 from their levels of the previous two seasons (Shepherd et al. 1991). (The other species of wading birds nesting at the site are not so dependent upon crayfish prey and, as such, were little affected by this aspect of the storm's impact.)

The immensity of the storm's impact became obvious to me on 18 May, when Jim Johnston and I spent 2 hours flying the coast between Pumpkinseed Island and Charleston searching for White Ibises and photographing hurricane damage. Overwashed beaches, windfall timber, and demolished houses were everywhere. South of Pumpkinseed Island, the South Carolina coast is riddled with impounded freshwater wetlands, and it was the storm's effect on these impoundments that drew most of our attention. In a normal year, the only way to separate such wetlands from adjacent brackish-water marshes during aerial observations is to note their sharper edges and less spontaneous geometry. But 1990 was not a normal year, and the presence or absence of tidal meanders was not the only way to distinguish impoundments from their more natural counterparts. Hurricane Hugo had color-coded the habitats below. Although brackish marshes remained a chlorophyllic green, dead and dying emergent vegetation in the region's freshwater impoundments had stained those sites anemic buffs and vibrant crimsons—the latter indicating the presence of immense blooms of an adventitious diatom. In 1990, these areas were clearly not serving as sources of much-needed crayfish prey.

A second line of evidence in support of the damage-to-feeding-sites hypothesis came from the birds themselves. Most of the White Ibises we saw at Pumpkinseed during the breeding season of 1990 were first seen flying north across Winyah Bay and onto the island. Many of these birds, which typically arrived in flocks of from several dozen to several hundred birds, circled the island for several minutes before taking off in the direction of nearby traditional freshwater feeding sites northwest of the colony site. Others sometimes roosted for several minutes to a few hours before departing. Subsequently, few of these flocks, which we believe comprised individuals returning to the site from wintering areas farther south, were ever seen again.

Although we never saw more than about 300 White Ibises on the island at any one time, we estimated that thousands of them had visited Pumpkinseed Island between April and June of 1990, presumably in search of an adequate breeding site. Their failure to stay and nest almost certainly reflects the fact that they were unable to detect sufficient fresh-water crayfish prey in the area.

Where these White Ibises went after visiting Pumpkinseed Island, I do not know. I do know that they did not breed elsewhere in South Carolina, even though many seemingly appropriate areas south of Charleston had been relatively undisturbed by the storm. Perhaps the birds failed to choose such sites because they had not been used in previous years. On the other hand, thousands of White Ibises did breed approximately 100 kilometers north of Pumpkinseed Island, near the storm-spared mouth of the Cape Fear River in coastal North Carolina, where University of North Carolina Professor Jim Parnell and his students have been studying them since the late 1970s.

When I called Jim in May of 1990, an intriguing story began to unfold. White Ibises had been breeding on Battery Island near the mouth of the Cape Fear River for over 20 years (see Chapter 3 for details). However, in 1990 they did so in a peculiar fashion. Rather than building nests in shrubbery at their traditional colony site, approximately 6,000 pairs of White Ibises first nested in grassy vegetation at a new site several miles up the river. When this initial attempt failed because of high tides several weeks later, 1,200 pairs of ibises nested on Battery Island in more traditional shrub vegetation.

Field ornithologists are possessive of their birds. And while Jim and I were on the phone, both of us spoke in terms of what "our" birds were or were not doing that year. After I hung up the phone, however, I began to wonder whether some of what I considered to be "my" birds, which are traditional grassy nesters, had in fact instigated the aborted attempt at ground nesting that Jim had just described, and hence had become "his" birds. Ibises are especially nomadic. Was it too farfetched to think that some of the White Ibises I had seen visiting and rejecting Pumpkinseed Island in April and May of 1990 had continued up the coast to Jim's study site? Why else would ibises at his site decide to breed in herbaceous vegetation after having nested in shrubs for all those years? Unfortunately, neither Jim nor I have spent much time banding ibises, and without individually marked birds, this intriguing possibility cannot be addressed. But even if some of the birds that attempted to breed at Jim's site were refugees from Pumpkinseed Island, still more than 10,000 pairs were unaccounted for, as these two sites had supported more than 20,000 pairs of ibises only 1 year earlier. The whereabouts of these birds during the breeding sabbatical of 1990 remains a mystery.

The Next Year

The breeding season of 1991 promised to be a watershed year. Although the lack of breeding in 1990 had proved to be something of a nuisance, it had also offered the opportunity to study the impact of a natural catastrophic event, something long-term studies are especially well suited to address. But what if the breeding sabbatical extended for 2 or 3 years? How would I feel about continuing the study if the White Ibises no longer bred regularly at the site? Furthermore, how long could I justify collecting zeros as data points? During the early 1980s, when I had committed myself to a long-term study of White Ibises, I had never considered that the birds, rather than I, might determine when my study ended. The precarious nature of long-term studies was beginning to sink in. To say that I nervously awaited the 1991 breeding season is something of an understatement.

In 1991, I made my first trip to Pumpkinseed Island on 23 March, about a week earlier than I had any right to expect to see nesting White Ibises. Nevertheless, I was disheartened to find that only 12 adults, none of which was approaching breeding color, were roosting at the site. On the other hand, I did see six flocks of from 25 to 55 adult White Ibises flying north and south over North Boundary Road between 22 and 25 March, and several of the lab's scientists reported seeing larger flocks several days earlier. In addition, more than 150 Great Egrets had already completed their clutches and were incubating them at the colony site, well ahead of last year's abbreviated schedule of events. Maybe the White Ibises would return.

I made my next trip to Pumpkinseed Island on 7 April. As graduate student Katie Golden and I approached the island, I excitedly pointed out two distant, multihundred-bird flocks engaging in unmistakable courtship flight about 1.5 kilometers northeast of the colony. However, when Katie and I stopped the boat to take a closer look at these birds, I realized I had been fooled. Both of the flocks turned out to consist entirely of Glossy Ibises.

When we reached the island 5 minutes later, the two of us breathed a sigh of relief as a cloud of close to 250 adult White Ibises, all of which were in full breeding color, exploded from a large patch of trampled needlerush within several meters of our landing site. The birds, which quickly resettled, appeared to be pair-bonding. Our cursory visit revealed that, in addition to this flock of White Ibises, over 400 Great Egrets and almost 100 Snowy Egrets were already incubating eggs, and that dozens of Tricolored Herons and Glossy Ibises were building nests. Everything appeared to be on schedule.

Even the crayfishes seemed to be back. Three nights of trapping in early April hinted that populations of this vital dietary component were recovering from the depressed levels of the previous year (see Shepherd et al. 1991). These observations, together with the fact that we were enjoying above-average winter-to-spring rainfall, indicated that any ibises that did decide to breed on Pumpkinseed Island in 1991 could expect to do well, at least if they bred early in the season. The only remaining variable to watch was the tides.

In the end, the 1991 breeding season was a disappointment. Crayfish numbers quickly plummeted, the flock of breeding-color White Ibises that Katie and I saw on 7 April had disappeared 2 weeks later, and not until the last few days of April did a relatively small group of about 1,200 individuals finally begin to lay eggs. Our annual islandwide ground count, which was conducted on 10 May, revealed 511 White Ibis nests with eggs and approximately 100 additional nests under construction.

Despite the presence of numerous stands of unoccupied and seemingly available Black Needlerush throughout the western half of the island, all but one of these nests had been built in Giant Cordgrass near the southeastern corner of the island in the middle of an area that White Ibises had avoided in most years. The single exception was a nest that had been placed in the middle of a group of Glossy Ibises that were nesting near the center of the island in bulrush. Most of the nests were well constructed and reasonably well elevated, and a pair of aerial counts bracketing the astronomical spring tide sets from 13 to 16 May indicated that 70% of them had survived these inundations. As luck would have it, a nor'easter that settled over the coast for several days in late May removed all but about 10% of the remaining nests. As a result, fewer than 40 White

Ibis nestlings fledged at Pumpkinseed Island during the summer of 1991. Although such a low number would have been unthinkable in 1989, ibis productivity was up from 1990, and there was little cause for complaint. In fact, there was reason for considerable optimism. White Ibises, or at least some of them, had returned to the site, and some had successfully raised young. I did not need to reevaluate the rationale for continuing my study. If anything, the 1991 field season strengthened my resolve to continue my work.

In the spring of 1992, as this manuscript was submitted for publication, approximately 2,500 pairs of White Ibises were once again raising young on a diet of crayfishes on Pumpkinseed Island.

The Storm Cloud's Silver Lining

Hurricane Hugo was a ruinous event that I wish had never occurred. Not only did the storm destroy the Baruch Institute's field lab and seriously disrupt the 1990 and 1991 field seasons, but it also erased much of Hobcaw Barony's idyllic charm. A previously picturesque trip to the coast is now a painful reminder of the storm's impact. Many of the forests ravaged by Hugo will not regrow in my lifetime. The fact that they were demolished by a natural event, rather than by obstinate human activity, offers little comfort.

These effects notwithstanding, Hurricane Hugo did provide a rare—and I hope once-in-a-lifetime—opportunity to study the impact of a natural catastrophic event on coastal ecological processes. Aside from enabling me to track the effect of a cataclysmic event on White Ibises in the area, the storm has forced me to expand the scope of my observations to more fully examine the breeding ecology of other species of wading birds nesting at the site. Although it will be some time before I will be able to reap many of the benefits of this new aspect of my work, such observations should ultimately render a better understanding of coastal processes and their impacts on coastal avifauna. In addition, studying the hurricane's impact on White Ibises and other wading birds should place me in a better position to assess the potential effects of analogous large-scale habitat perturbations resulting from human activities in the coastal areas.

12 A Lesson in White Ibis Conservation

The international ornithological community currently includes 6 of the world's 23 species of ibises in its list of threatened birds (Collar and Andrew 1988; see Table A2.1 in Appendix 2, Appendix 3). The White Ibis is not one of them. Nevertheless, two events in 1989 convinced me that Pumpkinseed Island's White Ibises were vulnerable to human development. The first was my trip to Trinidad. The second was Hurricane Hugo. Both confirmed the critical role of freshwater wetlands in the breeding ecology of coastal populations of White Ibises; both established the need for a broadly based habitat approach to conserve these populations, and both convinced me of the need to speak out for coastal wetland conservation (Bildstein et al. 1991).

Although most conservationists agree that preserving habitats is the best way to preserve the species occurring therein, convincing the general public that saving an entire habitat or functioning ecosystem is worthwhile has proved to be a considerable challenge. The difficulty is further exacerbated when the ecosystem in question is an open one that interacts with those adjacent to it. Consider, for example, the efforts surrounding Scarlet Ibis conservation in Trinidad and Tobago. Historically, conservationists have tended to preserve the habitats in which the targeted organisms concentrate and are most visible. Thus, because Scarlet Ibises are most conspicuous in and around their mangrove breeding colonies, it is not surprising that the government of Trinidad included managing of the Caroni Swamp as part of its efforts to preserve the Scarlet Ibis (Pannier and Dickinson 1989). However, as my findings in Trinidad in 1989 poignantly demonstrated, saving coastal mangrove forests alone without also protecting adjacent freshwater ecosystems inland is not enough.

Brackish coastal wetlands are, by definition, open ecosystems, and many of their organisms are constantly interacting with adjacent freshwater wetlands (Pannier and Dickinson 1989). Preserving such ecosystems alone will ensure neither their ecological integrity nor the preservation of their ibis inhabitants. Nowhere is the interconnectedness of coastal ecosystems more powerfully illustrated than in the ecology of coastal populations of White Ibises. The numbers of White Ibises breeding at the Pumpkinseed Island colony site dropped from more than 11,000 pairs in 1989 to none in 1990. Hurricane Hugo eliminated the breeding efforts of local populations of ibises not by any direct impact on the birds themselves, nor by any indirect impact on their prominent breeding colonies in coastal wetlands, but rather by an indirect effect on freshwater feeding sites further inland, far from where the birds are most conspicuous. Had it not been for my research, the role that the storm played in this precipitous decline may have gone unnoticed.

Coastal populations of White Ibises need both a "bedroom" and a "kitchen" to survive. Protecting their conspicuous coastal bedrooms will mean little if their less conspicuous inland kitchens are destroyed. Unfortunately, many coastal managers, decision makers, and administrators, both in the United States and elsewhere, remain oblivious to the fundamental ecological principle of the interconnectedness of coastal ecosystems. As a result, many of them attempt to manage the coastal ecosystems within their jurisdictions in a piecemeal manner. Until these individuals adopt a more regional or landscape approach—which would take into account such transboundary effects as I have documented for White Ibises—their efforts, however well intended, are likely to fail.

Tourism is South Carolina's second largest industry. Most tourists come to South Carolina to visit the coast. As a result, many coastal locations are experiencing population booms. For example, the greater Myrtle Beach or "Grand Strand" area, which is directly north of my study site, alone hosts 65 golf courses. The human population in the area is expected to triple between 1980 and the year 2000. Although brackish wetlands are relatively well protected in the state, many of the region's seasonal freshwater wetlands are being dredged, filled, and drained, not only for commercial and associated residential development but also for agricultural uses. Habitat losses such as these are certain to negatively affect the local populations of White Ibises.

The development of coastal South Carolina is a microcosm of worldwide coastal development. The earth's coastal zones have attracted human settlement for millennia. Indeed, history reveals that many of our so-called cradles of civilization evolved in these areas. Several early civilizations modified and developed the coastal zone in ways that remain evident even now. Today, people continue to seek out and settle in the world's coastal zones. Nearly half of the U.S. population lives within 80 kilometers of its coasts, and one estimate suggests that more than 70% of humanity lives within such regions. Often misunderstood and once viewed as coastal *wastelands*, coastal brackish and adjacent freshwater wetlands are of immediate value almost everywhere they occur. They are important transportation arteries for commerce and industry. They help regulate important hydrological processes, including recharging ground-water supplies, buffering against flooding and storm surges, storing nutrients, and helping to reduce sediment losses and coastal erosion. These wetlands provide essential nursery grounds for many commercially important shellfishes and finfishes, and critical habitat for numerous game and nongame animals, including many endangered species. They support large and growing tourism industries: nature study, fishing, hunting, and water sports, among others. They are, in fact, some of the most productive natural ecosystems on earth. But they are suffering under the strain of such use.

Burgeoning human populations stress the ecological functions of these ecosystems in many ways. Not only do we physically alter and pollute such sites, we also frequently deplete them of their native species while introducing exotic ones (Bildstein et al. 1991). Rising sea level, a global effect associated with planetary warming, also looms as a potentially significant threat to their ecological integrity. It should come as no surprise, then, that coastal areas are some of our most endangered ecosystems and that such sites frequently support a disproportionate share of an area's endangered species (see Reid and Trexler 1991). In coastal ecosystems, as in others, fundamental ecological principles and the Newtonian laws of thermodynamics conspire to produce an inevitable environmental corollary: *Increasing human population equals increasing change in the system.*

As ill-fated as the situation may appear, I remain guardedly optimistic. Recent advances in our understanding of how coastal ecosystems function, including the studies reported here, together with a growing realization of the importance of such habitats to humanity's own well-being, offer hope for the future. Knowledge is important because ignorance is so dangerous. One of the more enlightened shifts in the conservation movement of late has been the move from single-species to ecosystem management. Strict preservation and a hands-off approach are falling out of favor, and the prospect of living within healthy environments is rapidly gaining support. There has been a recent push toward incorporating local human populations and their activities into regional management schemes for sustaining ecosystems. All of these trends indicate that we may be fast approaching a time when we realize that preserving the functional integrity of coastal ecosystems is in the best interests of not only the species within those ecosystems but also us as well. Altruistic conservation, as laudatory as it may be, can use all of the human selfishness it can muster.

Should we choose to move in this direction, the future of Pumpkinseed Island's White Ibises will probably proceed naturally. Should we fail to do so, the future of Pumpkinseed's ibises will be the least of our worries.

Appendix 1

Names of Plants and Animals Mentioned in the Text and Appendixes

Common name	Scientific name

Plants

Common name	Scientific name
Black Mangrove	*Avicennia nitida*
Black Needlerush	*Juncus roemerianus*
Common Reed	*Phragmites communis*
Elderberry	*Sambucus canadensis*
Giant Cordgrass	*Spartina cynosuroides*
Giant Reed	*Arundo donax*
Groundsel Bush	*Baccharis halimifolia*
Live Oak	*Quercus virginiana*
Loblolly Pine	*Pinus taeda*
Marsh Elder	*Iva frutescens*
Marsh Mallow	*Hibiscus moscheutos*
Papyrus	*Cyperus papyrus*
Poison Ivy	*Rhus radicans*
Red Cedar	*Juniperus virginiana*
Red Mangrove	*Rhizophora mangle*
Saltmarsh Bulrush	*Scirpus robustus*
Saltwort	*Salicornia* species
Smooth Cordgrass	*Spartina alterniflora*
Southern Bald Cypress	*Taxodium distichum*
Tupelo Gum	*Nyssa aquatica*
White Mangrove	*Laguncularia racemosa*
Yellow Mangrove (= Button Mangrove)	*Conocarpus erectus*

Appendix 1

Common name	Scientific name

Invertebrates

American Oyster	*Crassostrea virginica*
Atlantic Mud Crab	*Panopeus herbstii*
Blue Crab	*Callinectes sapidus*
Brown Shrimp	*Penaeus aztecus*
Common Marsh Snail	*Melampus bidentatus*
Grass Shrimp	*Palaemonetes pugio*
Large Sandworm	*Nereis succinea*
Mangrove Land Crab	*Ucides cordatus*
Mangrove Tree Crab	*Aratus pisonii*
Marsh Periwinkle	*Littorina irrorata*
Mud Fiddler Crab	*Uca pugnax*
Mud Snail	*Ilyanassa obsoleta*
Red-jointed Fiddler Crab	*Uca minax*
Sand Fiddler Crab	*Uca pugilator*
Sandworms	*Nereis* species
Scissor-clawed Fiddler Crab	*Uca maracoani*
Southern Pine Beetle	*Dendroctonus frontalis*
White Shrimp	*Penaeus setiferus*

Fishes

Atlantic Silverside	*Menidia menidia*
Mullet	*Mugil* species
Mummichog	*Fundulus heteroclitus*

Reptiles and Amphibians

American Alligator	*Alligator mississippiensis*
Anolis Lizard	*Anolis carolinensis*
Copperhead	*Ankistrodon contortrix*
Eastern Cottonmouth	*Agkistrodon piscivorous*
Loggerhead Turtle	*Caretta caretta*
Tree frogs	*Hyla* species

Birds

Adelie Penguin	*Pygoscelis adeliae*
American Black Duck	*Anas rubripes*
American Flamingo	*Phoenicopterus ruber*
American Robin	*Turdus migratorius*

216

Common name	Scientific name

Birds (*continued*)

Common name	Scientific name
American White Ibis	*Eudocimus ruber albus*
(= White Ibis)	
Australian White Ibis	*Threskiornis molucca*
Australian Zebra Finch	*Poephila guttata*
Bald Eagle	*Haliaeetus leucocephalus*
Bald Ibis	*Geronticus calvus*
Barefaced Ibis	*Phimosus infuscatus*
Black-crowned Night-Heron	*Nycticorax nycticorax*
Black Ibis	*Pseudibis papillosa*
(see Whiteshouldered Ibis, subspecies)	
Black-necked Stilt	*Himantopus mexicanus*
Black Rail	*Laterallus jamaicensis*
Black Vulture	*Coragyps atratus*
Boat-tailed Grackle	*Quiscalus major*
Brewer's Blackbird	*Euphagus cyanocephalus*
Brown Pelican	*Pelecanus occidentalis*
Buffnecked Ibis	*Theristicus caudatus*
Carolina Parakeet	*Conuropsis carolinensis*
Caspian Tern	*Sterna caspia*
Cattle Egret	*Bubulcus ibis*
Clapper Rail	*Rallus longirostris*
Common Moorhen	*Gallinula chloropus*
Coturnix Quail	*Coturnix coturnix*
Dwarf Olive Ibis	*Bostrychia olivacea bocagei*
(subspecies of Olive Ibis)	
Eastern Reef Heron	*Egretta sacra*
Egyptian Plover	*Pluvianus aegyptius*
Eurasian Curlew	*Numenius arquata*
Eurasian Oystercatcher	*Haematopus ostralegus*
Fish Crow	*Corvus ossifragus*
Giant Ibis	*Thaumatibis gigantea*
Glaucous-winged Gull	*Larus glaucescens*
Glossy Ibis	*Plegadis falcinellus*
Great Auk	*Pinguinus impennis*
Great Blue Heron	*Ardea herodias*
(= Great White Heron)	
Great Egret	*Casmerodius albus*
Great White Heron	*Ardea herodias*
(= Great Blue Heron)	

Common name	Scientific name

Birds (*continued*)

Green-backed Heron	*Butorides striatus*
Green Ibis	*Mesembrinibis cayennensis*
Grey Heron	*Ardea cinerea*
Hadada Ibis	*Bostrychia hagedash*
Herring Gull	*Larus argentatus*
Laughing Gull	*Larus atricilla*
Least Bittern	*Ixobrychus exilis*
Little Blue Heron	*Egretta caerula*
Madagascar Crested Ibis	*Lophotibis cristata*
Magnificent Frigatebird	*Fregata magnificens*
Marsh Wren	*Cistothorus palustris*
Mottled Duck	*Anas fulvigula*
Mourning Dove	*Zenaida macroura*
Northern Bald Ibis	*Geronticus eremita*
(= Waldrapp Ibis)	
Northern Cardinal	*Cardinalis cardinalis*
Northern Harrier	*Circus cyaneus*
Olivaceous Cormorant	*Phalacrocorax olivaceous*
Olive Ibis	*Bostrychia olivacea*
(see Dwarf Olive Ibis, subspecies)	
Oriental Crested Ibis	*Nipponia nippon*
Oriental White Ibis	*Threskiornis melanocephalus*
Osprey	*Pandion haliaetus*
Passenger Pigeon	*Ectopistes migratorius*
Pileated Woodpecker	*Dryocopus pileatus*
Plumbeous Ibis	*Harpiprion caerulescens*
Prothonotary Warbler	*Protonotaria citrea*
Puna Ibis	*Plegadis ridgwayi*
Red-cockaded Woodpecker	*Picoides borealis*
Red-tailed Hawk	*Buteo jamaicensis*
Red-winged Blackbird	*Agelaius phoeniceus*
Ring-billed Gull	*Larus delawarensis*
Roseate Spoonbill	*Ajaia ajaja*
Royal Albatross	*Diomedea epomophora*
Royal Tern	*Sterna maxima*
Ruddy Turnstone	*Arenaria interpres*
Sacred Ibis	*Threskiornis aethiopicus*
Sandwich Tern	*Sterna sandvicensis*
Scarlet Ibis	*Eudocimus ruber ruber*
Sharptailed Ibis	*Cercibis oxycerca*

Common name	Scientific name

Birds (*continued*)

Snowy Egret	*Egretta thula*
Spotbreasted Ibis	*Bostrychia rara*
Strawnecked Ibis	*Threskiornis spinicollis*
Tricolored Heron	*Egretta tricolor*
Turkey Vulture	*Cathartes aura*
Waldrapp Ibis	*Geronticus eremita*
(= Northern Bald Ibis)	
Wattled Ibis	*Bostrychia carunculata*
Whimbrel	*Numenius phaeopus*
Whistling ducks	*Dendrocygna* species
Whitefaced Ibis	*Plegadis chihi*
White Ibis	*Eudocimus ruber albus*
(= American White Ibis)	
Whiteshouldered Ibis	*Pseudibis papillosa davisoni*
(subspecies of Black Ibis)	
Willet	*Catoptrophorus semipalmatus*
Wood Duck	*Aix sponsa*
Wood Stork	*Mycteria americana*
Yellow-crowned Night-Heron	*Nycticorax violaceus*

Mammals

Atlantic Bottlenose Dolphin	*Tursiops truncatus*
Cotton Rat	*Sigmodon hispidus*
Eastern Fox Squirrel	*Sciurus niger*
Eastern Gray Squirrel	*Sciurus carolinensis*
Feral Hog	*Sus scrofa*
Gray Fox	*Urocyon cinereoargenteus*
North American Porcupine	*Erethizon dorsatum*
Raccoon	*Procyon lotor*
River Otter	*Lutra canadensis*
White-tailed Deer	*Odocoileus virginianus*

Appendix 2

A Brief Pedigree of Ibises

The Ibis Family Tree

Depending upon one's taxonomic proclivities, the number of ibis species that currently exist is between 22 and 26. The most recent work on the subject (Hancock et al. 1992), which I follow, lists 23 ibis species (Table A2.1). This list includes three "white" ibises: the American White Ibis—which I refer to throughout the book as the White Ibis—as well as the Oriental White Ibis and Australian White Ibis. (The latter two species, which are rather closely related to the Sacred Ibis mentioned in Chapter 1, are so named because of their basically white body plumage, not because of any close relationship with American White Ibises.)

Ibis diversity is considerably greater in the tropics than elsewhere, but several species, including the endangered Oriental Crested Ibis, are found in temperate areas. One species, the Puna Ibis, inhabits cold and desolate Andean grasslands of high elevation (more than 4,000 meters above sea level) from central Peru through northwest Argentina. Ibises are currently found on all continents except Antarctica. North America normally hosts three species: the White, Glossy, and Whitefaced ibises. South America, a center of ibis diversity, is inhabited by nine species.

Traditionally, taxonomists have lumped all ibises, along with the world's six species of spoonbills, into a single family called the Threskiornithidae (Greek for "holy birds"). This taxonomic arrangement has been maintained in more recent classificatory schemes as well (Sibley et al. 1988). Some museum workers prefer the name Plataleidae (Bonaparte, 1838) to Threskiornithidae (Richmond, 1917) for consistency with past literature.

Although similarities in behavior, ecology, and overall physical structure seem to link ibises with other groups of wading birds, most notably the herons, egrets, bitterns, and storks, the exact relationships of these birds are in dispute. Traditional taxonomy places the family Threskiornithidae in the avian order Ciconiiformes, along with the families Ardeidae (herons, egrets, and bitterns), Cochleariidae (boat-billed herons), and Phoenicopteridae (flamingos) (Peters 1931). Although some recent classificatory schemes maintain that general arrangement (see Sibley et al. 1988, Sibley and Ahlquist 1990), others have suggested that ibises are

Table A2.1 Ibises of the world

Species	Distribution
Old World species	
Australian White Ibis	Indonesia, New Guinea, Australia
Bald Ibis*	Southern Africa
Black Ibis*[a]	India, Pakistan, Southeast Asia
Giant Ibis*	Vietnam, possibly Kampuchea and Thailand
Glossy Ibis	Nearly worldwide, including eastern North and South America
Hadada Ibis	Africa south of the Sahara
Madagascar Crested Ibis	Madagascar
Olive Ibis*[b]	Africa
Oriental Crested Ibis*	Japan(?), China
Oriental White Ibis	India, Pakistan, Sri Lanka, Southeast Asia
Sacred Ibis	Africa to west Asia, southwest Pacific islands
Spotbreasted Ibis	Liberia to Cameroon, Zaire
Strawnecked Ibis	Australia, Tasmania
Waldrapp Ibis*	Morocco
Wattled Ibis	Ethiopia, Eritrea
New World species	
Barefaced Ibis	South America
Buffnecked Ibis	Panama, South America
Glossy Ibis	Nearly worldwide, including eastern North and South America
Green Ibis	Southern Central America, South America
Plumbeous Ibis	Brazil, Argentina
Puna Ibis	Andean South America from Peru to Argentina
Sharptailed Ibis	Northern South America, Brazil
Whitefaced Ibis	Central South America and western North America
White Ibis and Scarlet Ibis (= two subspecies)	Eastern North America, Central America, northern South America, Brazil

Note: Asterisks denote those species that the International Council for Bird Preservation considers to be threatened in all or a portion of their range (Collar and Andrew 1988).

[a] Includes the threatened Whiteshouldered Ibis, a distinct subspecies restricted to Vietnam and Borneo.

[b] Includes the threatened Dwarf Olive Ibis, a distinct subspecies restricted to Sao Tome.

not at all closely linked to either flamingos or herons. Some researchers, for example, claim that flamingos are more closely related to geese than to other wading birds (Feduccia 1980, Olson and Feduccia 1980, Hagey et al. 1990). Others note that the posterior margin of an ibis's nostril is more characteristic of a shorebird (order Charadriiformes) (Olson 1979, Feduccia 1980); thus, Olson (1981) suggested that ibises are more closely related to that order than they are to Ciconiiformes.

Fossil remains shed little light on the subject (Feduccia 1980). As is true for most groups of birds, the fossil record for ibises is meager. A few researchers claim to have found extinct fossil "ibises" dating from the Eocene, 60 million years ago (Archibald et al. 1980). However, upon close examination, most of the specimens appear to have been either misidentified or inadequately documented (Olson 1981). Specimens that date back to the early Pliocene (approximately 5 million years ago) and that are indistinguishable from modern Sacred Ibises have been found, as has a close relative of Waldrapp and Bald ibises (Olson 1985). The oldest and best documented pre-Pliocene fossil ibis is that of a close relative of the modern Glossy Ibis, dating from the early Miocene (some 25 million years ago) of France. Yet another distinct relative of the Glossy Ibis is known from the late Pliocene (approximately 2 million years ago) of North America (Olson 1981). At least some researchers have suggested that the genus to which the White Ibis belongs is ancestral to one containing Glossy Ibises (Mayr and Short 1970). If this is true, then species similar, if not identical, to White Ibises probably existed at least 25 million years ago (Olson 1981). In any case, fossils dating from the last 1 million years do represent the White Ibis and many other living species (Olson 1981). Also represented from this time are several flightless ibises, whose fossilized remains have been found on Pacific and Caribbean islands (Olson and Wetmore 1976, Olson and Steadman 1977).

Family Traits

Ibises are distinguished from herons, egrets, storks, and other wading birds by their decurved and tactilely sensitive bills, an anatomical feature closely linked to the group's feeding techniques, which include rapid probing or sweeping for prey while walking on land or in shallow water. Most ibises are 30 to 60 centimeters tall (about 1 to 1.5 feet) and weigh between 450 and 2,500 grams (about 1 to 4 pounds). Several species, including the White Ibis, have mainly white plumage, whereas others have plumage that includes considerable amounts of grey, black, brown, scarlet, and iridescence (green, purple, and brown). Indeed, the family Threskiornithidae may display greater overall plumage variation than any other group of wading birds. In many ibis species, the young possess a distinctive juvenal plumage, at least for the first several months. Within species, adult plumage does not appear to differ between the sexes. In species where size has been examined in detail, males are typically larger than their mates, and they usually have disproportionately longer bills (Kushlan 1977d, Bildstein 1987). The bill, face, and legs often brighten dramatically during courtship, and the courting Oriental Crested

Ibis daubs the feathers on its shoulders and back with a mysterious black substance that it exudes from the skin around its neck.

Many herons and egrets possess a distinctive feather comb on the inner edge of their middle claw, and most produce powder down, a fine waxy substance resulting from the disintegration of specialized down feathers located in yellow patches on the bird's ventral surface. Both adaptations, which are lacking in White Ibises, apparently enable these species to scrupulously maintain their plumage free from parasites, food debris, and mud. Ibises, on the other hand, often allow their feathers to become quite stained. As a result, the White Ibises I watch appear quite drab and dingy each spring, especially in comparison to the more brilliantly plumed Great and Snowy egrets. Indeed, the difference is such that, at the colony site where I study ibis breeding behavior, the few Snowy Egrets that nest among the thousands of White Ibises can often be identified in aerial photographs taken from several hundred meters above the colony. Not surprisingly, there are relatively few artistic renditions of White Ibises, especially in comparison to those of most herons and egrets. Although it is not clear whether this lapse in personal hygiene costs or benefits White Ibises, one fact is clear: The species's inattention to this detail has enabled me to identify individuals much more easily than if the birds were more fastidious in their appearance.

Ibises are relatively compact, heavy-bodied wading birds that more closely resemble storks than either egrets or herons in the body mass supported by their wings. Possibly because of their heavier "wing-loading," ibises flap their wings more rapidly in flight than do egrets and herons, a fact reflected in the musculature of their forelimbs (Vanden Berge 1970). Even so, ibises fly at speeds similar to those of other wading birds (see Curren 1947, Pennycuick 1972, Urban 1974b, Campbell and Lack 1985, Pennycuick and De Santo 1989). Unlike most wading birds, ibises often fly in formation, either in V configuration similar to those of ducks and geese, or in long skeins like those of cormorants. Their ability to fly in these configurations appears to be learned (Petit and Bildstein 1986). Whether ibises derive an aerodynamic benefit by flying in formation is not known.

Ibises are generally considered water birds, and most species feed in wet areas, including marshes, swamps, and flooded agricultural fields, as well as along the edges of ponds, lakes, and streams. On the other hand, a few ibis species spend most of their time in open, dry areas, feeding on insects and other invertebrates, as well as on small vertebrates. Overall, ibises feed on a bewildering assortment of prey, ranging in size and type from minuscule aquatic and terrestrial invertebrates to small fishes, amphibians, reptiles, and mammals. As a group, ibises are extremely social—so much so that, in many species, individuals are rarely seen alone. Most species feed in large aggregations, frequently in excess of 100 birds, and often in the company of other species of wading birds. In the expansive freshwater wetlands of the Venezuelan llanos, for example, I have seen representatives of as many as seven species of ibises intermingled with many other wading birds and whistling ducks, feeding within several meters of each other (Frederick and Bildstein 1992).

Although a few species establish territories and nest alone, most ibises are colonial nesters. Ibis colonies are often enormous. In some species the nesting colony population regularly exceeds 10,000 ibis pairs, and there are credible reports of colonies in excess of 100,000 pairs. Colony sites are often shared with other species of wading birds, and most of these sites are traditional, even though they may not be used every year. Ibis species are generally considered to be monogamous—at least within a single breeding season—however, recent observations cast considerable doubt on the extent of mate fidelity within the group (Kushlan 1973a, Rudegeair 1975, Frederick 1985b, Lowe 1985).

Most ibises produce clutches with between two and six eggs, and all produce relatively helpless altricial young that require care for at least a month after hatching. In many species, nestlings often fight with each other over the food that is brought to them by their parents. In some instances such conflicts result in siblicide, or the sibling-caused death of one or more young.

Appendix 3

Threatened Ibises

The Waldrapp, Bald, Oriental Crested, and Giant ibises all are believed to be decreasing in abundance overall or undergoing substantial contractions in their ranges, and they are likely to continue to do so in the near future (Collar and Andrew 1988). The Sao Tome population of the Dwarf Olive Ibis and the Southeast Asian population of the Whiteshouldered Ibis, which some authorities consider to be distinct species, are also threatened. The population status of each is in flux, and the accounts that follow approximate conditions in early 1992.

Waldrapp Ibises. Kumerloeve (1984) reported seeing as many as 1,300 Waldrapp Ibises at a single Turkish colony site in 1953, and as recently as 1984, 350 to 400 Waldrapp Ibises, a species that is sometimes referred to as the Northern Bald or Hermit ibis, remained in the wild. However, all but 1 of the 13 colonies that were active in the mid 1980s have since disappeared, and the species is currently limited to breeding at a single site, the Souss-Massa estuary in Morocco. Despite infusions from captive populations, Asia Minor's Waldrapp Ibis colony in Birecik (mentioned in Chapter 1), which had dropped to fewer than 100 pairs by the early 1960s (Kumerloeve 1984), ceased to exist by the late 1980s; however, since then, there have been reports of isolated individuals at that site and in North Yemen.

There is a prospering population of more than 800 Waldrapp Ibises spread throughout the world's zoos, and there has been talk of reintroducing captively reared birds into portions of their former range, possibly in southern Spain, Switzerland, or North Africa. The successful introduction of several captively reared individuals into the Birecik colony in the early 1980s offers reason for hope in this regard. Unfortunately, it is likely to be more difficult to reintroduce birds into areas where there are no wild populations to pass along traditional behavioral patterns.

Bald Ibis. A close relative of the Waldrapp Ibis, the Bald Ibis is restricted to the other end of the African continent, where populations of between 5,000 and 8,000 birds occur in the highlands of South Africa, Lesotho, and Swaziland. The species requires protected-cliff nesting sites and large areas of grazed or recently burned grassland feeding sites (Manry 1985a, 1985b).

Dwarf Olive Ibis. Until recently, the elusive Dwarf or Sao Tome Olive Ibis had not been seen since a 1928 collecting expedition. In 1990, it was sighted 250 kilometers off the coast of West Africa on the tiny, formerly Portuguese colony of Sao Tome. Recently, reliable sightings from the forested mountainous interior of the island suggest that the species still survives at the site. Extant populations appear to be quite small.

Oriental Crested Ibis. The Oriental Crested Ibis originally ranged from eastern China into Korea, Japan, and even into portions of the former Soviet Union. It is currently considered the most endangered of all ibises. Extirpated from haunts in the former Soviet Union, in Korea, and more recently, in Japan, free-ranging individuals remain only in China, where as recently as the 1930s it was widely distributed in 14 provinces (Xiyang 1987). Today, fewer than several dozen individuals exist in several isolated pockets in a single province in China's Quinling Range (Xiyang 1987). Although once protected in Japan by the ruling class, Oriental Crested Ibises were hunted for food, sport, and as an agricultural pest (when they were abundant enough to trample newly planted rice paddies) in that country from 1886 to 1934. The species was declared a National Natural Monument in 1934. In 1952, it received an official designation as a Special Natural Monument. Even so, its breeding habitat was not protected in Japan until 1962, at which point only six birds remained in the wild in that country (Archibald and Lantis 1978). Currently, no free-ranging birds remain in Japan.

The survival of the Oriental Crested Ibis apparently hinges on the fate of China's remaining wild population, which probably numbers fewer than several dozen birds, as well as on a recent attempt to establish a viable captive population. In recent years the tiny wild population, which exists at two sites that are separated by about 40 kilometers in Yang County, has produced an estimated 15 young at 10 nests (Xiyang 1987). A single hand-reared chick that was artificially hatched at the Beijing Zoo in the summer of 1990 appears to be in good health (Anonymous 1990). Fieldwork suggests that if the species is to survive in the wild it needs to have immediate access both to tall trees, in which it builds its nests, and to rice paddies, in which it feeds. That the only known extant colonies of Oriental Crested Ibises are nesting in mature oriental oaks that are fortuitously growing in local graveyards does not bode success for the species (Xiyang 1987). Although the species is sometimes shot by local inhabitants, the greatest threat to its existence appears to be the loss of essential nesting sites and feeding habitat (Xiyang 1987).

Giant Ibis. The current status of the highly endangered Giant Ibis, a species known only from Mekong River wetlands in Vietnam, close to the Cambodian border, is unclear. The region receives little ornithological attention, and breeding has not been reported in recent years.

Whiteshouldered Ibis. The Whiteshouldered Ibis is a distinct subspecies of the Black Ibis and is currently restricted to Vietnam and Borneo. Its status remains largely unknown, although extant populations appear to be small.

Other ibis species. Although individual populations of other species of ibises are also threatened, none is currently considered to be threatened at the subspecies level.

References

Abramson, M. 1979. Vigilance as a factor influencing flock formation among Curlews *Numenius arquata*. *Ibis* 121:213–16.

Adams, D. A. 1963. Battery Island 1963. *Chat* 27:65–68.

Allen-Grimes, A. W. 1982. *Breeding biology of the White Ibis at Battery Island, N.C.* Master's thesis, Wilmington: University of North Carolina.

American Ornithologists' Union. 1983. *Check-list of North American birds*. 6th ed. Washington, D.C.: American Ornithologists' Union.

Anonymous. 1905. Hobcaw Barony. *The Carolina Field* 1(4):1–3.

———. 1990. Oriental Crested Ibis. *Specialist Group on Storks, Ibises and Spoonbills Newsletter* 3:3.

Antas, P. T. Z., P. Roth, and R. I. G. Morrison. 1990. Status and conservation of the Scarlet Ibis in Brazil. Pp. 130–36 in *The Scarlet Ibis (Eudocimus ruber): Status, conservation and research* (P. C. Frederick, L. G. Morales, A. L. Spaans, and C. S. Luthin, eds.). IWRB Spec. Publ. 11. Slimbridge, England: Inter. Waterfowl and Wetlands Res. Bur.

Archibald, G. W., and S. D. H. Lantis. 1978. Conservation of the Japanese Crested Ibis. *Proc. Colonial Waterbird Group* 1978:1–15.

Archibald, G. W., S. D. H. Lantis, L. R. Lantis, and I. Munetchika. 1980. Endangered ibises, Threskiornithidae: Their future in the wild and in captivity. *Int. Zoo Yearb.* 20:6–17.

Audubon, J. J. 1840–44. *The birds of America*. Vol. vi. London: Audubon & Chevalier (1991 reprint).

Bacon, P. R. 1970. *The ecology of the Caroni Swamp, Trinidad*. Port-of-Spain, Trinidad: Central Statistical Office Printing Unit.

Badolato, E. V., J. Bleiweis, J. D. Craig, and H. W. Fleming, Jr. 1990. *Hurricane Hugo: Lessons learned in energy preparedness*. Clemson, S.C.: Strom Thurmond Institute of Government and Public Affairs, Clemson University.

Ball, M. M., E. A Shinn, and K. W. Stockman. 1967. The geologic effects of Hurricane Donna in south Florida. *J. Geol.* 75:583–87.

Bancroft, G. T. 1989. Status and conservation of wading birds in the Everglades. *Am. Birds* 43:1258–65.

References

Barry, J. M. 1980. *Natural vegetation of South Carolina*. Columbia: University of South Carolina Press.

Bartram, W. 1791. *Travels through North and South Carolina, Georgia, east and west Florida, etc.* Philadelphia: James & Johnson.

Baruch, B. M. 1957. *Baruch: My own story*. New York: Henry Holt and Co.

Bateman, D. L. 1970. *Movement-behavior in three species of colonial-nesting wading birds: A radio-telemetric study*. Ph.D. diss., Auburn, Ala.: Auburn University.

Baynard, O. E. 1913. Home life of the Glossy Ibis *(Plegadis autumnalis*, Linn.). *Wilson Bull.* 25:103–17.

Beckett, T. A. 1965. Drum Island 1964. *Chat* 29:43–46.

Bedard, J., J. C. Therriault, and J. Berube. 1980. Assessment of the importance of nutrient recycling by seabirds in the St. Lawrence Estuary. *Can. J. Fish. Aquat. Sci.* 37:583–88.

Beebe, C. W. 1914. Notes on the ontogeny of the White Ibis, *Guara alba. Zoologica* 1:241–48.

Belcher, C., and G. D. Smooker. 1934. Birds of the colony of Trinidad and Tobago. *Ibis* 76:572–95.

Belser, C. G. 1989. A Scarlet Ibis or hybrid White Ibis × Scarlet Ibis in South Carolina. *Chat* 53:90–91.

Bertness, M. D. 1985. Fiddler crab regulation of *Spartina alterniflora* production on a New England salt marsh. *Ecology* 66:1042–55.

Best, L. B. 1977. Nesting biology of the Field Sparrow. *Auk* 94:308–19.

Bildstein, K. L. 1983. Age-related differences in the flocking and foraging behavior of White Ibises in a South Carolina salt marsh. *Colonial Waterbirds* 6:45–53.

———. 1984. Age-related differences in the foraging behavior of White Ibises and the question of deferred maturity. *Colonial Waterbirds* 7:146–48.

———. 1987. Energetic consequences of sexual size dimorphism in White Ibises *(Eudocimus albus). Auk* 104:771–75.

———. 1990. Status, conservation and management of the Scarlet Ibis *Eudocimus ruber* in the Caroni Swamp, Trinidad, West Indies. *Biol. Conserv.* 54:61–78.

Bildstein, K. L., G. T. Bancroft, P. J. Dugan, D. H. Gordon, R. M. Erwin, E. Nol, L. X. Payne, and S. E. Senner. 1991. Approaches to the conservation of coastal wetlands in the Western Hemisphere. *Wilson Bull.* 103:218–54.

Bildstein, K. L., E. Blood, and P. C. Frederick. 1992. The relative importance of biotic and abiotic vectors in nutrient processing in a South Carolina, U.S.A., estuarine ecosystem. *Estuaries* 15:147–57.

Bildstein, K. L., R. Christy, and P. DeCoursey. 1982. Size and structure of a South Carolina salt marsh avian community. *Wetlands* 2:118–37.

Bildstein, K. L., S. G. McDowell, and I. L. Brisbin. 1989. Consequences of sexual dimorphism in Sand Fiddler Crabs, *Uca pugilator:* Differential vulnerability to avian predation. *Anim. Behav.* 37:133–39.

Bildstein, K. L., W. Post, J. Johnston, and P. Frederick. 1990. Freshwater wetlands, rainfall, and the breeding ecology of White Ibises in coastal South Carolina. *Wilson Bull.* 102:84–98.

Bjork, R. 1986. *Reproductive ecology of selected Ciconiiformes nesting at Battery Island, N.C.* Master's thesis, Wilmington: University of North Carolina.

Blood, E. R., P. Anderson, P. A. Smith, C. Nybro, and K. A. Ginsberg. 1991. Effects of Hurricane Hugo on coastal soil solution chemistry in South Carolina. *Biotropica* 23:348–55.

Blood, E. R., W. T. Swank, and T. Williams. 1989. Precipitation, throughfall, and streamflow chemistry in a coastal Loblolly Pine stand. Pp. 61–78 in *Freshwater wetlands and wildlife, 1989* (R. R. Sharitz and J. W. Gibbons, eds.). Oak Ridge, Tenn.: USDOE Office of Scientific and Technical Information.

Boylan, P. 1922. *Thoth: The Hermes of Egypt.* Chicago: Ares Publishers (1987 reprint of 1922 ed. [1st ed.]).

Brown, J. L. 1987. *Helping and communal breeding in birds.* Princeton: Princeton University Press.

Bucher, E. H. 1992. The causes of extinction of the Passenger Pigeon. *Current Ornithol.* 9:1–36.

Burger, J. 1981. A model for the evolution of mixed-species colonies of Ciconiiformes. *Quart. Rev. Biol.* 56:143–67.

———. 1982. The role of reproductive success in colony site selection and abandonment in Black Skimmers *(Rhynchops niger). Auk* 99:109–55.

Burger, J., and M. Gochfeld. 1983. Feeding behavior in Laughing Gulls: Compensatory site selection by young. *Condor* 85:467–73.

Cade, T. J., and G. L. MacLean. 1967. Transport of water by adult sandgrouse to their young. *Condor* 69:323–43.

Caldwell, G. S. 1986. Predation as a selective force on foraging herons: Effects on plumage color and flocking. *Auk* 103:494–505.

Campbell, B., and E. Lack (eds.) 1985. *Dictionary of birds.* Vermillion, S.Dak.: Buteo Books.

Caraco, T. 1979. Time budgeting and group size: A test of theory. *Ecology* 60:618–27.

Carrick, R. 1962. Breeding, movements and conservation of ibises (Threskiornithidae) in Australia. *CSIRO Wildl. Res.* 7:71–88.

Catesby, M. 1731–47. *Natural history of Carolina, Florida and the Bahama Islands.* 2 vols. London.

Choate, E. A. 1973. *The dictionary of American bird names.* Boston: Gambit.

Christy, J. H. 1980. *The mating system of the Sand Fiddler Crab, Uca pugilator.* Ph.D. diss., Ithaca, N.Y.: Cornell University.

Christy, R. L., K. L. Bildstein, and P. DeCoursey. 1981. A preliminary analysis of energy flow in a South Carolina salt marsh: Wading birds. *Colonial Waterbirds* 4:96–103.

Clapp, R. B., M. K. Klimkiewicz, and J. H. Kennard. 1982. Longevity records of North American birds: Gaviidae through Alcidae. *J. Field Ornithol.* 53:81–124.

Clark, R. A., and A. Clark. 1979. The daily and seasonal movements of the Sacred Ibis at Pretoria, Transvaal. *Ostrich* 50:94–103.

Collar, N. J., and P. Andrew. 1988. *Birds to watch: The ICBP world checklist of threatened birds.* Washington, D.C.: Smithsonian Institution Press.

Connell, J. H. 1980. Diversity and the coevolution of competitors, or the ghost of competition past. *Oikos* 35:131–38.

Crane, J. 1975. *Fiddler crabs of the world.* Princeton: Princeton University Press.

References

Curren, C. H. 1947. Speed of a Great Blue Heron. *Auk* 64:309.

Custer, T. W., and R. G. Osborn. 1977. *Wading birds as biological indicators: 1975 colony survey.* Spec. Sci. Rpt. Wildl. 206. Washington, D.C.: U.S. Fish and Wildl. Serv.

Dame, R., T. Chrzanowski, K. Bildstein, B. Kjerfve, H. McKellar, D. Nelson, J. Spurrier, S. Stancyk, H. Stevenson, J. Vernberg, and R. Zingmark. 1986. The outwelling hypothesis and North Inlet, South Carolina. *Mar. Ecol.-Prog. Ser.* 33:217–29.

Dawkins, R. 1982. *The extended phenotype.* San Francisco: Freeman.

Dawson, T. J., D. Read, E. M. Russell, and R. M. Herd. 1984. Seasonal variation in daily activity patterns, water relations and diet of emus. *Emu* 84:93–102.

De Santo, T. L., S. G. McDowell, and K. L. Bildstein. 1990. Plumage and behavioral development of nestling White Ibises. *Wilson Bull.* 102:226–38.

Desfayes, M. 1987. Evidence for the ancient presence of the Bald Ibis *Geronticus eremita* in Greece. *Bull. Brit. Ornithol. Cl.* 107:93–94.

Douglas, D. S. 1968. Salt and water metabolism of the Adelie Penguin. *Antarctic Res. Ser.* 12:167–90.

Dujardin, J.-L. 1990. Status and conservation of the Scarlet Ibis in French Guiana. Pp. 107–14 in *The Scarlet Ibis (Eudocimus ruber): Status, conservation and research* (P. C. Frederick, L. G. Morales, A. L. Spaans, and C. S. Luthin, eds.). IWRB Spec. Publ. 11. Slimbridge, England: Inter. Waterfowl and Wetlands Res. Bur.

Edmunds, M. 1974. *Defence in animals.* Essex: Longman.

Ensor, D. M., and J. G. Phillips. 1972. The effect of age and environment on extrarenal excretion in juvenile gulls *(Larus argentatus* and *L. fuscus). J. Zool. Lond.* 168:119–26.

Etchecopar, R. D., and F. Hue. 1967. *The birds of North Africa from the Canary Islands to the Red Sea.* Edinburgh.

Evans, P. R. 1973. Avian resources of the North Sea. Pp. 400–12 in *North Sea science* (E. D. Goldberg, ed.). Cambridge: Harvard University Press.

Feduccia, A. 1980. *The age of birds.* Cambridge: Harvard University Press.

ffrench, R. 1966. The Scarlet Ibis. *Biol. J. Biol. Soc. Univ. W.I., St. Augustine* 1:30–36.

———. 1978. Birds of the Caroni Swamp and marshes. *Living World (J. Field. Nat. Cl. Trinidad & Tobago)* 1977:42–44.

———. 1984. *The Scarlet Ibis in Trinidad.* Port-of-Spain, Trinidad: Ministry of Agriculture, Lands and Food Production, UNFAO.

———. 1985. A new look at our Scarlet Ibis. *Trinidad Nat.* 6(5):30–34, 55, 59.

———. 1991. *A guide to the birds of Trinidad and Tobago.* 2d ed. Ithaca, N.Y.: Comstock Publ.

ffrench, R., and F. Haverschmidt. 1970. The Scarlet Ibis in Surinam and Trinidad. *Living Bird* 9:147–65.

Forestry Division, Organization of American States. 1979. *Management and development plan, Caroni Swamp National Park.* Port-of-Spain, Trinidad: Trinidad and Tobago Forestry Division.

Fox, D. L. 1975. Carotenoids in pigmentation. Pp. 162–82 in *Flamingos* (J. Kear and N. Duplaix-Hall, eds.). Berkhamsted, England: T & AD Poyser.

Francis, E. 1978. White Ibis in Transylvania County, N.C. *Chat* 42:81.

Frederick, P. C. 1985a. Intraspecific food piracy in White Ibis. *J. Field Ornithol.* 56:413–14.

———. 1985b. *Mating strategies of White Ibis (Eudocimus albus).* Ph.D. diss., Chapel Hill: University of North Carolina.

———. 1986. A self-tripping trap for use with colonial nesting birds. *N. Am. Bird Bander* 11:94–95.

———. 1987a. Chronic tidal-induced nest failure in a colony of White Ibises. *Condor* 89:413–19.

———. 1987b. Extrapair copulations in the mating system of White Ibis *(Eudocimus albus). Behaviour* 100:171–201.

———. 1987c. Responses of male White Ibises to their mate's extrapair copulations. *Behav. Ecol. Sociobiol.* 21:223–28.

Frederick, P. C., and K. L. Bildstein. 1992. Foraging ecology of seven species of neotropical ibises (Threskiornithidae) during the dry season in the llanos of Venezuela. *Wilson Bull.* 104:1–21.

Frederick, P. C., and M. W. Collopy. 1989. The role of predation in determining reproductive success of colonially nesting wading birds in the Florida Everglades. *Condor* 91:860–67.

Frederick, P. C., L. G. Morales, A. L. Spaans, and C. S. Luthin, eds. 1990. *The Scarlet Ibis (Eudocimus ruber): Status, conservation and recent research.* IWRB Spec. Publ. 11. Slimbridge, England: Inter. Waterfowl and Wetlands Res. Bur.

Frix, M. S., M. E. Hostetler, and K. L. Bildstein. 1991. Intra- and interspecies differences in responses of Atlantic Sand *(Uca pugilator)* and Atlantic Mud *(U. pugnax)* fiddler crabs to simulated avian predators. *J. Crustacean Biol.* 11:523–29.

Gardner, L. R., W. K. Michener, E. R. Blood, T. M. Williams, D. J. Lipscomb, and W. H. Jefferson. 1991a. Ecological impact of Hurricane Hugo—salinization of a coastal forest. *J. Coastal Res.* 8:301–17.

Gardner, L. R., W. K. Michener, B. Kjerfve, and D. A. Karinshak. 1991b. The geomorphic effects of Hurricane Hugo on an undeveloped coastal landscape at North Inlet, South Carolina. *J. Coastal Res.* 8:181–86.

Gentry, R. C. 1971. Hurricanes, one of the major features of air–sea interaction in the Caribbean Sea. In *Symposium on investigation and resources of the Caribbean and adjacent regions.* Paris: UNESCO.

Gibbs, H. L., P. J. Weatherhead, P. T. Boag, N. B. White, L. M. Tabak, and D. J. Hoysak. 1990. Realized reproductive success of polygynous Red-winged Blackbirds revealed by DNA markers. *Science* 250:1394–97.

Girard, G. T., and W. K. Taylor. 1979. Reproductive parameters for nine avian species at Moore Creek, Merritt Island National Wildlife Refuge, Florida. *Florida Sci.* 42:94–102.

Goss-Custard, J. D. 1977. The ecology of the Wash. III. Density-related behaviour and the possible effects of a loss of feeding grounds on wading birds (*Charadrii*). *J. Appl. Ecol.* 14:721–39.

Goss-Custard, J. D., S. E. A. Le Vit dit Durell, and B. J. Ens. 1982. Individual differences in aggressiveness and food stealing among wintering Oystercatchers, *Haematopus ostralegus* L. *Anim. Behav.* 30:917–28.

Gould, S. J. 1977. *Ontogeny and phylogeny.* Cambridge: Harvard University Press.

References

Gray, W. M. 1990. Strong association between West African rainfall and U.S. landfall of intense hurricanes. *Science* 249:1251–56.

Greenway, J. C. 1958. *Extinct and vanishing birds of the world.* Spec. Publ. No. 13. New York: American Committee for International Wild Life Protection.

Greig, S. A., J. C. Coulson, and P. Monaghan. 1983. Age-related differences in foraging success in the Herring Gull *(Larus argentatus). Anim. Behav.* 31:1237–43.

Grzimek, B. 1968. *Grzimek's animal life encyclopedia.* vol 7. New York: Van Nostrand Reinhold.

Haeckel, E. 1866. *Generalle Morphologie der Organismen.* Berlin: Reimer.

Hagey, L. R., C. D. Schteingart, H-T. Ton-Nu, S. S. Rossi, D. ODell, and A. F. Hofmann. 1990. B-phocacholic acid in bile: Biochemical evidence that the flamingo is related to an ancient goose. *Condor* 92:593–97.

Hamilton, W. D. 1971. Geometry for the selfish herd. *J. Theor. Biol.* 31:12–45.

Hamilton, W. J. III, and F. H. Heppner. 1967. Radiant solar energy and the function of black homeotherm pigmentation: An hypothesis. *Science* 155:196–97.

Hammatt, R. B. 1981. *Reproductive biology in a Louisiana estuarine heronry.* Master's thesis, Baton Rouge: Louisiana State University.

Hancock, J. A., J. A. Kushlan, and M. P. Kahl. 1992. *Storks, ibises, and spoonbills.* London: Academic Press.

Hayes, M. O. 1978. Impact of hurricanes on sedimentation in estuaries. Pp. 323–46 in *Estuarine interactions* (M. L. Wiley, ed.). New York: Academic Press.

Henderson, E. G. 1981. *Behavioral ecology of the searching behavior of the White Ibis (Eudocimus albus).* Master's thesis, Columbia: University of South Carolina.

Hicks, S. D., H. A. Debaugh, and L. E. Hickman. 1983. *Sea level variations for the United States, 1855–1980.* NOAA report. Rockville, Md.: USDC.

Hislop, G., and C. James. 1990. Status and conservation of the Scarlet Ibis in Trinidad and Tobago. Pp. 115–23 in *The Scarlet Ibis (Eudocimus ruber): Status, conservation and recent research* (P. C. Frederick, A. L. Spaans, L. G. Morales, and C. S. Luthin, eds.). IWRB Spec. Publ. 11. Slimbridge, England: Inter. Waterfowl and Wetlands Res. Bur.

Holmes, R. T., and F. W. Sturges. 1973. Annual energy expenditure by avifauna of a northern hardwoods ecosystem. *Oikos* 24:24–29.

Holmgren, V. C. 1972. *Bird walk through the Bible.* New York: Seabury Press.

Houlihan, P. F. 1986. *The birds of ancient Egypt.* Atlantic Heights, N.J.: Humanities Press.

Howell, T. R. 1979. Breeding biology of the Egyptian Plover, *Pluvianus aegyptius. Univ. Calif. Publ. Zool.* 113:1–76.

Hughes, M. R. 1968. Renal and extrarenal excretion in the common tern, *Sterna hirundo. Physiol. Zool.* 41:210–19.

———. 1984. Osmoregulation in nestling Glaucous-winged Gulls. *Condor* 86:390–95.

Hutchinson, G. E. 1950. Biochemistry of vertebrate excretion. *Bull. Am. Mus. Nat. Hist.* 96:1–554.

James, C., N. Nathi-Gyan, and G. Hislop. 1984. *IWRR/ICBP Neotropical Wetlands*

Project: National report, Trinidad and Tobago. Port-of-Spain, Trinidad: Forestry Division, Ministry of Agriculture, Lands and Food Production.

James, F. C., and C. H. McCullough. 1985. Data analysis and the design of experiments in ornithology. *Current Ornithol.* 2:1–63.

Jenni, D. A. 1969. A study of the ecology of four species of herons during the breeding season at Lake Alice, Alachua County, Florida. *Ecol. Monogr.* 39:245–70.

Johnston, J. W., and K. L. Bildstein. 1990. Dietary salt as a physiological constraint in White Ibis breeding in an estuary. *Physiol. Zool.* 63:190–207.

Jones, L. P. 1971. *South Carolina: A synoptic history for laymen.* Lexington, S.C.: Sandlapper Store, Inc.

Joseph, E. L. 1838. *History of Trinidad.* Trinidad: H. J. Mills.

Kahl, M. P., Jr. 1962. Bioenergetics of growth in nestling Wood Storks. *Condor* 64:169–83.

Kana, T. W., B. J. Baca, and M. L. Williams. 1988. Charleston case study. Pp. 37–59 in *Greenhouse effect, sea level rise, and coastal wetlands* (J. G. Titus, ed.). Washington, D.C.: U.S. Environmental Protection Agency.

Kenward, R. E. 1978. Hawks and doves: Factors affecting success and selection in Goshawk attacks on Woodpigeons. *J. Anim. Ecol.* 47:449–60.

———. 1987. *Wildlife radio tagging.* New York: Academic Press.

Kharitonov, S. P., and D. Siegel-Causey. 1988. Colony formation in seabirds. *Current Ornithol.* 5:223–72.

Kjerfve, B., and J. A. Proehl. 1979. Velocity variability in a cross-section of a well-mixed estuary. *J. Mar. Res.* 37:409–18.

Koenig, W. D. 1985. Dunking of prey by Brewer's Blackbirds: A novel source of water for nestlings. *Condor* 87:444–45.

Koenig, W. D., and R. L. Mumme. 1987. *Population ecology of the cooperatively breeding Acorn Woodpecker.* Princeton: Princeton University Press.

Krebs, J. R. 1978. Colonial nesting in birds, with special reference to the Ciconiiformes. Pp. 299–314 in *Wading birds* (A. Sprunt IV, J. C. Ogden, and S. Winckler, eds.). New York: National Audubon Society.

Krebs, J. R., M. H. MacRoberts, and J. M. Cullen. 1972. Flocking and feeding in the Great Tit *(Parus major):* An experimental study. *Ibis* 114:507–30.

Kumerloeve, H. 1984. The Waldrapp, *Geronticus eremita* (Linnaeus, 1758): Historical review, taxonomic history, and present status. *Biol. Conserv.* 30:363–73.

Kushlan, J. A. 1973a. Promiscuous mating behavior in the White Ibis. *Wilson Bull.* 85:331–32.

———. 1973b. White Ibis nesting in the Florida Everglades. *Wilson Bull.* 85:230–31.

———. 1974. *The ecology of the White Ibis in southern Florida, a regional study.* Ph.D. diss., Coral Gables, Fla.: University of Miami.

———. 1976. Site selection for nesting colonies by American White Ibis, *Eudocimus albus,* in Florida. *Ibis* 118:590–93.

———. 1977a. Differential growth of body parts in the White Ibis. *Auk* 94:164–67.

———. 1977b. Foraging behavior of White Ibises. *Wilson Bull.* 89:342–45.

————. 1977c. Population energetics of the American White Ibis. *Auk* 94:114–22.

————. 1977d. Sexual dimorphism in the White Ibis. *Wilson Bull.* 89:92–98.

————. 1978. Feeding ecology of wading birds. Pp. 249–97 in *Wading birds* (A. Sprunt IV, J. C. Ogden, and S. Winckler, eds.) New York: National Audubon Society.

————. 1979a. Feeding ecology and prey selection in the White Ibis. *Condor* 81:376–89.

————. 1979b. Prey choice by tactile-foraging wading birds. *Proc. Colonial Waterbird Group* 3:133–42.

Kushlan, J. A., and K. L. Bildstein. 1992. *White Ibis.* The birds of North America. Washington, D.C.: American Ornithologists' Union.

Lack, D. 1954. *The natural regulation of animal numbers.* London: Oxford University Press.

————. 1966. *Population studies of birds.* London: Clarendon.

————. 1968. *Ecological adaptations for breeding in birds.* London: Chapman and Hall.

Lasiewski, R. C. 1972. Respiratory function in birds. Pp. 287–342 in *Avian biology.* Vol. 2 (D. S. Farner, J. R. King, and K. C. Parkes, eds.). New York: Academic Press.

LeGrand, H. E., Jr. 1990a. Bird sightings in the Carolinas associated with Hurricane Hugo. *Chat* 54:73–78.

————. 1990b. Southern Atlantic coast region. *Am. Birds* 44:252–56.

Leotaud, A. 1866. *Oiseaux de l'île de la Trinidad.* Port-of-Spain, Trinidad: Chronicle Publications Office.

Likens, G. E., F. H. Borman, R. S. Pierce, J. S. Eaton, and N. M. Johnson. 1977. *Biogeochemistry of a forested ecosystem.* New York: Springer-Verlag.

Lissaman, P. B. S., and C. A. Schollenberger. 1970. Formation flights of birds. *Science* 168:1003–05.

Lowe, K. W. 1985. *The feeding and breeding biology of the Sacred Ibis Threskiornis aethiopicus in southern Victoria.* Ph.D. diss., Melbourne: University of Melbourne.

Loyacano, H. A., Jr. 1967. *Acute and chronic effects of salinity on two populations of red swamp crawfish, Procambarus clarki.* Master's thesis, Baton Rouge: Louisiana State University.

Ludlum, D. M. 1989. Weatherwatch. *Weatherwise* 42:341–42.

Lugo, A. E., M. Applefield, D. J. Pool, and R. B. Mcdonald. 1983. The impact of Hurricane David on the forests of Dominica. *Canadian J. For. Res.* 13:201–11.

Luthin, C. S. 1983. Breeding ecology of neotropical ibises (Threskiornithidae) in Venezuela, and comments on captive propagation. In *Proc. J. Delacour/I.F.C.B. symp. breeding birds in captivity.* Hollywood, Ca.: International Foundation for the Conservation of Birds.

————. 1985. The bird that is being loved to death. *Trinidad Nat.* 6(5):18–21.

Lyster, S. 1985. *International wildlife law.* Cambridge, England: Grotius.

MacLean, A. A. E. 1986. Age-specific foraging ability and the evolution of deferred breeding in three species of gulls. *Wilson Bull.* 98:267–79.

MacLean, G. L. 1983. Water transport by sandgrouse. *BioScience* 33:365–69.

Mallet, M. 1977. The Waldrapp Ibis. Pp. 26–31 in *The Jersey Wildlife Preservation*

Trust, Twelfth Annual Report. Jersey, Channel Islands: Jersey Wildlife Preservation Trust.

Manry, D. E. 1982. Habitat use by foraging Bald Ibises *Geronticus calvus* in western Natal. *S. Afr. J. Wildl. Res.* 12:86–93.

———. 1985a. Distribution, abundance and conservation of the Bald Ibis *(Geronticus calvus)* in southern Africa. *Biol. Conserv.* 33:351–62.

———. 1985b. Reproductive performance of the Bald Ibis *Geronticus calvus* in relation to rainfall and grass burning. *Ibis* 127:159–73.

Martin, R. P., and R. B. Hamilton. 1985. Wading bird predation at crawfish ponds. *Louisiana Agriculture* 28(4):3–5.

Mayr, E., and L. L. Short. 1970. *Species taxa of North American birds*. Publ. Nuttall Ornithol. Club 9. Cambridge, Mass.

McColl, J. G., and J. Burger. 1976. Chemical input by a colony of Franklin's Gulls nesting in cattails. *Am. Midl. Nat.* 96:270–80.

McCraith, B. J. 1992. *A long-term study of temporal variation in the foraging behavior of White Ibises and the effect of White Ibis probing behavior on pore water residence times at the North Inlet Estuary, South Carolina*. Master's thesis, Rock Hill, S.C.: Winthrop College.

McNabb, G. C. 1978. White Ibis near Rosman, N.C. *Chat* 42:81.

McVaugh, W., Jr. 1972. The development of four North American herons. *Living Bird* 11:155–73.

———. 1975. The development of four North American herons. II. *Living Bird* 14:163–83.

Meanley, B. 1985. *The marsh hen: A natural history of the Clapper Rail of the Atlantic Coast salt marsh*. Centreville, Md.: Tidewater.

Mitcham, S. A., and G. Wobeser. 1988a. Effects of sodium and magnesium sulfate in drinking water on Mallard ducklings. *J. Wildl. Dis.* 24:30–44.

———. 1988b. Toxic effects of natural saline waters on Mallard ducklings. *J. Wildl. Dis.* 24:45–50.

Mock, D. W. 1981. White–dark polymorphism in herons. *Proc. 1st Welder Wildl. Fed. Symp.* 1:145–61.

Montague, C. 1980. A natural history of temperate western Atlantic fiddler crabs (genus *Uca*) with reference to their impact on the salt marsh. *Contrib. Mar. Sci.* 23:25–55.

Morison, S. E. 1942. *Admiral of the ocean sea: A life of Christopher Columbus*. Boston: Little, Brown and Co.

Morse, D. H. 1970. Ecological aspects of some mixed-species foraging flocks of birds. *Ecol. Monogr.* 40:119–68.

Murphy, R. C. 1936. *Oceanic birds of South America*. New York: Macmillan Co.

NOAA. 1985. *Local climatological data for Georgetown, South Carolina (30 year summary, 1951–1980)*. Asheville, N.C.: National Climatic Data Center.

O'Connor, R. J. 1984. *The growth and development of birds*. New York: Wiley.

Odum, E. P. 1989. *Ecology and our endangered life-support systems*. Sunderland, Mass.: Sinauer.

Olson, S. L. 1979. Multiple origins of the Ciconiiformes. *Proc. Colonial Waterbird Group* 1978:165–70.

———. 1981. The generic allocation of *Ibis pagana* Milne-Edwards, with a review of fossil ibises (Aves: Threskiornithidae). *J. Vert. Paleont.* 1:165–71.

———. 1985. Early Pliocene ibises (Aves, Plataleidae) from south-western Cape Province, South Africa. *Ann. S. Afr. Mus.* 97(3):57–69.

Olson, S. L., and A. Feduccia. 1980. Relationships and evolution of flamingos (Aves: Phoenicopteridae). *Smithson. Contrib. Zool.* 316:1–73.

Olson, S. L., and D. W. Steadman. 1977. A new genus of flightless ibis (Threskiornithidae) and other fossil birds from cave deposits in Jamaica. *Proc. Biol. Soc. Wash.* 91:972–81.

Olson, S. L., and A. Wetmore. 1976. Preliminary diagnosis of two extraordinary new genera of birds from Pleistocene deposits in the Hawaiian Islands. *Proc. Biol. Soc. Wash.* 89:247–58.

O'Neill, R. V., D. L. DeAngelis, J. B. Waide, and T. F. H. Allen. 1986. *A hierarchical concept of ecosystems.* Princeton: Princeton University Press.

Onuf, C. P., J. M. Teal, and I. Valiela. 1977. Interactions of nutrients, plant growth and herbivory in a mangrove ecosystem. *Ecology* 58:514–26.

Osborn, R. G., and T. W. Custer. 1978. *Herons and their allies: Atlas of Atlantic coast colonies, 1975 and 1976.* FWS/OBS-77/08. Washington, D.C.: U.S. Fish and Wildl. Serv.

Padgett, C. A., and W. D. Ivey. 1959. Coturnix Quail as a laboratory research animal. *Science* 129:267–68.

Page, G., and D. F. Whitacre. 1975. Raptor predation on wintering shorebirds. *Condor* 77:73–83.

Palmer, R. S., ed. 1962. *Handbook of North American birds.* Vol. 1. New Haven: Yale University Press.

Pannier, F., and J. Dickinson. 1989. *Manglares.* Caracas, Venezuela: Fundacion para la Defensa de la Naturaleza (FUNDENA).

Parnell, J. F., ed. 1968. Briefs for the files. *Chat* 32:79–81.

Parnell, J. F., and R. F. Soots, Jr. 1979. *Atlas of colonial waterbirds of North Carolina estuaries.* University of North Carolina Sea Grant Publ. UNC-SG-78-10. Chapel Hill.

Peaker, M., and J. L. Linzell. 1975. *Salt glands in birds and reptiles.* Cambridge: Cambridge University Press.

Pennycuick, C. J. 1972. Soaring behavior and performance of some East African birds observed from a motor-glider. *Ibis* 114:178–218.

Pennycuick, C. J., and T. De Santo. 1989. Flight speeds and energy requirements for White Ibises on foraging flights. *Auk* 106:141–44.

Peters, J. L. 1931. *Check-list of birds of the world.* Vol. 1. Cambridge: Harvard University Press.

Peters, W. D., and T. C. Grubb, Jr. 1983. An experimental analysis of sex-specific foraging in Downy Woodpecker, *Picoides pubescens. Ecology* 64:1437–43.

Petit, D. R., and K. L. Bildstein. 1986. Development of formation flying in juvenile White Ibises *(Eudocimus albus). Auk* 103:244–46.

———. 1987. Effect of group size and location within the group on the foraging behavior of White Ibises. *Condor* 89:602–09.

Pollard, J. E., S. M. Melancon, and L. S. Blakey. 1982. Importance of bottomland hardwoods to crawfish and fish in the Henderson Lake area, Atchafalaya Basin, Louisiana. *Wetlands* 2:73–86.

Porcher, R. D. 1976. *A history of the land use of Hobcaw Barony.* Report to the Belle W. Baruch Forest Science Institute of Clemson University, Georgetown, S.C.

Post, W. 1990. Nest survival in a large ibis–heron colony during a 3-year decline to extinction. *Colonial Waterbirds* 13:50–61.

Pritchard, D. 1967. Observations of circulation in coastal plain estuaries. Pp. 37–44 in *Estuaries* (G. Lauff, ed.). Publ. No. 83. Washington, D.C.: American Association for the Advancement of Science.

Pulliam, H. R. 1973. On the advantages of flocking. *J. Theor. Biol.* 38:419–22.

Ramo, C., and B. Busto. 1982. Son *Eudocimus ruber* y *E. albus* distintos especies? *Donana Act. Vertebr.* 9:404–08.

———. 1985a. Comportamiento reproductivo del corocoro (*Eudocimus ruber*) en los llanos de Venezuela. *Mem. Soc. Cienc. Nat. La Salle* 123:77–113.

———. 1985b. *El Corocoro Rojo y su mundo.* Caracas, Venezuela: Mediciencia Editora.

———. 1987. Hybridization between the Scarlet Ibises (*Eudocimus ruber*) and the White Ibis (*Eudocimus albus*) in Venezuela. *Colonial Waterbirds* 10:111–14.

Ramsamujh, B. 1990. Status and conservation of the Scarlet Ibis in Guyana. Pp. 95–99 in *The Scarlet Ibis (Eudocimus ruber): Status, conservation and research* (P. C. Frederick, L. G. Morales, A. L. Spaans, and C. S. Luthin, eds.). IWRB Spec. Publ. 11. Slimbridge, England: Inter. Waterfowl and Wetlands Res. Bur.

Raven, P. 1986. The size of minnow prey in the diet of young Kingfishers *Alcedo atthis. Bird Study* 33:6–11.

Raven, P. H., and G. B. Johnson. 1989. *Biology.* St. Louis: Times Mirror/Mosby College Publ.

Recher, H. F., and J. A. Recher. 1969. Comparative foraging efficiency of adult and immature Little Blue Herons (*Florida caerulea*). *Anim. Behav.* 17:320–22.

Reid, W. V., and M. C. Trexler. 1991. *Drowning the national heritage: Climate change and U.S. coastal biodiversity.* Washington, D.C.: World Resources Institution.

Reimold, R. J., and F. C. Daiber. 1967. Eutrophication of estuarine areas by rainwater. *Chesapeake Sci.* 8:132–33.

Risser, P. G., ed. 1972. *A preliminary compartment model of a tallgrass prairie, Osage site, 1970.* U.S.I.B.P. Grassland Tech. Rep. 159. Washington, D.C.

Robertson, W. B., Jr., L. L. Breen, and B. W. Patty. 1983. Movement of marked Roseate Spoonbills in Florida, with a review of present distribution. *J. Field Ornithol.* 54:225–36.

Robin, P. 1973. Comportement des colonies de *Geronticus calvus* dans le sud marocain, lors des periodes de secheresse. *Bonner Zool. Beitr.* 24:317–22.

Rogers, G. C., Jr. 1970. *The history of Georgetown County, South Carolina.* Columbia: University of South Carolina Press.

Roze, U. 1989. *The North American Porcupine.* Washington, D.C.: Smithsonian Institution Press.

Rudegeair, T. J. 1975. *The reproductive behavior and ecology of the White Ibis (Eudocimus albus).* Ph.D. diss., Gainesville: University of Florida.

References

Rutgers, A., and K. A. Norris. 1970. Scarlet Ibis. Pp. 85–88 in *Encyclopedia of aviculture*. Vol. 1. London: Blanford Press.

Ryder, R. A. 1967. Distribution, migration and mortality of the White-faced Ibis in North America. *Bird Banding* 38:257–77.

Schmidt-Nielsen, K. 1959. Salt glands. *Scien. Am.* 200(1):109–16.

———. 1983. *Animal physiology: Adaptation and environment*. 3d ed. Cambridge: Cambridge University Press.

Schmidt-Nielsen, K., C. B. Jorgensen, and H. Osaki. 1958. Extrarenal salt excretion in birds. *Am. J. Physiol.* 193:101–07.

Schmidt-Nielsen, K., and Y. T. Kim. 1964. The effect of salt intake on the size and function of the salt gland of ducks. *Auk* 81:160–72.

Scholander, P. F. 1957. The wonderful net. *Scien. Am.* 196(4):96–107.

Schreiber, R. L., A. W. Diamond, R. T. Peterson, and W. Cronkite. 1989. Waldrapp: Last in the line of Abu Mengel. Pp. 244–45 in *Save the birds* (R. L. Schreiber, A. W. Diamond, R. T. Peterson, and W. Cronkite, eds.). Boston: Houghton Mifflin.

Shepherd, P., T. Crockett, T. L. De Santo, and K. L. Bildstein. 1991. The impact of Hurricane Hugo on the breeding ecology of wading birds at Pumpkinseed Island, Hobcaw Barony, South Carolina. *Colonial Waterbirds* 14:150–57.

Shields, M. A. 1985. *An analysis of Fish Crow predation on eggs of the White Ibis at Battery Island, North Carolina*. Master's thesis, Wilmington: University of North Carolina.

Shields, M. A., and J. F. Parnell. 1985. Fish Crow predation on eggs of the White Ibis at Battery Island, North Carolina. *Auk* 103:531–39.

Shoemaker, V. H. 1972. Osmoregulation and excretion in birds. Pp. 527–74 in *Avian biology*. Vol. II (D. S. Farner and J. R. King, eds.). New York: Academic Press.

Sibley, C. G., and J. E. Ahlquist. 1990. *Phylogeny and classification of birds: A study in molecular evolution*. New Haven: Yale University Press.

Sibley, C. G., J. E. Ahlquist, and B. L. Monroe, Jr. 1988. A classification of the living birds of the world based on DNA–DNA hybridization studies. *Auk* 105:409–23.

Siegel-Causey, D., and S. P. Kharitonov. 1990. The evolution of coloniality. *Current Ornithol.* 7:285–330.

Silliman, J., G. S. Mill, and S. Alden. 1977. Effect of flock size on foraging activity in wintering Sanderlings. *Wilson Bull.* 89:434–38.

Simpson, M. B. 1988. Status of the Scarlet Ibis in South Carolina: Historical records from John Abbot and Alexander Wilson. *Chat* 52:4–5.

Skutch, A. F. 1986. *Helpers at birds' nests*. Iowa City: University Iowa Press.

Smith, H. A. M. 1913. The baronies of South Carolina. *The South Carolina Historical and Genealogical Magazine* 14:61–80.

Snow, B. K. 1974. The Plumbeous Heron of the Galapagos. *Living Bird* 13:51–72.

Sokal, R. R., and F. J. Rohlf. 1969. *Biometry*. San Francisco: Freeman.

Spaans, A. L. 1975. On the present breeding status of the Scarlet Ibis, *Eudocimus ruber*, along the north-eastern coast of South America. *Biol. Conserv.* 7:245–53.

———. 1990. Problems in assessing trends in breeding populations of Scarlet Ibises and other ciconiiform birds. Pp. 1–6 in *The Scarlet Ibis (Eudocimus ruber): Status, conservation and recent research* (P. C. Frederick, A. L. Spaans, L. G. Morales, and C. S. Luthin, eds.). IWRB Spec. Publ. 11. Slimbridge, England: Inter. Waterfowl and Wetlands Res. Bur.

Spendelow, J. A., and S. R. Patton. 1988. *National atlas of coastal waterbird colonies in the contiguous United States: 1976–1982.* U.S. Fish and Wildl. Serv. Biol. Rep. 88(5), Washington, D.C.

Spil, R. E., M. W. Van Walstijn, and H. Albrecht. 1985. Observations on the behaviour of the Scarlet Ibis, *Eudocimus ruber,* in Artis Zoo, Amsterdam. *Bijdragen tot de Dierkunde* 55:219–32.

Sprunt, A. 1944. Northward extension of the breeding range of the White Ibis. *Auk* 61:144–45.

Staaland, H. 1967. Anatomical and physiological adaptations of nasal glands in Charadriiformes birds. *Comp. Biochem. Physiol.* 23A:933–44.

Stahlecker, D. W. 1989. White-faced Ibis breeding in Rio Arriba County: Second verified nesting location for New Mexico. *New Mexico Ornithol. Soc. Bull.* 17:2–6.

Stangel, P. W., J. A. Rodgers, Jr., and A. L. Bryan. 1991. Low genetic differentiation between two disjunct White Ibis colonies. *Colonial Waterbirds* 14:13–16.

Steele, B. B. 1984. Effects of pesticides on reproductive success of White-faced Ibis in Utah, 1979. *Colonial Waterbirds* 7:80–87.

Stephens, J. L. 1950. White Ibis found nesting in North Carolina. *Chat* 14:49–50.

Stinner, D. H. 1983. *Colonial wading birds and nutrient cycling in the Okefenokee Swamp ecosystem.* Ph.D. diss., Athens: University of Georgia.

Stoddard, P. K., and M. Beecher. 1983. Parental recognition of offspring in the Cliff Swallow. *Auk* 100:795–99.

Storer, J. H. 1948. *The flight of birds.* Cranbrook Inst. Sci. Bull. No. 28. Bloomfield Hills, Mich.

Swanton, J. R. 1946. *The Indians of the southeastern United States.* Washington, D.C.: Smithsonian Institution Press.

Tanner, W. F. 1961. Mainland beach changes due to Hurricane Donna. *J. Geophys. Res.* 66:2265–66.

Taplin, L. E., G. C. Grigg, P. Harlow, T. M. Ellis, and W. A. Dunson. 1982. Lingual salt glands in *Crocodylus acutus* and *C. johnstoni* and their absence from *Alligator mississippiensis* and *Caiman crocodilus. J. Comp. Physiol.* 149:43–47.

Technau, G. 1936. Die Nasendruse der Vogel. *J. Ornithol.* 84:511–617.

Teixeira, D. M., and R. Best. 1981. Adendas a ornitologia do Territorio Federal do Amapa. *Bol. Mus. Paraense Emilio Goeldi, nova serie* 104:1–25.

Thomas, B. T. 1984. Maguari Stork nesting: Juvenile growth and behavior. *Auk* 101:812–23.

Urban, E. K. 1974a. Breeding of Sacred Ibis *Threskiornis aethiopica* at Lake Shala, Ethiopia. *Ibis* 116:263–77.

———. 1974b. Flight speeds and wingflapping rate of Sacred Ibis. *Auk* 91:423.

Valiela, I., J. M. Teal, and W. J. Sass. 1975. Production and dynamics of salt marsh vegetation and the effects of experimental treatment of sewage sludge. *J. Appl. Ecol.* 12:973–81.

References

Vanden Berge, J. C. 1970. A comparative study of the appendicular musculature of the order Ciconiiformes. *Am. Midl. Nat.* 84:289–362.

Ward, P., and A. Zahavi. 1973. The importance of certain assemblages of birds as "information center" for finding food. *Ibis* 128:195–213.

Waterman, M., D. Close, and D. Condon. 1971. Straw-necked Ibis *(Threskiornis spinicollis)* in South Australia: Breeding colonies and movements. *S. Austral. Ornithol.* 6:7–11.

Wayne, A. T. 1922. Discovery of breeding grounds of the White Ibis in South Carolina. *Bull. Charleston Mus.* 17:17–30.

Weiner, A., and Z. Glowackinski. 1975. Energy flow through a bird community in a deciduous forest in southern Poland. *Condor* 77:233–42.

Wiens, J. A. 1973. Pattern and process in grassland bird communities. *Ecol. Monogr.* 43:237–70.

Wilson, A. 1840. *Wilson's American ornithology.* Boston: Otis, Broaders, and Co.

Wilson, E. O. 1978. *On human nature.* Cambridge: Harvard University Press.

Woodall, P. F. 1985. Waterbird populations in the Brisbane Region, 1972–1983, and correlates with rainfall and water heights. *Austral. Wildl. Res.* 12:495–506.

Wrege, P. H. 1980. *Social foraging strategies of White Ibis.* Ph.D. diss., Ithaca, N.Y.: Cornell University.

Wylie, F. E. 1979. *Tides and the pull of the moon.* New York: Berkley Books.

Xiyang, T. 1987. Five more Crested Ibises have taken wing. Pp. 39–56 in *Living treasures.* New York: Bantam Books.

Zelickman, E. A., and A. N. Golovkin. 1972. Composition, structure, and productivity of neritic plankton communities near the bird colonies of the northern shores of Novaya Zemlya. *Mar. Biol.* 17:265–74.

Zucker, I. H., R. C. Huskey, C. E. C. Haack, and J. P. Gilmore. 1979. Functional maturation of the salt gland of the goose. *Comp. Biochem. Physiol.* 62A:627–30.

Zwarts, L. 1980. Intra- and inter-specific competition for space in estuarine bird species in a one-prey situation. *Proc. XVII Int. Ornithol. Congr.* (1978):1045–50.

Index

Index